DEMOCRACY AND HUMAN RIGHTS IN LATIN AMERICA

DEMOCRACY AND HUMAN RIGHTS IN LATIN AMERICA

Edited by
Richard S. Hillman, John A. Peeler,
and Elsa Cardozo Da Silva

Westport, Connecticut
London

Library of Congress Cataloging-in-Publication Data

Democracy and human rights in Latin America / edited by Richard S. Hillman, John A.
Peeler, and Elsa Cardozo Da Silva.
   p.   cm.
   Includes bibliographical references and index.
   ISBN 0–275–97482–0 (alk. paper)
   1. Democracy—Latin America.   2. Human rights—Latin America.   3. Latin
America—Politics and government—20th century.   4. United States—Foreign
relations—Latin America.   5. Latin America—Foreign relations—United States.   6.
Democratization—Government policy—United States.   I. Hillman, Richard S., 1943–   II.
Peeler, John A.   III. Cardozo Da Silva, Elsa.
JL966.D4538   2002
321.8′098—dc21   2001036318

British Library Cataloguing in Publication Data is available.

Library of Congress Catalog Card Number: 2001036318
ISBN: 0–275–97482–0

First published in 2002

Praeger Publishers, 88 Post Road West, Westport, CT 06881
An imprint of Greenwood Publishing Group, Inc.
www.praeger.com

Printed in the United States of America

The paper used in this book complies with the
Permanent Paper Standard issued by the National
Information Standards Organization (Z39.48–1984).

10 9 8 7 6 5 4 3 2 1

Contents

Preface

Richard S. Hillman

This book is the product of the efforts of a concerned group of academics who are engaged in the promotion of a more humane world through their scholarship and other activities. While each has lived in and studied Latin America, their observations and analyses of human progress in that important region have much to contribute to understanding other parts of the world.

Latin American experiences, especially in the areas of democratization and human rights protection, are particularly relevant for developing countries that are attempting to build stable political and economic systems in order to provide a decent standard of living and incorporate previously excluded populations into the national mainstream. The past record, of course, is far from acceptable.

The advent of the twenty-first century, however, appears to be a time of great potential progress for the institutionalization of democratic human rights regimes that would reduce human pain and suffering. The number of countries in Latin America and elsewhere that are experimenting with democracy has never been greater. Clearly, the path toward fulfilling the expectations raised by these experiments is not an easy one; it is fraught with difficult obstacles deriving from the historical legacy as well as contemporary challenges. Nevertheless, democracy and human rights have definitely entered the political lexicon and discourse throughout the world.

These considerations were on the minds of the over 100 scholars who participated in the twenty-first annual conference of the Middle

Atlantic Council of Latin American Studies (MACLAS) sponsored by the Institute for the Study of Democracy and Human Rights at St. John Fisher College in Rochester, New York, on April 7–8, 2000. Among the papers presented, each sparking lively discussion and debate, many stood out by virtue of their consistency with the central theme of the conference: democracy and human rights in Latin America. This book includes some of the papers chosen by the editors for expansion into complete chapters. Unfortunately, space limitations prohibited the inclusion of all the worthy papers, but we did want to make available to the public at least some of the ideas contained in the conference's deliberations. We believe they are of great moment in a world that is just beginning to accept democracy and human rights as fundamental virtues.

I am deeply indebted to my coeditors, John A. Peeler and Elsa Cardozo Da Silva, who helped coordinate the MACLAS conference and whose support, collegiality, and friendship have been inspirational. They are both true scholars and gentlepersons. I am convinced that our close teamwork was catalytic in bringing this project to fruition. Of course, the authors of the chapters contained in this book are to be commended for their excellent work and commitment to the highest ideals of the academy. Without their close collaboration we would not be able to offer this volume. Their patience is also appreciated.

We are grateful to the U.S. Department of State, which provided funding for the creation of the Institute for the Study of Democracy and Human Rights as an integral part of the College and University Affiliations Program (under which St. John Fisher College and the Central University of Venezuela have engaged in academic exchanges since 1997). MACLAS officers and members also deserve our thanks for providing the context in which our deliberations on democracy and human rights in Latin America could take place. Finally, we wish to express our gratitude to editors Michael Hermann and Seth Reichgott, whose helpful comments enhanced the final version of the book.

DEMOCRACY AND HUMAN RIGHTS IN LATIN AMERICA

CHAPTER 1

Introduction

Richard S. Hillman, John A. Peeler,
and Elsa Cardozo Da Silva

Many questions about democracy and human rights have emerged at
the advent of the twenty-first century, a time in which the prospects
for progress in these areas have never been greater. Yet there are significant challenges that must be understood if advances are to be
achieved. This book is designed to respond to these questions and
discuss the challenges with particular reference to Latin America, where
democratic regimes have alternated with authoritarian governments
and the human rights record is inconsistent at best.

Moreover, as in any region of the world, governmental and social
institutions are products of political culture. The attitudes, values, and
beliefs that legitimize these institutions develop over time and are
transmitted from generation to generation. They may be promoted,
supported, and nurtured but not imposed by external agents. Democracy and human rights in Latin America, therefore, may reflect universal principles but will also be idiosyncratic.

Democracy, or "rule of the people," is, minimally, a governmental
system that provides for peaceful competition for positions of power
at regular intervals, open participation in the election of leaders and
policies, and civil and political liberties that ensure the legitimacy of
competition and participation (Diamond, Hartlyn, Linz, and Lipset

1999, ix). This definition assumes that people's interests will be represented, and that majority power will be checked in order to ensure that minority rights are respected and no one individual or group is dominant. The latter considerations generally require institutionalized opposition, normally through political parties. Substantive and procedural conceptions of democracy may be distinguished. Electoral procedures, for example, do not necessarily produce substantive protection of human rights when they are designed in practice to serve the interests of an elite. Especially in the advanced industrial democracies of Western Europe and North America, much attention is now being paid to the issue of "deepening" democracy—making democratic practice fit more closely the democratic ideal.

On the other hand, in Latin America the first priority has been the mere establishment of minimal democracy. Latin American political institutions have been characterized as a "hybrid" combination of democratic and authoritarian systems, with elitist, hierarchical, authoritarian, corporatist, and patrimonial strains (Wiarda and Kline 1996, 11). As a result of conflicts between these strains and democratic principles, regimes in the region have undergone a series of difficult transitions and their future is uncertain (Peeler 1998). This is problematic because there is a definitive connection between democracy and human rights: A functioning democracy will, by definition, be respectful of human rights.

The Universal Declaration of Human Rights (U.N. General Assembly 1948) recognizes rights and entitlements that one has by virtue of being human. In the same way that political culture informs democratization patterns, cultural relativity requires that the protection of universal rights and entitlements avoid the extremes of either cultural imperialism or cultural homogenization. Again, the issue may be understood in terms of degrees. The essential linkage between procedural democracy and substantive human rights, however, remains. Only when supported by "rights-protective political attitudes and institutions" will elections produce liberal democratic regimes (Donnelly 1998, 159).

The latter consideration signals the complexity of promoting democracy and human rights. U.S. foreign policies regarding democracy building and human rights protection abroad are a case in point. While ample rhetoric has been articulated in support of these ends, real policies have been inconsistent. Security and economic interests have often prevailed over interest in democracy and human rights. Throughout the twentieth century, the United States supported dictatorships and intervened in the domestic affairs of other countries "for purposes far removed from the promotion of democracy" (Carothers 1999, 5).

Nevertheless, since President Woodrow Wilson proclaimed that the United States was fighting World War I "to make the world safe for democracy," the championing of democracy became an ideal integral to U.S. international relations. The Holocaust during World War II, in which millions of innocent civilians were murdered by Germany, propelled the issue of human rights to the forefront of world politics. The Cold War was considered a struggle to preserve the "Free World." Although for the most part this consisted of opposition to communism, human rights became the cornerstone of President Jimmy Carter's foreign policy and continued to gain global legitimacy as treaties and conventions were signed throughout the world.

Today, democratic rule does not appear to be threatened by military takeover, as it has been through most of Latin American history. Nevertheless, the region's governments are overwrought by crises of weak economies unable to provide relief to declining living standards, deteriorating public services and infrastructure, social malaise occasioned by increasing crime and persistent corruption, and human rights violations. An important current issue among students of human rights concerns whether the concept should be expanded to include additional rights such as a clean environment or access to adequate medical care, and what this implies for our conception of democracy itself.

While this movement toward a fourth generation of human rights is taking place in the world, it is not surprising that among Latin Americans there is growing governmental and social emphasis on human rights of the second and third generations. Based on the assumption that minimal civil and political rights are either granted or "negotiable," focus has shifted to the needs of vast numbers of economically disadvantaged people in the region as well as the empowerment of those who have been historically excluded or neglected by dominant social groups.

Political systems that are neither truly authoritarian nor completely democratic are conducting elections that have produced neo-*caudillos*, or a new type of populist who promises to solve the problems and improve the quality of life (Hillman 1994). In other words, Latin America's governmental institutions have become discredited and "many citizens appear willing to give up some measure of democracy and accept authoritarian governments that they believe can solve their problems" (Hakim 2000, 107). An alternative explanation views the strong leadership pattern as a culturally relative variant of democratic governance, one that combines centralized and referenda democracy.

In either case, the basic questions about democracy, human rights, and their promotion remain. In the spirit of seeking a more comprehensive understanding of these matters, the Institute for the Study of Democracy and Human Rights at St. John Fisher College in Rochester, New York, hosted the twenty-first annual meeting of the Middle Atlantic Council of Latin American Studies on April 7 and 8, 2000. Twenty panels and plenary sessions covered a wide array of topics related to the general conference theme: democracy and human rights in Latin America. Over 100 academic participants from Argentina, Brazil, Canada, the Caribbean, Chile, Mexico, Venezuela, and the United States as well as observers (faculty and students) engaged in lively discussions, including one in which two former ambassadors participated and one in which the U.S. ambassador to Venezuela gave a keynote address.

This book is based on selected papers presented at the conference. Each chapter represents the analysis of an expert who has had ongoing engagement with the topic under review. Although a general consensus pervades the chapters, there are significant differences regarding particular matters. Both commonalities and divergences are apparent in the chapters and summarized in the conclusion.

Part I contains three critical perspectives on democracy and human rights in Latin America. Louis N. Bickford, associate director of the Global Studies Program at the University of Wisconsin, Madison, raises issues of general concern to democracy and human rights in discussing the meanings of "the past" for the human rights movement in Chile in Chapter 2. Elsa Cardozo Da Silva, professor of international relations at the Central University of Venezuela, compares and contrasts democratic governance in Venezuela and Colombia in Chapter 3. Chapter 4 contains an appraisal of human rights in Brazil by Isabel Ribeiro de Oliveira, professor of political science at the Federal University of Rio de Janeiro.

Part II analyzes the promotion of democracy and human rights. Chapter 5, by Christopher Sabatini, director of the Latin American and the Caribbean Program of the National Endowment for Democracy, discusses the international promotion and defense of democracy at a time when democratic governance is under stress. In Chapter 6, María Teresa Romero, professor of international relations at the Central University of Venezuela, offers a critique of U.S. efforts to promote democracy in Venezuela. Irwin P. Stotzky, director of the Center for the Study of Human Rights and professor of law at the University of Miami School of Law, treats international military intervention to restore a democratically elected government in Haiti in Chapter 7. Chapter 8, by Edward Drachman, professor of political science at the State University of New York at Geneseo, concludes that U.S. policy toward Fidel Castro should be rethought in terms of "best business practices" in order to effectively promote political and economic reform in Cuba.

Our conclusion outlines the trends and prospects suggested by the analyses contained in the previous parts of the book. Clearly, the challenges facing democracy and human rights in Latin America are formidable and require eternal vigilance.

BIBLIOGRAPHY

Brown, Seyom. 2000. *Human Rights in World Politics*. New York: Longman.

Carothers, Thomas. 1999. *Aiding Democracy Abroad: The Learning Curve*. Washington, D.C.: Carnegie Endowment for International Peace.

Diamond, Larry, Jonathan Hartlyn, Juan J. Linz, and Seymour Martin Lipset. 1999. *Democracy in Developing Countries: Latin America*. 2d ed. Boulder, Colo.: Lynne Rienner.

Donnelly, Jack. 1998. *International Human Rights*. 2d ed. Boulder, Colo.: Westview Press.

Hakim, Peter. 2000. "Is Latin America Doomed to Failure?" *Foreign Policy* 117 (Winter): 104–117.

Hillman, Richard S. 1994. *Democracy for the Privileged: Crisis and Transition in Venezuela*. Boulder, Colo.: Lynne Rienner.

Peeler, John A. 1998. *Building Democracy in Latin America*. Boulder, Colo.: Lynne Rienner.

The Universal Declaration of Human Rights. 1948. U.N. General Assembly Resolution 217.

Wiarda, Howard J., and Harvey F. Kline. 1996. *Latin American Politics and Development*. 4th ed. Boulder, Colo.: Westview Press.

PART I

CRITICAL PERSPECTIVES
ON DEMOCRACY
AND HUMAN RIGHTS

CHAPTER 2

Preserving Memory:
The Past and the Human Rights
Movement in Chile

Louis N. Bickford

The introduction to this book makes clear the importance of a critical perspective on the political evolution of movements toward the recognition and protection of human rights (HR). This chapter explores the ways in which the Chilean human rights movement (HRM) since 1990 approaches the past, with particular focus on the ways in which the construction of collective memory has become a major area of concern, and an important battleground, for human rights activists.[1]

To the degree that a human rights movement exists at all in Chile today, it is in large part dedicated to "addressing" or "confronting" the past. This chapter addresses four questions: What does it mean to "confront the past"? How do human rights activists do this, exactly? Why did this focus emerge as a dominant concern? Why does it matter?

To get at these four questions, this chapter primarily draws on my involvement in a three-year project funded by the Ford Foundation's Santiago office to examine human rights archives in the Southern Cone. During this project I became aware that a concerted and robust effort to create "memory repositories" in the form of human rights archives was, in itself, a conscious form of activist truth-telling. By creating counterhegemonic sources of documented truth, the HRM sought to influence the future telling of history and to influence the shape and content of "collective memory."

In addition, this chapter draws on a blossoming literature that might be called "legacies of authoritarianism."[2] This literature provides some useful material to conceptualize the development of the HRM in Chile since 1990. Finally, a small but interesting literature within social movement theory has addressed the ways in which all social movements inevitably decline over time (see Freeman and Johnson 1999). This literature, although it has tended to focus on the United States, has much to teach us about the ways in which the Chilean HRM has declined since 1990.

THE HUMAN RIGHTS MOVEMENT IN CHILE, 2000

By virtually all accounts, the HRM in Chile today is going through a period of relative inactivity compared to its famously vibrant period in the 1970s and 1980s, although recent developments in the Pinochet case have led to increased vitality and visibility.[3] In fact, we may now be seeing a renaissance of the Chilean HRM after a decade-long hiatus in which it has been searching for a new mission under putative democracy. For the past ten years, from an organizational point of view, the eight or nine largest human rights organizations (HROs) in Chile—not to mention dozens of smaller groups, including neighborhood and regional HROs—have been weak, underfunded, and minimally staffed; they have garnered low levels of popular enthusiasm and been practically invisible as agenda setters or influential voices in Chilean society (except, perhaps, on the specific issue of Pinochet's possible prosecution).

On one level, this is hardly a surprise at all. Social movements—almost by definition—decline over time (see Freeman and Johnson 1999). Moreover, it may be more useful to see the Chilean HRM beginning in 1973 not as a human rights movement, per se, but as an antiauthoritarian movement; it might then have been expected almost automatically to vanish after its primary goal—the elimination of authoritarianism—was achieved in 1990. There are also other explanations for why the Chilean HRM has faded in glory and influence, such as Garth and Dezalay's argument that international support and allegiances (especially, but not only, through funding) were key to the HRM's vibrancy, and when these partnerships dissolved, the HRM was left without necessary resources (Garth and Dezalay 2001).

Although the HRM in Chile has been relatively weak, it has not ceased to exist entirely. At least six of the major and historically most important HROs still exist in some form, and each of these is still active. These include the Vicaria de la Solidaridad (which has downsized to become a human rights archive), the Chilean Commission of Human Rights (CCHR), the Corporación de Promoción y Defensa de los

Derechos del Pueblo (CODEPU), the Fundación Para la Protección de la Infancia Dañada por los Estados de Emergencia (PIDEE), the Agrupación de Familiares de Detenidos-Desaparecidos (AFDD), and the Fundación de Ayuda Social de los Iglesias Cristianas (FASIC).[4]

These groups are involved in numerous activities, including human rights education, international networking, and developing activities around access to justice and social and economic rights, but an important part of the work of these organizations has to do with "addressing the past" and fighting impunity based on past human rights abuses.

WHAT DOES IT MEAN TO "CONFRONT THE PAST": PAST AS PAST AND PAST AS PRESENT

The past is an important part of the human rights movement in at least two ways. First, the human rights movement is concerned with reclaiming the past as a kind of shared public space ("the past as past"). That is, it is concerned with fighting against dominant, state-constructed narratives of historical truth and replacing these with narratives that include, or even center on, the experiences of victims of repression. The human rights movement is also concerned with the past as a conscious strategy in an effort to democratize the present ("the past as present"). This is best summed up in the idea of a battle against impunity (see Basombrío 2000; Sieder 1995). The basic notion here is that democratization requires confronting the past and an examination of the past is a useful strategy for deepening democracy.

In both cases (and obviously these overlap) it is widely accepted by the human rights community in Chile that the Chilean Truth and Reconciliation Commission of 1990 was not enough in terms of addressing the past. Human rights activists call for both expanding the truth and more than truth (i.e., "justice").[5] Perhaps more than anything else, they call for *remembering*. Why put so much energy into remembering the past? In Chile, human rights activists usually give the following reasons:

1. *The moral imperative.* Human rights activists argue that there is a moral imperative to remember, to validate and acknowledge victims as victims. They suggest that this is the first step toward healing the nation and toward justice, which can only be based on truth.

2. *The past is impossible to ignore.* Another argument is that the past is impossible to ignore or forget—it will always surface—so it is better to allow it to surface in constructive and healing ways. The other alternative is what might be called "eruptions" of memory, in which anger and frustration seethes beneath the surface of political life and then erupts at various moments.[6] The American author William Faulkner put it well: "The past is not dead and gone; it isn't even past" (quoted in Shriver 1995, 4).

3. *Strengthening democracy.* Activists also argue that democracy cannot be built on a foundation of lies, and that an assertive, organized, and concerted effort to remember the past can lead to a stronger democracy. Truth heals individuals (citizens) and the collectivity as a whole (the citizenry), the building blocks of democracy. In addition, activists argue that the pursuit of justice for past crimes will help strengthen democratic institutions, such as the judiciary. Testing and pushing these institutions by seeking to process human rights claims through them, it is argued, can lead to their strengthening and maturity.

4. *Accountability.* Democratization can be enhanced by creating mechanisms of accountability (the opposite of impunity). This is done by bringing past human rights offenders to trial or by finding ways to hold them accountable for their crimes.

5. *Building a democratic culture.* Here an argument is made that only by highlighting the sad and horrible truths about the past can we hope to build a democratic culture in the future. The fundamental operating assumption is basically educational: If HR activists can help educate the population about past evils they can help create a cultural shift to a more humane set of shared values.

6. *Nunca Mas.* Finally, there is an argument that remembering creates deterrence: Only remembering is likely to prevent these things from happening again in the future. Chilean human rights activist Sola Sierra puts it this way: "Remembering helps the people of a country avoid committing the same crimes, calling things by their name; a criminal is a criminal. . . . The worst thing that could happen in Chile . . . would be for forgetting to do away with this problem" (available at http://www.derechoschile.com).

These six justifications (whether for reclaiming the past as historical memory–public space, or for using the past as a strategic tool within the HRM) infuse the human rights movement in Chile (as well as, in slightly different ways, in Argentina and Uruguay). These six justifications further translate into three basic lines of activity that occupy the bulk of the day-to-day work and long-term planning of the HROs discussed in this chapter.

Prosecuting Offenders

On the most obvious level, addressing the past means retroactive justice.[7] Publicly accusing and prosecuting the perpetrators of human rights abuses is among the top priorities for the HRM as a whole in Chile, and this strategy has met with some success. Especially since the detainment of Pinochet in London, a number of military figures have been detained or arrested.[8] The logic behind this strategy is fairly obvious: It includes retribution, basic concepts of justice, punishment for evil deeds, an opportunity for victims to publicly tell their stories and be acknowledged, and a chance for society to take a moral stand through its public institutions. Further, the prosecution of perpetrators—through the judicial system—is seen as strengthening (potentially vulnerable or corrupted) political institutions and protecting democracy.

Sites, Ceremonies, and Commemorative Space

Writing about Argentina, Marguerite Feitlowitz (1998) explains the importance, especially among victims of human rights abuses but also, arguably, for the soul of the nation as a whole and collective healing, of efforts "to recuperate places that were stolen, rededicate public spaces, and convert death centers into places that resonate with life" after the end of authoritarian rule (p. 170). In addition to "taking back" places like torture centers, in Chile this has also meant smaller expressions of memory, such as the creation of roadside shrines (*animitas*) to the fallen and commemorative plaques.[9] Since the end of authoritarianism in Chile (as well as in Argentina and Uruguay), commemorative activities resulting in "expressions of memory" have been a major thrust within the HRM. A few examples include the Memorial del Detenido Desaparecido y del Ejecutado Político, located in the Santiago General Cemetery, which is an imposing and visually impressive commemorative space to those killed or disappeared during the authoritarian period, and the Parque por la Paz (Peace Park), a commemorative public space for reflection aimed at remembering human rights violations and victims during the authoritarian period, located at the site of an important detention and torture center, Villa Grimaldi (also known as Cuartel Terranova) in the Peñalolén neighborhood of Santiago; ongoing projects to build a Memory Museum in Argentina; and the multimeaning Jewish Holocaust Monument in Uruguay.[10]

Archiving as Human Rights Strategy

The third main activity, related to monuments and commemorative activities, is a recent push by human rights groups in these countries to collect documents to archive.[11] It has become increasingly apparent to many people that human rights organizations that functioned during the military years amassed huge collections of documentary materials that themselves represent a kind of national patrimony telling the story of a particular period. Human rights groups have thus been frantically collecting their documents, trying to organize them and preserve them (such as on microfilm) (see Hutchison 1999). This effort to preserve documentary materials is a key human rights strategy in Chile, as it is seen as a counterhegemonic source of history. Archives, seen in this sense, are not simply repositories of paper, but become active elements in the reconstruction of a national narrative. Their existence—and the energy put into them by human rights organizations—is further evidence that one of the major battlegrounds of the human rights struggle in the 1990s was the struggle over the "master narrative" of what happened a few decades earlier. Archives play an important role in this (see Bickford 1999, 2000).

Throughout its history, the HRM has sought to document and publicize human rights abuses. In fact, documentation has been at the core of the global human rights movement since at least 1961, when a group of lawyers, journalists, writers, and others created the *Appeal for Amnesty*, which told the stories of six "prisoners of conscience" from different countries and of different political and religious backgrounds, all jailed for peacefully expressing their political or religious beliefs, and called on governments everywhere to free such prisoners (the *Appeal* later led to the creation of Amnesty International).

Archiving is, in essence, an extension of documenting human rights atrocities. In the most basic sense, archiving means choosing the most relevant and important of a wide range of documents that might be preserved. The list begins most obviously with legal documents (such as habeas corpus briefs or writs filed on behalf of disappeared persons), but also includes testimonials of victims, family members, and witnesses to atrocities; contemporary accounts in published sources (including both newspapers and movement publications); and countless types of other materials, including pamphlets, posters, position papers, mimeos, video and audiotapes, and meeting agendas or notes taken by members of human rights groups.

Whether stated as such or not, the HRM's current emphasis on archiving the past is based on an interesting set of assumptions about history and the construction of social memory. First, the creation of an "official story," a state-generated narrative about the past, is seen as a part of a larger "project"—if not an outright conscious strategy—by dominant or hegemonic forces to interpret the past in ways that benefit certain groups in society. What we might call "hegemonic truth" thus becomes the enemy of human rights advocates because the pursuit of such "truth" is seen as a "complex and purposefully selective process of historical recollection," which is a "bid for hegemony" by powerful groups in society.[12]

In this sense, from the perspective of the HRM the primary and most frightening alternative to its demand for "remembering" is not "forgetting" per se, but instead the acceptance (or victory) of the official narrative. In fact, an argument that is often posed as a debate between remembering and forgetting is really frequently an argument about choosing among multiple different interpretations of Chile's past. Were the people who were disappeared Communist troublemakers and subversives who threatened the foundations of the republic? Or were they idealistic innocents fighting for a better society who were subjected to unjustifiably harsh repression? Or were they leftist insurgents who were on the brink of building true socialism? Or were they all of these? Or none?

WHY DID THE PAST EMERGE AS SUCH A KEY CONCERN?

Although there are reasons that the HRM would have been likely to focus on the past, as it has done, it was not inevitable. Given the multiple and diverse challenges associated with deepening Chilean democracy, the human rights movement might have taken an entirely different direction after 1990. For example, it might have focused on strengthening basic liberties or expanding freedoms such as freedom of expression under polyarchic rule; challenging police brutality; seeking to improve economic, social, and cultural rights; fighting against gender, racial, or class discrimination; or battling for enhanced consumer rights in a neoliberal economy. But very few of these activities have emerged as important concerns of any of the major human rights organizations in Chile.[13] To understand why the past has remained a more central concern than any of these other areas, it is necessary to look at the formation of the movement.

Chile experienced massive human rights violations during the 1970s and 1980s, resulting in the death or disappearance of thousands, not to mention numerous cases of torture.[14] It was largely in reaction to these violations that a strong human rights movement emerged. Although the HRM may have had certain antecedents (e.g., labor organizations) before the advent of "bureaucratic authoritarianism" in the 1970s, it was clearly pushed to an entirely new level during—and because of—military rule. In this sense, we can say that the dictatorship contributed directly to the creation (ironically) of a strong HRM, although this was clearly not a desirable result from the perspective of military rulers. Nonetheless, the human rights movement can be considered a legacy of authoritarianism.[15]

The definition of a "legacy" of authoritarianism is not entirely clear. In general, this term has been defined according to an assumption of path-dependency; that is, the idea that a set of institutions or a behavioral pattern changed or became firmly entrenched as a direct result of a specific regime (authoritarian rule, in this case). This assumption assumes that history was "diverted" at an identifiable moment or period in time and that it took a different "path" because of authoritarian rule.[16] For example, we might say that the neoliberal economic model in much of the Southern Cone was a direct result of authoritarian rule, or we might suggest that a cultural hesitancy to speak out publicly on political issues in Chile was a result of seventeen years of dictatorship. The term "legacy," at least as it is used in the phrase "legacies of authoritarianism," tends to connote a "negative" result.

The fact that the HRM in Chile can be seen as a (positive) legacy of authoritarianism is significant because it means that the particular ways in which the movement was constituted—and the ways in which it has attempted to reconstitute itself in a postauthoritarian context— are greatly influenced by its origins under military rule. This creates enormous problems and challenges for the movement as a whole.

FORMATION OF THE CHILEAN
HUMAN RIGHTS MOVEMENT

It is well established that simple grievance is insufficient to launch a social movement.[17] On the contrary, certain other conditions must obtain before grievance can be translated into collective action. First, certain already existing mobilizing structures must be in place that can absorb and push collective action, such as black churches before the U.S. civil rights movement or the existence of organizational networks, including consciousness-raising groups, which led to an outburst of feminist activity in the mid-1960s.[18] Second, the role of a crisis is important: Often a movement will emerge out of the ether of a nonorganized grievance because of the dramatization of a problem. This dramatization, such a military coup d'etat or the milder example of Rosa Parks on a Montgomery bus, can serve to crystallize and focus discontent. In the presence of mobilizing structures, this can then catalyze action. Finally, fragmentation of elite groups—especially if certain elite groups are able to provide resources (either funding or legitimacy) to movement actors—allows for movements to divide elite opinion and launch action. In the United States, for example, a segment of the policy-making elite strongly favored the 1973 Vocational Rehabilitation Act, even though this pitted them against business interests. However, the elite legitimation thus given to the disabled-peoples movement helped strengthen that movement enormously by the early 1980s.

The dynamics of movement formation is important because it locates social movements in a particular organizational framework with specific goals. Moreover, organizational cultures then grow. Formal organizations often have written constitutions or bylaws governing them; all movement groups have mechanisms for recruitment and maintenance (e.g., sustainability), as well as preferred ways of pursuing goals and making strategic choices. Often, moreover, groups are strongly influenced by strong individuals who lead them, frequently those who initiate them. If social movement organizations do not have well-thought-out mechanisms for passing organizations on to new generations, this can result in stagnation and "founders' syndrome" (i.e., when initial founders cling to the organization and are unable to adapt to new circumstances).

When the military staged a coup in 1973 in Chile, military leaders were on some level deeply aware of the importance of mobilizing structures for social movements, and they set out to destroy or take control of as many of these as possible. Universities were raided, academic departments eliminated, and academic administrators replaced with military appointees. The labor movement was totally destroyed and its leaders were imprisoned, disappeared, or sent into exile. The only three sets of major mobilizing structures the military was unable to demolish or co-opt were shantytown neighborhoods, families, and the church. The first of these was too unwieldy to control, and the other two represented sacred space.[19] The institutionality of the human rights movement thus began in neighborhoods and, especially, in first the church and then the family. Courageous church leaders, as well as lay leaders of various denominations, were able to provide the earliest institutional structures for the launching of the human rights movement.[20]

In the face of massive repression, the human rights struggle was largely built around resisting, delegitimatizing, rejecting, denying, struggling against, or saying no to authoritarian rule. With organizational bases in the church and then through the emergence of family-based organizations, the formation of the human rights movement was almost entirely focused on opposition.

Although the movement adopted the vocabulary of human rights, in fact the movement was dedicated to (1) opposing authoritarianism and (2) protecting the lives and security of potential and actual victims. In a sense, the movement was based largely on one "human right": the right to life and security of the person. These two core elements of the Chilean human rights movement became deeply embedded in its institutional structure, its mission and mandate, and, by extension, its strategies and goals.

During the entire seventeen-year period of dictatorship, the Chilean human rights movement would fortify—as opposed to diversify—both these organizational and strategic antecedents. The formation of the movement had set a tone that would become difficult to change: The human rights movement was "about" defeating dictatorship and protecting life. When these two goals were accomplished with the transition to democracy in 1990, the human rights movement was faced with a difficult challenge: rethink its purpose or vanish from the scene. The deeply embedded emphasis of the movement on "la batalla en contra del terror" (Fruhling, quoted in Orellana and Hutchison 1991, 99) thus had effects along three axes.

Framing

A vitally important component of formation is strategic framing: how a social movement manages to use "specific metaphors, symbolic representations, and cognitive clues to render or cast behavior and events in an evaluative mode and to suggest alterative modes of action" (McAdam, McCarthy, and Zald 1999, 262; also see Morris and Mueller 1992). Framing is in essence a competitive process in which different political frames compete for primacy in the public sphere. Successful social movements are able to (1) draw on existing cultural repertoires (see Tilly 1993; Tarrow 1994) to "win" the competitive process, at least with relevant constituencies if not with the population at large, by utilizing established narratives and myths, values, cultural themes, folklore, and ideology; (2) disseminate a specific frame, especially by attracting media attention, either because of the appeal of the way the issue has been framed or because of alliances with sympathetic media outlets; and (3) adapt the frame, and build on it, as circumstances change (Gamson and Meyer 1999).

In one recent formulation (Payne 2000), framing can be seen as a four-step process: naming, blaming, aiming, and claiming. "Naming" refers to identifying a problem as such, "blaming" means identifying the source of grievance, "aiming" is taking aim at a specific target that will solve the problem, and "claiming" means being able to demonstrate progress and claim victory over adversaries and thus keep the movement going by keeping constituents enthusiastic.

The Chilean human rights movement framed its mission in the starkest terms possible and was able to capture the attention of allies around the world. By naming the problem "human rights" (instead of "antiauthoritarian" or "prodemocracy," for example) the new movement was able to appeal directly to a nascent global struggle for human rights, thus fitting nicely into the cultural repertoire of a growing cosmopolitan liberal consensus about human rights norms, as well as an expanding international framework for addressing violations of human rights. As Garth and Dezalay (2001) put it,

The connection between Chile and the emergence of the international human rights movement emerged in part because of the central role that Chile had already been playing in northern political struggles. Chile was a focus of international contestation and concern about Allende and democratic transitions to socialism, and it remained very much in the news after Pinochet came to power. The Peace Committee—kept alive initially through the umbrella of the church—maintained links with *Le Monde*, *Time*, the U.N., Amnesty International, *The New York Times* and others who were coming by every day to report on the Chilean situation. Chile was news—the hot case of the day, reflected in the strong international presence. This attention helped to internationalize the strategies that the activists utilized. The people at [COPACHI] soon learned of Amnesty International, the International Commission of Jurists, the Organization of American States, and the international human rights instruments that had been created under U.N. auspices and were, in some cases, just coming into effect. The Vicariate soon became recognizable as a human rights organization.

Once authoritarian repression was named as a problem of "international human rights," the additional step of blaming (the dictatorship) allowed for a clear-cut strategy for solving it. Aiming could thus be facilitated in large part through what Keck and Sikkink (1998) call the "boomerang effect"; that is, petitioning other governments and intergovernmental organizations to exert pressure on the Chilean government. Moreover, framing the issue in this way attracted the attention of another set of institutions: international funders, in particular the Ford Foundation.[21] Increased funding helped lead to an assertive presence in Chile, the formation of important international alliances, and, most important, certain measurable victories, not least of which was Jimmy Carter's human rights policy beginning in 1976 and, a little more than a decade later, the replacement of Reagan's ambassador to Chile. In the long run, framing the issue in this way and appealing to an international audience helped the human rights movement contribute to the defeat of dictatorship.[22]

But framing the issue in this way also created problems for the human rights movement in a postauthoritarian context. By creating a binary and oppositional framework which identified the source of the problem (blaming) as the military regime, the human rights movement was cast adrift when this problem was removed. Although using the vocabulary of the international human rights movement was an excellent strategic tool, it is unclear to what degree the broader elements of human rights were incorporated into the Chilean movement.

The existence of a clear enemy meant that the HRM was less likely to branch out into multiple issue areas, especially those that could not be attributed to military rule. HROs did, in fact, have many different priorities, but the overarching goal of ending dictatorship was so strong that other issue areas often seemed irrelevant, impractical, or low priority. In this sense, the struggle for civil liberties, for example, or for social and economic rights, can be more accurately seen as the "struggle to end dictatorship so that civil rights can be improved" or the "struggle to rid ourselves of dictatorship so that we can work towards a more equitable society." The socialist and Communist parties did not nec-

essarily help diversify this focus, as they frequently called for revolution first and human rights second. Thus, the HRM during most of the
1970s and 1980s was, arguably, less a human rights movement as much
as it was a counterauthoritarian (or counterhegemonic) movement that
used the vocabulary of human rights. As one activist put it, "We were
fighting against the dictatorship, pure and simple. 'Human rights' gave
us a rich and useful framework—and one with which, of course, we
fully agreed—but we were not fighting as much for human rights as
we were for the end of Pinochet" (personal interview 1999).

This means that once the dictatorship was in fact over, the HRM
could, on one hand, claim victory. On the other hand, ironically, this
meant that the HRM's essential motivating force had been weakened.
Like many social movements, such as, arguably, the U.S. civil rights
movement (McAdam 1999), the HRM's decline was marked by its success in achieving its goal.

Institutionality

With its goals set toward toppling authoritarian rule, and with the
disarticulation of civil society well underway, the HRM was never able
to "take a breath" and consider its own institutionality, particularly in
terms of funding and local capacity building. A large influx of resources
from liberal governments and foundations, responding to the demand
of what was clearly a struggle for justice painted in stark terms, allowed HROs to build a strong but potentially ephemeral set of institutions. In each country, HROs specialized and carved out niches (such as
symbolic protest or legal advocacy), but the dependence of HROs on these
resources meant that they were never able to develop alternative sources
of viability. When dictatorships fell, so did HR institutions, as international funding dissipated. But it was not just funding that created this
problem. HROs—driven by a just mission and the complexities of the
context—had often chosen goal-oriented mechanisms to use the funding. The flip side to this was that they had often not been able to put
energy into developing broad bases of support, they were at times
internally hierarchical and unable to develop stakeholdership in staff
members, and they had frequently not been able to communicate among
themselves as to the most efficient division of labor among different
groups, thus setting a precedent that—although workable at the time,
given the context—would cause problems in the future.[23]

Forward-Looking Strategies

Because they were so concerned with the moment, and because it
was impossible to envision the details of a democratic future, it was

often difficult for HROs to develop long-term strategies for how to act after the end of authoritarianism. This is not surprising, but it did turn out to be problematic once democracy arrived. In effect, it meant that HROs found it difficult to adapt. The default strategy after democracy would thus become looking at the past.

A complicating factor here, of course, was the (arguably unavoidable) centrality of the experiences of victims. The victims of human rights abuses were, obviously, at the core of any struggle for human rights in Chile. The experiences of the victims were so dramatic and so evil that they could easily translate into anger and sadness, two powerful emotions that would help animate the struggle in Chile. When the dictatorship ended, the centrality on the experiences of victims remained.

TERROR AND DISMEMBERMENT OF CIVIL SOCIETY

At the same time as the HRM was emerging and fighting the dictatorship, authoritarian rulers were taking steps to destroy the fabric of a democratic civil society. The result was that civil sector actors, including HROs, found it difficult to reconfigure themselves into viable forces after the end of authoritarianism.

One of the primary goals of military rulers was, quite explicitly, to eliminate politics from the scene. The correct task of government was thought to be administration, and politics was thought to be a hindrance to good administration. As such, bureaucratic authoritarian rulers sought the efficient, administrative, and deideologized state, and they were willing to use repressive power to achieve it.

From just two examples, the university system and organized labor, it is clear that the underlying legal, social, and political foundations of a democratic society were severely undermined during the dictatorships in the region. Universities, for instance, were dramatically altered after the military took control. Entire departments were destroyed or repressed, student groups were demobilized, and academic administrators were replaced by military appointments. Organized labor was, of course, violently repressed, as were other civil-sector actors and organizations.

In addition to destroying existing civil-sector organizations, the military government was able to reduce political opportunities for future activity by removing access points into the political process that could serve as incentives for civil-sector participation. Without institutions to "invite" the participation of interested groups and individuals, civil society was further isolated. Thus, the authoritarian regime left a number of institutional legacies that would make it difficult for the HRM to reconstitute itself along interest-group lines. Interest groups require access points into governmental processes. With most vestiges of corporatism removed (which, in Chile, had included certain mechanisms for labor to be involved in decision making), and with no or few pluralist institutions in place, there would be few "opportunity structures" for a newly constituted HRM after 1990.[24]

THE TRANSITION

The literature on transitions to democracy establishes the importance of the mode of transition from authoritarian to democratic rule as a key moment in the recent history of new democracies.[25] For the purposes of this chapter, what is important is the "pacted" nature of the Chilean transition; specifically, the negotiations between the military and the Concertación leading up to the smooth transition and the handing over of the presidential mantle on March 11, 1990.

Although the Chilean human rights movement and other social movements (such as those generated by the popular sectors) had contributed greatly to the downfall of the military regime, these groups were largely not included in the discussions—which often took place behind closed doors—between representatives of the outgoing and incoming regimes between 1988 and 1990.[26]

The incoming government of Patricio Aylwin had a strong human rights platform, based on the twin pillars of "truth" and "reconciliation" that led to the creation of the Truth and Reconciliation Commission.[27] But there were at least three effects of the government's role. First, the government took control of human rights discourse on a national stage. By establishing a blue-ribbon commission on truth, the Aylwin government highlighted human rights and memory as central concerns. This created heightened awareness of the linkage between a discourse of rights, on the one hand, and a discourse of memory, truth, past atrocities, and history on the other. But the government's central role in establishing the truth commission and setting the tone of many discussions about the past also meant that HR activists were somewhat displaced. Those who were still committed to the struggle often found themselves interacting with the democratic government, which changes the dynamic of an oppositional force considerably.[28] In interviews, HR activists explained that on the one hand they were thrilled to have the government "on their side" for once, but at the same time,

Having the government's involvement actually diminished some of our energy, as I think we began to think that the struggle was really over and the government would take care of all our problems. This was stupid of us, of course, but at the time we were very excited about our victory against Pinochet. We were proud that *our* government was so involved in human rights. (personal interview 1998)

At a July 1999 conference in Peru, human rights leaders from all over Latin America convened to discuss the status and future of the human rights movement in the region.[29] The discussion emphasized five "policy arenas" that the human rights movement could seek to influence under a democratic system: the political policy arena (state and governmental institutions, law, regulations, and international institutions, such as the United Nations or World Bank), the private sector (multinational corporations, local business practices), civil society (strengthening the power and voice of nongovernmental organizations [NGOs] and popular organizations), political culture (creating cultural norms that favor human rights), and individual consciousness (fostering individual self-worth, and thus leading people to make demands in terms of their rights). These five policy arenas were seen as wholly different than the situation under authoritarianism, where speaking of policy arenas would have made little sense. Indeed, political life was so dominated by the military government that it is not surprising that the movement would have a basically two-level approach to fighting it: contestation on the national level and influence on the international level.

The nine major human rights organizations in Chile remain, in general, deeply connected to the authoritarian period. By prioritizing justice for past human rights abuses, they have made inroads into challenging state impunity and holding perpetrators of what Carlos Nino (1996, following Arendt) calls "radical evil" accountable for their actions. They have, in this sense, contributed to Chilean democratization by demanding that the rule of law apply to perpetrators from Pinochet down. Some (SERPAJ, AFDD, and, most significant, the Chilean Commission on Human Rights) have virtually disbanded. The Vicaria—once one of the world's most important human rights groups—has become a human rights archive with two full-time staff members. Others (e.g., PIDEE, FASIC) have attempted to develop human rights education, but with tiny staffs and little expertise in this field. The policy arenas discussed at the Peru conference continue to represent future challenges for most human rights groups in Chile. In the meantime, the past remains the primary focus of contestation.

CONCLUSION

The Latin American human rights movement faces major challenges, especially concerning its role in postauthoritarian contexts. Born under dictatorship, the human rights movement in the Southern Cone has thus far been comparatively timid about using its once-powerful voice to criticize the region's still-incomplete democracies. This is changing, however. Two major events in the past decade—specifically, the confessions of Francisco Scilingo in Argentina and the arrest of

Pinochet in London—have helped revitalize the movement and give it added energy.[30] Still, the past remains the primary battleground for the articulation of human rights concerns.

In Chile, the rise of the HRM was a direct result of severe repression under dictatorship, and the HRM was greatly influenced by these origins.[31] It came to life at a moment when civil society was under attack and severely repressed. At the same time, the HROs themselves became organized according to the logic of "no to dictatorship," which made it difficult for them to adapt to the multiple issues they would face under democratic rule. They were never fully able to develop sustainable institutionality that would last beyond the fall of dictators, nor were they practiced in other elements of the human rights struggle, and had never been able to articulate forward-looking strategies for the next stage under political democracy.

It is an enormous challenge for social movements to adapt to changed circumstances, and the Chilean HRM is no exception. It has withered substantially (although it may now be on the brink of a renaissance). What remains is a smaller but still committed group of activists and HROs dedicated to a focus on the past (either past as past or past as present): They continue to struggle against authoritarianism, which has always been—and continues to be—at the core of the mission of the HRM.

An important part of the remaining movement is focused on archives and building archives as a source of counterhegemonic truth. By creating human rights archives, HR activists suggest that they can help construct a narrative of the past that gives adequate emphasis to the pain and suffering of victims of human rights abuses. Archives are thus seen as both an activist tool (i.e., because they contain living documents, documents that are still relevant to the pursuit of justice) and a source of ammunition on a broader and more complex battlefield, the battlefield of historical memory.

As the movement seeks to built itself anew under current conditions, it faces, and will continue to face, enormous challenges. Perhaps most important among these is, as Argentine activist Martín Abegú (quoted in Basombrío 2000) puts it, "building a human rights movement that transcends its beginnings yet maintains the legitimacy derived from those earlier struggles."

NOTES

1. A version of this chapter was presented at the Latin American Studies Association meeting in Miami, Florida, March 16–18, 2000.

2. Some representative texts that have attempted to capture the idea of "legacies," even when they do not necessarily use the term, include Jelin and

Hershberg (1996), Corradi, Fagen, and Garreton (1992), Malamud-Goti (1996), Nino (1996), and Feitlowitz (1998). In addition, there is large nonacademic literature on this subject, including Rosenberg (1996), and Weschler (1998).

3. This is clear from numerous interviews and firsthand observation, and also raised in, for example, Garth and Dezalay (2001). Also see Orellana and Hutchison (1991). Keck and Sikkink's (1998, 79–121) examination of the human rights advocacy networks is also instructive.

4. There are at least two other organizations that are worth mentioning, although one—*Servicio Paz y Justicia* (SERPAJ)—has virtually disappeared altogether and the other—the Association of Relatives of Politically Executed Persons (AFEP)—is very small and specialized.

5. Although practically no one in Chile contests the number 3,000—the approximate number of officially documented cases of death or disappearance—HR activists often point out that, first, the number could be larger and, second, the number does not include torture victims or other victims who were not killed.

6. For a good theoretical exploration of the idea of "eruptions," see Wilde (1999).

7. See Nino (1996) for an explanation of this concept historically, globally, and in Argentina.

8. Including, for example, retired Gen. Humberto Gordon, a former head of the Central Nacional de Inteligencia (CNI; secret police); Brigadier Gen. Arturo Alvarez Scoglia, former director of the Army Intelligence Directorate (DINE); Sergio Arellano Stark, indicted for his responsibility in the so-called Caravan of Death case involving the aggravated kidnapping of nineteen political prisoners in October 1973; and Humberto Leiva Gutierrez and Hugo Salas Wenzel, both charged as authors of the deaths in 1987 of twelve members of the Manuel Rodríguez Patriotic Front (FPMR) in the case known as Operation Albania.

9. For Chile, the places used as torture and detention centers during military rule are listed in the Rettig report. An excellent adaptation of the information from the Rettig report, plus some additional "sites of memory," can be found at the Derechos Chile Web site (http://www.derechoschile.com). There is an *animita* to the *degollados*, a group of five men who had their throats slit in 1985, on the side of the highway in Quilicura near the national airport, and one near the bullet-pocked wall of a cemetery (Parque del Recuerdo) in the northern part of Santiago. There are small commemorative plaques at the Colegio de Profesores de Chile (2394 Moneda), the Colegio de Medicos (Esmaraldo 678), and the Clinica San Juan Sotero del Rio (Matcuna and Huerfanos). Other examples of these kinds of expressive gestures include a small memorial park in La Reina (near Tobalaba and J. Rivera). Similar efforts were made in various regions, such as in the cities of Concepción, Temuco, and Antofagasta.

10. More information on Villa Grimaldi can be found in both the Rettig report and at the Derechos Chile Web site (http://www.derechoschile.com).

11. This activity received an added boost in the region when the Ford Foundation convened an international workshop to discuss archiving human rights documents. My involvement in organizing this workshop makes it difficult

for me to evaluate it neutrally, but I have recently done a follow-up report, six months later. One impact of this workshop concerns the convocational power of the Ford Foundation to highlight an area of interest, draw attention to it, and encourage activity. Everyone I interviewed told me that the preservation of human rights documents is now on the agenda in a way that it was not before. One activist went so far as to suggest a paradigm shift in thinking about documents within human rights organizations. Another suggested that the workshop served as a consolidating moment, consolidating a theme that had existed before but could now be considered an important line of activity within the human rights movement in Latin America.

12. These are the words of Raphael Samuel (1994), who is actually discussing British museums and the "heritage" movement. The words—and Samuel's ideas in this book—seem appropriate for the current discussion.

13. There are clearly exceptions to these general statements. For example, Human Rights Watch undertook an extensive study on freedom of expression in Chile, and cases of censorship of journalists—such as Alejandra Matus, who wrote an exposé of the Chilean judiciary—have aroused much ire and action.

14. The minimum scope of these human rights abuses are clearly documented in the major publication on the subject: the Chilean Truth and Reconciliation Report (or Rettig Commission Report). In addition, Human Rights Watch/ Americas, Amnesty International, the Inter-American Commission on Human Rights of the Organization of American States (OAS), various United Nations agencies, the International Commission of Jurists, the U.S. State Department, and Freedom House, among others, have all documented these violations.

15. I am grateful to Alex Wilde for first bringing this idea to my attention during numerous discussions in Chile in 1998, although he may or may not agree with the direction in which I take this core notion.

16. For a discussion of path dependency and "critical junctures," see Collier and Collier (1993).

17. Much of the following paragraphs has been influenced by McAdam, McCarthy, and Zald (1999).

18. Jo Freeman (Freeman and Johnson 1999, 20) points out that strain from women from 1955 to 1965 was as great, if not greater, than after 1965, yet the women's movement as we know it today really began after organizational networks had emerged and movement activists were able to pull these together into a bona fide movement.

19. Although the military did raze certain poor sectors and, in a feat of perverse urban planning, managed by 1990 to push shantytowns to the distant outskirts of the city.

20. The Comite de Cooperacion para la Paz en Chile (COPACHI) was formed as early as October 1973 to provide assistance to victims of repression. Other organizations, such as La Vicaria and FASIC, would emerge soon afterward.

21. Keck and Sikkink (1998) provide an excellent overview of the ways in which the Ford Foundation helped contribute to the emerging human rights movement in Chile.

22. This is one of the key points made by two recent works on human rights and democratic transitions: Barahona de Brito (1997), and Brysk (1994).

23. This was further complicated by suspicion and ideological divisions.

24. For a discussion of opportunity structures and interest groups, see McCann (1986). For a discussion of post–1990 political institutions in Chile and pluralist openings for political participation in Chile, see Bickford (1998).

25. This literature is obviously voluminous. Some representative texts of this literature include O'Donnell and Schmitter (1986), Karl and Schmitter (1991), and Huntington (1996).

26. This is another key point made by Barahona de Brito (1997) and Brysk (1994).

27. The results of the Truth and Reconciliation Commission have been published in English and Spanish. Also see Barahona de Brito (1997), Garretón (1995), Hayner (1994), and Zalaquett (1993).

28. For example, projects such as the Truth Commission, the Memorial Wall, and the early stages of the creation of the Villa Grimaldi Peace Park all involved, to a greater or lesser degree, individual members of the government and/or direct participation by the government per se (as in the case of the Truth Commission).

29. Much of the following is taken from Yamin (1999).

30. Horcaio Verbitsky's (1996) book, *The Flight* (*El Vuelo*), is the best source on Scilingo, and Feitlowitz's (1998) chapter on the "Sciligo Effect" is exceptional.

31. Other factors also have to be considered, such as increasing global acceptance of human rights norms, the role of the church, and the role of revolutionary movements in articulating grievance.

BIBLIOGRAPHY

Abuelas de la Plaza de Mayo. 1990. *Niños Desaparecidos en Argentina desde 1976*. Buenos Aires: Abuelas de la Plaza de Mayo.

Barahona de Brito, Alexandra. 1997. *Human Rights and Democratization in Latin America*. Oxford: Oxford University Press.

Basombrío, Carlos. 2000. "Looking Ahead: New Challenges for Human Rights Advocacy." *ANCLA* 34: 7–11.

Bickford, Louis. 1995. "Civil Society and Its Applicability in the Third World." *Labour, Capital and Society* 28 (2): 203–214.

———. 1998. *Public Participation, Political Institutions and Democracy in Chile, 1990–1997*. Santiago: FLACSO.

———. 1999. "The Archival Imperative." *Human Rights Quarterly* 21 (4): 1097–1122.

———. 2000. "Human Rights Archives and Research on Historical Memory: Argentina, Chile, and Uruguay." *Latin American Research Review* 35 (2): 160–182.

Brünner, Jose Joaquín, and Guillermo Sunkel. 1992. *Conocimiento, Sociedad y Política*. Santiago: FLACSO.

Brysk, Alison. 1994. *The Politics of Human Rights in Argentina*. Stanford, Calif.: Stanford University Press.

Caldeira, Teresa. 1996. "Crime and Individual Rights: Violence in Latin America." In *Constructing Democracy: Human Rights, Citizenship and Society in Latin America*, edited by Elizabeth Jelin and Eric Hershberg. Boulder, Colo.: Westview Press.

Castells, Manuel. 1983. *The City and the Grassroots*. Berkeley and Los Angeles: University of California Press.

Collier, Ruth Berins, and David Collier. 1993. *Shaping the Political Arena: Critical Junctures, the Labor Movement, and Regime Dynamics in Latin America*. Princeton, N. J.: Princeton University Press.

Corradi, J. E., P. W. Fagen, and M. A. Garreton, eds. 1992. *Fear at the Edge: State Terror and Resistance in Latin America*. Berkeley and Los Angeles: University of California Press.

Eckstein, Susan, ed. 1989. *Power and Popular Protest: Latin American Social Movements*. Berkeley and Los Angeles: University of California Press.

Escobar, Arturo, and Sonia Alvarez, eds. 1992. *The Making of Social Movements in Latin America: Identity, Strategy, and Democracy*. Boulder, Colo.: Westview Press.

Feitlowitz, Marguerite. 1998. *A Lexicon of Terror: Argentina and the Legacies of Torture*. New York: Oxford University Press.

Freeman, Jo, and Victoria Johnson, eds. 1999. *Waves of Protest: Social Movements since the Sixties*. New York: Rowan and Littlefield.

Gamson, William A., and David S. Meyer. 1999. "Framing Political Opportunities." In *Comparative Perspectives on Social Movements: Political Opportunities, Mobilizing Structures, and Cultural Framings*, edited by Doug McAdam, John D. McCarthy, and Mayer Zald. Cambridge Studies in Comparative Politics. Cambridge: Cambridge University Press.

Garretón, Manuel Antonio. 1995. "Derechos Humanos y Democratización." In *Hacia una nueva era política*. Santiago: Fondo de Cultura Económica.

Garth, Bryant, and Yves Dezalay. (2001). "Constructing Law Out of Power: Investing in Human Rights as an Alternative Political Strategy." In *Global Cause Lawyering*, edited by Stuart Scheingold and Austin Sarat. New York: Oxford University Press.

Hayner, Priscilla. 1994. "Fifteen Truth Commissions—1974–1994: A Comparative Study." *Human Rights Quarterly* 16: 597–655.

Huntington, Samuel. 1996. "Democracy for the Long Haul." *Journal of Democracy* 7 (2): 3–13.

Hutchison, Liz. 1999. *Rapporteur's Report. Preserving Historical Memory: Documents and Human Rights Archives in the Southern Cone*. Santiago: Ford Foundation Office of the Andes and the Southern Cone.

ILAS (Instituto Latinoamericano de Salud Mental y Derechos Humanos). 1996. *Reparación, Derechos Humanos y Salud Mental*. Santiago: ILAS.

Jelin, Elizabeth, and Eric Hershberg, eds. 1996. *Constructing Democracy: Human Rights, Citizenship and Society in Latin America*. Boulder, Colo.: Westview Press.

Karl, Terry Lynn, and Philippe Schmitter. 1991. "Modes of Transition in Latin America, Southern and Eastern Europe." *International Social Sciences Journal* 128: 269–284.

Keane, John, ed. 1988. *Civil Society and the State: New European Perspectives*. London: Verso.

Keck, Margaret, and Katheryn Sikkink. 1998. *Activists Beyond Borders*. Ithaca, N.Y.: Cornell University Press.

Linz, Juan, and Alfred Stepan. 1996. *Problems of Democratic Transition and Consolidation*. Baltimore: Johns Hopkins University Press.

Loveman, Brian. 1992–1993. "Protected Democracies and Military Guardianship: Political Transitions in Latin America, 1978–1993." *Journal of Inter-American Studies and World Affairs* 36(2): 105–189.

Mainwaring, Scott, Guillermo O'Donnell, and Samuel Valenzuela, eds. 1992. *Issues in Democratic Consolidation: The New South American Democracies in Comparative Perspective*. Notre Dame, Ind.: University of Notre Dame Press.

Malamud-Goti, Jaime. 1996. *Game without End: State Justice and the Politics of Justice*. Norman: University of Oklahoma Press.

McAdam, Doug. 1999. "The Decline of the Civil Rights Movement." In *Waves of Protest: Social Movements since the Sixties*, edited by Jo Freeman and Victoria Johnson. New York: Rowan and Littlefield.

McAdam, Doug, John D. McCarthy, and Mayer Zald, eds. 1999. *Comparative Perspectives on Social Movements: Political Opportunities, Mobilizing Structures, and Cultural Framings*. Cambridge Studies in Comparative Politics. Cambridge: Cambridge University Press.

McCann, Michael. 1986. *Taking Reform Seriously: Perspectives on Public Interest Liberalism*. Ithaca, N.Y.: Cornell University Press.

Morris, Aldon, and Carol McClurg Mueller, eds. 1992. *Frontiers in Social Movement Theory*. New Haven, Conn.: Yale University Press.

Nino, Carlos Santiago. 1996. *Radical Evil on Trial*. New Haven, Conn.: Yale University Press.

O'Donnell, Guillermo, and Philippe Schmitter. 1986. *Transitions from Authoritarian Rule: Tentative Conclusions about Uncertain Democracies*. Baltimore: Johns Hopkins University Press.

Orellana, Patricio, and Elizabeth Quay Hutchison. 1991. *El Movimiento de derechos humanos en Chile, 1973–1990*. Santiago: Centro de Estudios Políticos Latinoamericanos.

Oxhorn, Philip. 1995. *Organizing Civil Society: The Popular Sectors and the Struggle for Democracy in Chile*. University Park: Pennsylvania State University Press.

Payne, Leigh. 2000. *Uncivil Movements: The Armed Right Wing and Democracy in Latin America*. Baltimore: Johns Hopkins University Press.

Rettig Guissen, Raúl. 1991. *Informe de la Commission Nacional de Verdad y Reconciliación*. Santiago: Government of Chile.

Rosenberg, Tina. 1996. *The Haunted Land: Facing Europe's Ghosts after Communism*. New York: Vintage Books.

Salamon, Lester, and Helmut Anheier. 1994. *The Emerging Sector: The Non-Profit Sector in Comparative Perspective*. Baltimore: Johns Hopkins University Press.

Samuel, Raphael. 1994. *Theaters of Memory*. London: Verso.

Schedler, Andres. 1998. "What Is Democratic Consolidation." *Journal of Democracy* 9: 2.

Shriver, Donald. 1995. *An Ethic for Enemies: Forgiveness in Politics*. New York: Oxford University Press.

Sieder, Rachel, ed. 1995. *Impunity in Latin America*. London: Institute of Latin American Studies.

Sikkink, Kathryn. 1996. "The Emergence, Evolution, and Effectiveness of the Latin American Human Rights Network." In *Constructing Democracy: Human Rights, Citizenship and Society in Latin America*, edited by Elizabeth Jelin and Eric Hershberg. Boulder, Colo.: Westview Press.

Stepan, Alfred. 1988. *Rethinking Military Politics: Brazil and the Southern Cone*. Princeton, N.J.: Princeton University Press.

Tarrow, Sidney. 1994. *Power in Movement: Social Movemetns, Collective Action and Politics*. Cambridge: Cambridge University Press.

Tilly, Charles. 1993. Modular Collective Action and the Rise of the Social Movement." *Politics and Society* 21: 69–90.

Valenzuela, J. Samuel. 1992. "Democratic Consolidation in Post-Transitional Settings." In *Issues in Democratic Consolidation: The New South American Democracies in Comparative Perspective*, edited by Scott Mainwaring, Guillermo O'Donnell, and Samuel Valenzuela. Notre Dame, Ind.: University of Notre Dame Press.

Varas, Augusto. 1997. "Democratización y políticas públicas." In *Cambio Social y Políticas Públicas*, edited by Raúl Urzúa. Santiago: Centro de Analísis de Políticas Públicas.

———. 1997. "Los nuevos desafíos democraticos: Fiscalización y poder ciudadano." *Vida y Derecho* 19: 8.

Verbitsky, Horacio. 1996. *The Flight: Confessions of an Argentine Dirty Warrior*. New York: New York Press.

Vilas, Carlos. 1997. "Participation, Inequality and the Whereabouts of Democracy." In *The New Politics of Inequality in Latin America*, edited by Douglas Chalmers, Carlos M. Vilas, Katherine Hite, Scott B. Martin, Kerlahne Pilster, and Monique Segarra. New York: Oxford University Press.

Weschler, Lawrence. 1998. *A Miracle, a Universe: Settling Accounts with Torturers*. Chicago: University of Chicago Press.

Wilde, Alex. 1999. "Irruptions of Memory: Expressive Politics in Chile's Transition to Democracy." *Journal of Latin American Studies* 31: 473–500.

Yamin, Alicia. 1999. *Facing the 21st Century: Challenges and Strategies for the Latin American Human Rights Community: A Rapporteur's Report*. Washington, D.C.: WOLA. Much of this report can be found on the Web site: http://www.wola.org/hrworkshopintro.html.

Zalaquett, José. 1993. Introduction to the English Edition. *Report of the Chilean Commission on Truth and Reconciliation*. Notre Dame, Ind.: Notre Dame University Press.

CHAPTER 3

Venezuela and Colombia: Governability as the Social Construction of Democracy

Elsa Cardozo Da Silva

Since the mid-1990s the fragility of Latin American democracies has become apparent in what appears to be a new cycle of democratic deconsolidation. Venezuela and Colombia are very interesting cases because both countries have enjoyed the advantage of relatively lasting democratic stability, but also demonstrate the fragility and potential deconsolidation of their democratic institutions. Venezuela and Colombia have been suffering strong pressures over ineffective and discredited institutions, weakened democratic practices, and fragile social commitment to democratic values.

In accordance with the theme propounded in the introduction to this book, I discuss commonalities in these cases in order to improve our understanding of the current challenges and democratic prospects of each country. In so doing, I explore recent and current problems in the social construction of democracy in Colombia and Venezuela. First, I review the concept of governability from the perspective of its social construction. Second, I identify similarities in these two Andean countries, whose democracies, until recent times considered stable and strong, have begun to show enormous fragility.

The argument is presented in four sections: (1) an approach to the regional situation, (2) a review of the discourse of democracy and its governability, (3) an analysis of the vicious circle created by the over-extension of consociational systems of social negotiation, and (4) an approach to the present opportunities for the social construction of democracy.

THE CURRENT SITUATION IN THE REGION

Virtually all major political actors in new democracies publicly declare their allegiance to democratic norms, yet some actors behave in ways seemingly designed to undermine those norms.

(Peceny 1999, 99)

There has been extensive and intense academic attention and debate concerning the problems of democratic governability (DG). The "fault-lines" of this debate are democratic post-transitions, the difficulties for politicians to learn how to manage redemocratization, the generalized discontent with democracy, and the political management of economic reform (Wiarda 1995; Hadenius 1997; Agüero and Stark 1998; McCoy 2000a). Moreover, there is an enormous gap between the academic and political discourse, on the one hand, and the practical consequences of it, on the other. A major contribution of this debate has been to show how democratic governability is an issue that comprises both a wide range of aspects and a broad diversity of reflection. Among the many approaches to the present and future of democratic governability, the literature that deals with the analysis of consolidation and deconsolidation is of particular relevance to this chapter.

The cycle of democratization that could be reaching its end—or at least is in serious distress—commenced in the 1970s and extended worldwide. In Latin America it began with the return to civilian rule and elected governments through fair and competitive processes, as well as with the adoption of programs for economic adjustment and reform. The Andean countries were part of this dynamic, since elections marked the return of civilian governments in Ecuador (1978), Peru (1980), and Bolivia (1982). Also, economic reforms oriented by neoliberal criteria were early initiated in Bolivia and extended to all the Andean countries within the particular conditions of each economy. Venezuela and Colombia, with their longer democratic experience, were part of this cycle, since both countries initiated economic and political reforms, although at a dissimilar pace as well as at different moments and through varying forms. Figure 3.1 shows economic, social, and political data for five Andean countries.

All those efforts notwithstanding, the aggravation of sociopolitical and economic pressures over fragile democratic institutions continued. From 1992 onward, even the officers of international multilateral organizations such as the International Monetary Fund, the World

Bank, and the Inter-American Development Bank would recognize that the region's suffering derived from much more than economic deficits (Naím 1995; BID 1997, 1998, 1999). Indeed, it was impossible to ignore the social and political consequences of the policies introduced in the 1980s and 1990s: "It was not merely 'growth without redistribution.' It amounted to growth with further polarization and an expansion of poverty" (Robinson 1999, 48). The political analysts placed new emphasis on the study of both the obstacles for democratic consolidation and the factors that could lead to deconsolidation even in apparently stable democracies (Hillman 1994; Torres-Rivas 1995; Stokes 1995; Wiarda 1995).[1]

Currently there is scant reason to believe that the proportions of the problem presented in the *Latinobarómetro* 1998 study will be ameliorated any time soon. The study found that one-third of Latin Americans remained unsatisfied with democracy, while at least one-third was indifferent to or explicitly in favor of the establishment of authoritarian governments (Welch and Carrasquero 1998; Hakim 2000, 107; BID 1999). The final decade of the twentieth century offers us a terribly negative balance: economic growth that is less than half the rate obtained between 1960 and 1970; more than half the national income concentrated in a seventh part of the population, which makes Latin America the region with the worst income distribution in the world; the deterioration of public services and of the capabilities of the state to deal with education, health, security, and justice; as well as a lack of enough qualified human resources when compared to countries of similar income (Hakim 2000, 105–109; Robinson 1999, 45–50; BID 1999).

As a matter of fact, diverse authors as well as opinion and attitudinal studies have issued warnings about the predisposition of a growing number of people to concede crucial aspects of democratic values and procedures to authoritarian governments that they increasingly believe offer stability, order, and prosperity (Hakim 2000; Hadenius 1997).

In a variety of different ways this temptation has been more and more conspicuous in Latin America, and certainly in the Andean countries. Among them, Colombia and Venezuela have very interesting profiles that—despite their specific manifestations—make the two of them important cases that illustrate a sustained process of deconsolidation that is very difficult to overcome. Both were stable sociopolitical and economic systems during almost all the second half of the twentieth century. The model of consociational democracy was chosen to create this stability: In the two countries there were explicit arrangements among the elites to build governability from a system of alternation, democratic freedoms, and competence. Indeed, the stability reached through the consociational arrangements (Pacto de Punto Fijo in Venezuela and Frente Nacional in Colombia) created certain pat-

Figure 3.1
Andean Countries: Economic, Social, and Political Data

	Venezuela	Colombia	Perú	Ecuador	Bolivia
Human Development Rank / Index 1998 (1)	65 / 0.770	68 / 0.754	80 / 0.737	91 / 0.722	114 / 0.643
Population: Total in millions / urban % (1998) (1)	23.2 / 86.8	40.8 / 74.1	24.8 / 72.0	12.2 / 61.1	8.0 / 63.2
Latest return to democracy (2) and constitutional reform (3)	1958 / 1999	1958 / 1991	1980 / 1992	1978 / 1998	1982 / 1994
Share of income or consumption (1987-1998): Poorest 20% / Richest 20% (1)	3.7 / 53.1	3.0 / 60.9	4.4 / 51.2	5.4 / 49.7	5.6 / 48.2
Adult illiteracy (% age 15 and above)(1998)(1)	8.0	8.8	10.8	9.4	15.6
Per capita income 1980 / 1998 (1995 US $) (1)	3,995 / 3,499	1,868 / 2,392	2,777 / 2,392	1,547 / 1,562	1,016 / 964
Average rate of change GDP per capita 1975-1998 (1995 US $) (1)	-0.8	1.7	-0.4	0.8	-0.2
Average rate of change GDP per capita 1975-1998 (1995 U.S. $) (1)	-0.8	1.7	-0.4	0.8	-0.2
Life expectancy at birth (years) 1970-75 / 1999-2000 (1)	65.7 / 72.4	61.6 / 70.4	55.5 / 68.3	58.8 / 69.5	46.7 / 61.4

34

Access to information flows: Televisions / computers / internet hosts (per 1,000 people, 1996-1998) (1)	185 / 43 / 0.34	217 / 28 / 0.44	144 / 18 / 0.19	293 / .. / 0.13	115 / .. / 0.08
Public expenditure as % of GNP: Education 1995-97/ health 1996-98 / military 1998 (1)	5.2 / 1.0 / 1.3	4.4 / 1.5 / 2.6	2.9 / 2.2 / ..	3.5 / 2.5 / ..	4.9 / 1.1 / 1.8
Average annual rate of deforestation (1990-95) / Carbon dioxide emmissions as % of world total (1)	1.1 / 0.6	0.5 / 0.3	0.3 / 0.1	1.6 / 0.1	1.2 / ..
Democracy ratings in 1980-81 and 1999-2000: Political rights, civil liberties (4)	1,2,F / 4,4,PF	2,3,F / 4,4,F	2,3,F / 5,4,PF	2,2,F / 2,3,F	7,5,NF / 5,5,PF

(1) UNDP 2000.

(2) Cardozo Da Silva 1995.

(3) FUNEDA 1999.

(4) Freedom House 2000. "The characters representing scores are, from left to right, political rights, civil liberties, and freedom status. Each of the first two is measured on a one-to-seven scale, with one representing the highest degree of freedom and seven the lowest. 'F', 'PF', and 'NF' respectively stand for 'free', 'partly free', and 'not free'. Countries whose political rights and civil liberties fall between 1.0 and 2.5 are designated 'free'; between 3.0 and 5.5 'partly free' and between 5.5 and 7.0 'not free'."

terns of governance among elite groups, patterns that undoubtedly
survived the formal term of each pact (Peeler 1985, 25; Hillman 1994;
Hillman and Cardozo Da Silva, 1997).

Certainly, since the 1960s both Colombia and Venezuela maintained
a certain degree of economic stability, regular and uninterrupted electoral processes, and even institutional attempts to reform the state.
Nevertheless, a dynamics of deconsolidation of democracy developed
and accelerated since the 1980s in both cases. The particular blend of
objective and subjective conditions that surround their processes requires a very refined analysis, one that can contribute to the understanding of the way each society is managing to deal with its own
circumstances.

Following is an exposition of basic common characteristics behind
the particularities of the two processes, with the purpose of contributing to a better comprehension of fundamental obstacles and opportunities for the construction of democracy.

THE SOCIAL DISCOURSE OF DEMOCRACY
AND DEMOCRATIC GOVERNABILITY

"When *I* use a word," Humpty Dumpty said, in rather a scorn-
ful tone, "it means just what I Choose it to mean—neither more
nor less."

"The question is," said Alice, "whether you *can* make words
mean so many different things."

"The question is," said Humpty Dumpty, "which is to be the
master—that's all."

(Lewis Carroll, *Through the Looking Glass*, cited by Dahl 1998, 100)

Democracy as a Social Construction

The most interesting and promising approaches to democracy and
democratic governability focus on cultural, normative, and institutional conditions that favor democracy (Diamond 1994). It is by means
of these conceptual lenses that the structural, material, or objective
conditions promoting democratic practices are better understood. This
is especially important when studying consolidation and deconsolidation of democracy. While transitions can and have usually happened
in the midst of very undetermined and uncertain political processes
dominated by strategic decisions of a few, consolidation "involves a
recursive process that approximates the political dynamics anticipated
by a constructivist approach" (Peceny 1999, 98). This approach assumes
that the conditions that characterize and reproduce democracy are
neither "given" nor "objective." Therefore, our perspectives on de-

mocracy should consider both the meanings that social actors give to those conditions and the identities of such actors.[2]

The aspect to emphasize, therefore, is the social process involved in the construction of democracy. From this perspective, and following Peceny's (1999) argument, it is possible to illuminate certain basic things to be considered in the cases of Venezuela and Colombia. First, the construction of democracy requires that actors perceive democracy as the legitimate and normal way of conducting politics in such a way that the daily practice reinforces its legitimacy and strengthens its institutions. Second, it invites us to pay special attention to the values and attitudes of the elite, "arguably those who have the most to gain in engaging in strategic deception" (Peceny 1999, 99). These two considerations provide very important orientations for the exploration of the Venezuelan and Colombian cases.

Certainly, the social constructivist approach helps to reintroduce the problems of democratic governability with a more comprehensive, complex, and critical perspective about the present obstacles to and possibilities for democratic governments in Venezuela and Colombia. The review of the discourse on democratic governability—both political and academic—deserves attention to the concepts of democracy and governability.

Democracy: Conceptions and Meanings

Beyond the basic idea of democracy as the government of the people, there is, as Sørensen (1993) reminds us, a broad range of conceptions between the restricted Schumpeterian democracy as a political method to select political leaders through elections and David Held's (1997) idea of democratic autonomy as the creation of social, economic, cultural, physical, and political conditions to offer to each person the opportunity to determine the development of his or her own life.

In spite of that variety, there is a classic set of criteria that help us— as both citizens and analysts—to identify certain arrangements, practices and institutions that are typical of modern representative democracies.[3] Robert A. Dahl (1998, 85) has presented those conditions in his writings on "poliarchy": elected officials; free, fair, and frequent elections; freedom of expression; alternative sources of information; associational autonomy; and inclusive citizenship. Those criteria are crucial for a "political democracy" (Sørensen 1993, 11–13), so that even the political qualification of a country as a democracy goes far beyond the mere realization of elections. The minimum components for a political democracy are civic competence and participation, as well as the political and civic freedom that allow for the citizens to be equally entitled to express, formulate, and promote their preferences among them and before their government (Dahl 1989; Sørensen 1993).

From the perspective of Latin American societies, the discontent with democracy refers to a long list of deficits in its social, cultural, economic, and political outcomes. The main risk—quite apparent in the current processes of Venezuelan and Colombian societies—is the persistence of a rhetorical approach to democracy and democratic governability. Such a perspective proclaims the virtues of democracy while also creating a huge gray zone by socially promoting responses and behaviors that do not contribute to the social reconstruction of democratic institutions. Therefore, the generalized discontent with the limited achievements of political democracy—except in papers, books, and analysis—tends to promote behaviors that undermine the concept and the practice of democracy.

Indeed, democracy is usually considered and evaluated through both its basic components—associated with democratic autonomy—and the socially specific conditions from which it is adapted by each society (Domínguez and Lowenthal 1996; Achard and Flores 1997). Here, the cultural dimensions are tremendously important, and in the cases of Venezuela and Colombia, as well as in all of Latin America and the Hispanic Caribbean, the recursive process visible in cycles of democratic and authoritarian rule has been well analyzed from the perspective of the hybrid culture, one that accounts for the mixture of premodern and modern ideas and practices, *caudillismo*, authoritarianism and militarism mixed with civilian rule, and republican practices (Wiarda 1990, 31–57; Hillman 1997, 345–350). This is the perspective from which the concept of democratic governability will be revisited.

Democratic Governability:
Its Social Construction and Negotiation

Since the 1970s, political and academic discourse have given special importance to democratic governability. Specifically, governability has been understood as the capacity of a government to act under two conditions: legitimacy and efficacy (Arbós and Giner 1996). That is why democratic governability emerged as such an important consideration in the last third of the twentieth century: the transitions to democracy and the socioeconomic and political pressures for their renewal—which was the case in Venezuela and Colombia—made apparent the problems of efficacy and legitimacy of the two governments (Jácome 1997).

Accordingly, the concept of governability was enriched, precisely through the pressure of social and economic dynamics.[4] Beyond the basic concept, the idea of the social construction of democracy permits elaboration of the notion of democratic governability in a way that provides certain criteria to compare the current situations of Colombia and Venezuela.

- DG means governmental control, but is more than that, since it is associated to the idea and practice of good government, of government for the people.[5]
- DG is not just a "top-down" dynamic, though it presupposes the effective existence of regulations and governmental controls that allow for high-quality decision making.
- DG is not just a "bottom-up" dynamic, though it includes and incorporates it in different moments of decision making.
- DG doesn't mean harmony; it is actually constructed upon the recognition of social conflict as a result of the encounter of private of individual interests in the public space.
- DG is not built up in just the public sphere of human action, since individuals and organizations acting privately affect the public interests and relations, and collective interchanges affect private interests and relations.
- DG is not just a dynamic within societies, but has increasingly extended to the relations among societies, as well as to international and transnational relations.
- DG is not just a political phenomenon in the more restrictive form of governments–citizens relations, since it incorporates all manifestations of social life, from economics to culture; political and civil society.
- DG is, in brief, a social negotiation system that creates and recreates an integrative dynamics, one that privileges the creation over the claiming of values.

In essence, democratic governability is part of the dynamic that contributes to the social construction of democracy beyond restrictive political, national, and public limits. That dynamic operates as a social negotiation system that has the possibility to create and recreate democratic practices. It is a complex negotiation, since it incorporates not only diverse counterparts—individuals and groups—but also different levels of societal, national, international, and transnational interaction. It is a multilateral, multilevel negotiation through which democracy can be socially constructed.

Venezuela and Colombia are both in a process in which the old arrangements (social negotiation systems) have been decaying and moving toward collapse. Although in each society this appears in different ways, there is a similar challenge to construct a new pattern of social relations, one that is hopefully democratic. What would make this dynamic a democratic one? The most important condition is the social predisposition to negotiate, to engage in dialogue, and to construct certain rules to deal with diversity and conflict, oriented by the objective of creating and recreating a language of cooperation, not just among elites but among the whole society (Barragán 1990).

With these ideas in mind, the next section of this chapter proposes how the future of democracy in Venezuela and Colombia depends on the construction of a new social negotiation system.

COLOMBIAN AND VENEZUELAN DEMOCRACY: THE PRESENT AND FUTURE OF NEGOTIATIONS

[El reto es] situarse en el presente, en referencia al pasado, para pensar el futuro (The challenge is to conceive of the present with reference to the past in order to construct the future).

(Mires 1997, 126–128)

The current governability problems of Venezuela and Colombia could be considered very different and incomparable. The most commonly referred to characteristics of contemporary Colombia are overwhelming violence, wars, and a fragile state. The most often mentioned troubles in Venezuela are the breakdown of the party system, the centralization and militarization of politics, and the ambiguity of the democratic revolution (*revolución democrática*) announced by a president who emerged from a military group after leading a *golpe de estado*.

There are, however, many similarities in these two cases. Exploring those similarities can be a useful exercise in understanding the processes behind specific manifestations of democratic deconsolidation. This is not a reflection on the reasons that in the past created the present situation, certainly an important question; here the emphasis will be on the present and future trends of two processes of social renegotiation of principles, rules, and procedures. The exploration of those processes is presented through the basic components of a negotiation: context, agenda, counterparts, process, results, and consequences.

The Context:
Overextended or Nonexistent Social Arrangements?

Both Venezuela and Colombia have experienced relatively long periods of democratic political stability. In the case of Colombia, an oligarchic democracy prevailed between 1910 and 1949, until an explosion of generalized social violence gave rise to the dictatorship of Laureano Gómez from 1950 to 1953 and the military regime of Gustavo Rojas Pinilla from 1953 to 1957 (Wilde 1978, 30; Sánchez and Orjuela 1997; Ramírez 1999). In July 1957 the Pact of Sitges between Conservatives and Liberals created the Frente Nacional, whose central concern was the building of a consociational system that institutionalized the relations among the parties and attempted to prevent violence. That pact and its rules for *convivencia* were submitted to plebiscite and approved in December 1957.

In Venezuela, the long nineteenth-century-style dictatorship of Juan Vicente Gómez from 1908 to 1936 was followed by two transitional governments that failed to work out strong vehicles for the political participation of new sociopolitical actors. A civil–military coup evolved into a brief democratic experience called the *Trienio* from 1945 to 1948, but the coup of November 1948 reinitiated ten years of dictatorship in the form of a military government. The main organized social actors learned from the experience of the *Trienio* that they needed a more comprehensive arrangement to establish and maintain a democratic regime. The Pacto de Punto Fijo, signed in October 1958, was the agreement among Venezuelan elites to create a consociational system in order to prevent conflict and promote consensus (Martz and Myers 1971; Rey 1989; Urbaneja 1992; Hillman 1994; Coppedge 1996). Elites included in the new system were the military, the church, the entrepreneurial and labor sectors, and the political parties. The Communist Party was excluded.

Both pacts were primarily intended to contribute to the construction of a democracy conceived and defended by elites. A secondary objective of the pacts was to be socially extended and legitimated. Therefore, the pacts consisted not only of a declaration of general principles to promote consensus and *convivencia*, but also of certain specific rules that—beyond the literal and temporary effects of the pacts—created in practice a social system of negotiation among elites with strong mediation by political parties.

Indeed, while the Frente Nacional was to operate as a system of *paridad y alternancia*, allowing for Conservatives and Liberals not to be excluded from government for sixteen years, its patterns of negotiation among elites extended until the present. The Pacto de Punto Fijo also extended its basic arrangements well beyond the end of the coalition governments in 1960s and created in practice certain principles, rules, and styles of negotiation among elites and by the whole society that somehow also prevailed until the present (Jácome 2000; McCoy 2000a).

This is the common context of the present process of deconsolidation of democracy in both countries: Neither Venezuela nor Colombia have overcome the degradation of an old system of negotiation that overextended in time, generated broad vacuum areas, and became an obstacle for the social construction of democracy that would benefit the majority within their respective societies. Such a "context" has been absent not only due to the social practice of elites, but also due to political orientations within the rest of these societies.

The Agenda:
From Representation, to Delegation, to Participation

The consociational system of negotiation created in both countries by the mid twentieth century is still alive, but only barely. Although the issues of public and government concern are not exactly the same, the broad themes have been quite similar since the 1980s.

In general, both Colombia and Venezuela have had the issue of institutional reform on their respective public and government agendas. In both cases constitutional assemblies were formed (in 1990–1991 in Colombia and in 1999 in Venezuela) as attempts to create a new institutional fabric through new constitutions.[6] In spite of the many differences between the two processes, they have certain important features in common that illustrate the prevailing negotiation dynamics: Both assumed that the changes in the constitutional arrangement would be crucial for the transformation of social dynamics, both proposed a more social and participatory democracy, and both maintained the main rules that established a strong presidentialist regime and centralized control and management of the government agenda.

Those arrangements—certainly recent in Venezuela, though considered since the 1980s—along with the very social political processes that preceded and followed the constitutional assemblies reveal an agenda that, to begin with, includes as a broad theme the very essence of democratic legitimacy and efficacy.

In the case of Colombia the agenda includes the internal war, which involves guerrilla movements, the illegal drug problem, the paramilitary, regional and rural violence, and "everyday" violence; the deterioration of the institutional and social fabric; a severe economic recession; and the need for international support to effectively deal with the peace process (Kline 1996). In Venezuela the agenda includes the prevalence of a conflictive and increasingly polarized sociopolitical scenario; continuity in the deterioration of the institutional framework, since even the new constitutional arrangement has already been seriously challenged and weakened; a severe economic recession in spite of rising oil prices; and the need to generate trust in the *revolución democrática* on the part of governments, international organizations, private investors, and businesspeople (Cardozo Da Silva 2000).

In both cases the government agendas—in spite of different attempts to recover legitimacy and efficacy for the government and the most important political institutions—are failing to deal with the multiple dilemmas that socioeconomic pressures pose to the main strategic decisions about economics and social issues. Moreover, the very process of agenda setting has followed the logic of "delegative" democracies (O'Donnell 1994; Jácome 1997) and come to be perceived as the agenda of the few: elites, oligarchy, political parties, technocrats, and multilateral financial institutions.

The crucial challenge as socially expressed in both societies is to create a new dynamics of participation, but it must be more than a demagogic exercise or a mere plebiscite. It is important to analyze who the social actors are and the possibilities for them to become legitimate and efficacious counterparts in the social renegotiation of democracy.

The Actors: Rivals, Neglected Participants, or Counterparts?

Colombia appears to have maintained the same traditional actors in their roles within the consociational arrangement. In contrast, Venezuela seems to have discarded the old roles: What is left of the discredited traditional political parties suffers harsh criticism, generalized disdain, and lack of credible programmatic renewal. However, this is a very superficial approach.

The new presidents of each country, with quite diverse biographies, won their respective elections with the support of heterogeneous and weak alliances that have been falling apart. Moreover, both presidents have been losing their initial high rates of popularity. The political parties and groups that support them—Gran Alianza por el Cambio in Colombia and Polo Patriótico in Venezuela—are not consistent political coalitions and, in fact, are in a process of fragmentation.

Looking back at previous elections, there has been growing abstention in electoral processes. This phenomenon is more traditional in Colombia and relatively newer in Venezuela. The growing abstentionism nevertheless shows how political parties, central ingredients in a consociational system of negotiation, are not representative enough to negotiate any credible social arrangement. It is impossible to ignore that while in Colombia this has meant the weakening of the president, in Venezuela it has been conducive to a process of centralization and personalization of presidential power. This continues to be true in Venezuela, where the election of the constitutional assembly through a uninominal system gave control of 123 of 131 positions to candidates from outside the traditional party system proposed by the president. Hence, more than 90 percent of the posts went to less than 40 percent of the voters. Also, other traditional counterparts in the classical consociational system, such as business, the church, and the armed forces, continue to exert pressure. Their legitimacy and efficacy in both Colombia and Venezuela have been seriously challenged.

The "antipolitical mood" that created the fantasy of democracy without political parties continues to be generalized. This mood is certainly more apparent in Venezuela than it is in Colombia. The political dynamics from 1995 to 2001 in Venezuela, especially during the Chávez administration, has resuscitated the idea of strong leadership directly connected to the masses through popular consultation and with increasingly weak institutional mediation and balance.

In Colombia, the extension and intensification of many forms of violence are extreme expressions of the rejection of the most traditional sociopolitical counterparts and of the lack of credibility of institutional channels to deal with sociopolitical conflict. Certainly, actors such as guerrilla groups, the paramilitary, and organizations related to the illegal drug business enormously complicate the set of actors and interests. They are major pressures as well as obstacles in the attempt to democratically construct a new social arrangement.

The presence of other actors trying to participate in a social negotiation system that is struggling with its own transformation is undoubtedly relevant. It should be recognized that a dynamics of enrichment of civil society and local life is also present in the two countries. Many groups and organizations have sought inclusion in the Colombian and Venezuelan civil societies, related to specific issues in the societal agenda of each country: human rights and judiciary development, the peace process, community development, promotion of democracy and civic education, and free market promotion.[7]

Regional dynamics in both countries, although historically more intense in Colombia, present new and not well-attended opportunities and pressures to the societies and their central governments. More actors, encouraged to participate at the local levels and very diverse in their interests, are nevertheless tempted to develop a mere instrumental relationship with the central government and society as a whole.

Also, both countries need to take part in regional, hemispheric, and global negotiations. This is another area in which important differences in approaches and styles should be understood (Cardozo Da Silva 1998). However, those differences shouldn't hide the fact that the social negotiation systems of Venezuela and Colombia include explicit and tremendously important negotiations with "external" counterparts: governments, societies, and international organizations, as well as private investors and entrepreneurs. For both the *revolución Democrática* and the "Plan Colombia" international and transnational counterparts are of crucial interest. The role of international counterparts is and will continue to be very important, both for these two societies and for the sake of regional and hemispheric social, economic, and political development (Serbin 1997; Carmona Estanga 1997). Finally, there continues to be a very narrow group of national counterparts in the two countries: Players and stakes continue to be very concentrated in certain elites, though under growing sociopolitical pressure. In the Venezuelan case, the breakdown of traditional political parties and their arrangements has meant a new concentration of political power. The new elite practices clientelism and patronage just as the old elite did.

It is not only the two governments but also the two societies that are still in the conflictive process of working out a renewed or an entirely new set of local, national, regional, and global partnerships. In the meantime, beyond counterparts, there continue to be social rivals and self-neglected participants who compete under the old rules. Their attitudes and practices derive from a game that pretends to have changed.

The Process and Strategies:
Consociational or Not Consociational, Is That the Question?

Departing from the idea of basic similarities in the social weakness of democracy in Venezuela and Colombia, and also from the characterization of a still narrow and closed set of counterparts, my main argument is that the dynamics of deconsolidation provoked by the degradation of the old consociational negotiation system has continued.

Neither the Chávez nor the Pastrana administrations, neither the Colombian nor the Venezuelan societies as a whole, have changed the inertia of deconsolidation that is historically associated in Venezuela with the February 18, 1983, the February 27, 1989, and the coup attempts of 1992, and in Colombia with the attack on the Supreme Court in 1985 and the "Proceso-8000" against President Samper between 1994 and 1997. The general characteristics of the traditional consociational negotiation process that continue are the following: relatively few counterparts constitute concentrated strategic decision-making processes; centrality of political negotiations and deals among political parties, leaders, and their political movements in the making of policies; generalized emphasis in the control of social conflict rather than in its management; and people's expectations of government responses, including patronism and clientelism on the part of the masses. These old ways were complemented during the 1990s by the strategic growing importance of the military and the search for broader national and international legitimacy.

Concerning processes and strategies, certain differences deserve to be mentioned. Pastrana, with a legacy of commitment to the rules of the game reinitiated in 1957, is working hard to adjust the old system of social negotiation and to renew some kind of consociational arrangement; Chávez is working hard to eliminate *puntofijismo* and has been defying it in what is left of political parties, unions, public institutions, and projects, and certainly in relations with traditional social counterparts in the negotiation system, except for the military, including international partners such as the United States and Colombia. In the process, however, this administration could be creating its own consociational arrangement, exclusive on its own terms, tremendously centralized, and closer every day to the risk of a "tyranny of the majority" (McCoy 2000b).

Both societies and their governments have been experiencing diverse grades of social distress and conflict, political polarization, and even economic recession, though still within the limits of an old way of undertaking the social negotiation of conflict and institutional building. The main failure of the old game that continues to shadow the present has been *elitización* of politics and the discouragement of the process of social construction of democracy. The culture and practices of delegative democracy still prevail in the elites as well as in the whole society, but in different ways (Jácome 2000).

Daily practices of important social actors in the two countries tend to undermine the legitimacy and efficacy of democracy. Hence, there continues to be a strong temptation for old or new elites and central players to engage in strategic deception even within the frameworks of their own programs for change.[8] These practices contribute to a vicious circle that persists despite increasing challenges.

RESULTS, CONSEQUENCES, AND POSSIBLE FUTURES: HOW TO BUILD DEMOCRACY

Despite the many shortcomings signifying the practice of political democracy, there might be light in the tunnel. Democratic government seems to evolve in a process of learning by doing: by people experiencing and being accustomed to the special institutions and the norms of behaviour associated with the principles of popular rule. In other words: it is by addressing and working out the crises of democracy that we may eventually lay the ground for the victory of this form of government.

(Hadenius 1997, 11)

Both Venezuela and Colombia are societies attempting to rebuild their governability. Both see as a point of departure a system of social negotiation that is no longer efficacious but is culturally resistant to a new social dynamics. Building governability, as well as democratization, is a top-down and bottom-up process; governmental and societal; public and private; individual and collective; and local, national, international, and transnational.

Regarding the negotiation systems in general, it is clear that in Colombia the elites are trying to resolve economic and political problems in a way that allows for the traditional social negotiation system to survive. In Venezuela, while the government has been challenging and fighting against *puntofijismo*, there has been a process of adaptation that is promoting a new arrangement under the ruins of the old system, although it still preserves in its practices structural traits of the traditional consociational system.

The immediate results of these two ways of dealing with tremendously complex obstacles to democratic (and even nondemocratic) governability can translate into popular support for government leaders while the society perceives them as legitimate and efficacious counterparts. A sound use of that social support has the potential to promote trust in the creation of socially desirable democratic arrangements, practices, and institutions, as the social mood surrounding constitutional assemblies reflected at different moments in both countries. However, it also has the potential, given the volatility of popular support, the complexity of the task, and the limited accomplishments of the two governments on critical issues, to accelerate deconsolidation and sociopolitical chaos.

The current situation in the two societies shows a tendency toward radicalization and polarization, although in diverse forms. In Colombia, sustained efforts to negotiate with guerrilla groups, especially the adjudication of 42,000 square kilometers of territory with the Fuerzas Armadas de Liberación Nacional (FARC), the largest group, along with the beginning of new negotiations with the smaller but equally aggressive Ejército de Liberación Nacional (ELN) and the new commitment to struggle with the illegal drug problem, have created major pressures from other social actors, and even tensions between the government and the military. The alliance with the United States and the international presidential activism on behalf of the "Plan Colombia," has explicitly incorporated new counterparts into government peace negotiations, a crucial issue on the Colombian domestic and international agendas. Pastrana's government, in the process of working out the adaptation of the traditional social negotiation system, has used a rather conciliatory style.

In Venezuela, the activism of the president, his concentration on political issues, and the lack of effective attention to economics has not provided the expected improvement to the socioeconomic situation, notwithstanding the rise in oil prices since mid-1999. The attempts to lure international investment and to gain trust for the *revolución democrática* and its leader, and thereby trying to incorporate new counterparts into the negotiation system, has not been successful after a year and a half of government, when judged from the perspective of economic dynamism and growth. In the process of drastically changing the rules of the game, the style of the president has been one of confrontation, not only with traditional domestic elites, mainly associated with political parties, but also with traditional international partners (Cardozo Da Silva 2000).

Looking toward the future, there are two aspects worthy of consideration as a preliminary conclusion of this analysis: first, the need for a less governmental and more societal approach to democratic governability, and second, the method for serving this need.

Despite new developments in civil society, both countries have continued to deal with the problems of governability according to a very "governmental" approach in a form that—as usual, though for different reasons—discourages the social construction of democracy. There is not much to learn from the past. Instead, there is much to forget and forgive so that the societies of Colombia and Venezuela can put into effective practice the minimum rules for political democracy and democratically construct their own broad democratic arrangements, practices, and institutions.

The questions to deal with, from now on, are if, how, and what kind of democracies can be built by societies that appear to value democratic principles and possess a comprehensive idea of socioeconomic democracy. The challenge is to translate those ideas into at least a limited practice of democracy. These questions do not admit to a mere theoretical reflection: They require consideration in light of the conditions that prevail in each society. In the process of changing from a vicious cycle of lack of trust to one of trust and cooperation, there are two social practices that are slowly creating and recreating new patterns of democratic behavior: national decentralization and regional integration.

Integration among societies is creating, beyond economic arrangements, broad and shared references and practices that could favor from above and from below, directly and indirectly, through positive and negative incentives, the creation of democracy by each society. Both Venezuela and Colombia have dense networks of relations among them and with other societies that can be better incorporated as legitimate counterparts, supportive of the negotiation of a renewed set of social arrangements. Here the role of the United States is very significant, as a state and as a society.

Decentralization is a relatively recent but very important social dynamic, directly connecting everyday life to local decision making, management, and accountability. It is not a substitute for the democratization of central governments, but is ostensibly a new way to deal with politics that is gaining momentum and influence in local and national politics.

Two questions remain for the short- and mid-term future: Will democracy reemerge from a "negative consensus," as has happened in the past after authoritarian responses to socioeconomic chaos took place? Could it emerge as a "positive consensus," before the current deconsolidation goes further? The challenge is to socially promote a positive consensus from the present circumstances, which include both a huge shadow of the past and the new light of local and global practices.

NOTES

This chapter reflects research projects accomplished as part of the affiliation program between St. John Fisher College and the Central University of Venezuela between 1997 and 2000.

1. The succession of political crises since 1992 reveals generalized discontent and institutional limitations: the self-coup by Alberto Fujimori in April 1992 and the practices of a government that has increasingly concentrated power in a president decisively supported by the military; the Chiapas revolt, the attempt in Tijuana, and the financial breakdown in Mexico between 1993 and 1994; the coup attempts against the Venezuelan government in February and November 1992, as well as the impeachment of President Pérez that threw him out of power in 1993, followed by the acceleration of institutional weakening and the electoral triumph of the antiestablishment candidate and former *golpista* Hugo Chávez in 1998; the institutional stress in Colombia during the government of president Samper and the deepening of violence and many wars fought in Colombian territory; the Brazilian financial crisis and political stress since 1998; the coup attempts in Guatemala in 1993 and in Paraguay in 1996 and 1999; the overthrow of the Ecuadorian president in 2000; the discourse of opposition against neoliberal economics and democratic achievements in every single electoral campaign, as well as the growing evidence of sociopolitical conflict in the whole region; and tensions among civilians and military, in many countries associated with the postauthoritarian transition, the fight against drug production and trafficking, and the need for control of social discontent, combined with the weaknesses of civilian institutional support.

2. Identities, interests, and relations are created and recreated by intersubjective practices among social actors. On the one hand, collective meanings define the structures that organize actions; on the other, social actors acquire their interests and identities through their participation in those collective meanings (Wendt 1999, 437–438).

3. Dahl (1998) explains, "Political arrangements sound as if they might be rather provisional, which they could well be in a country that has just moved away from non democratic rule. We tend to see practices as more habitual and therefore more durable. We usually think as institutions as having settled in for the long haul, passed from one generation to the next. As a country moves from a non democratic to a democratic government the early democratic arrangements become practices, which in due time turn into settled institutions" (pp. 83–84).

4. Governability, which involves both principles and concrete decisions and policies, can be understood in many different ways, so it is not necesarily democratic. Arbós and Giner (1996, 9–12) identify three main currents of thought around governability, and each one connects politics to economics in a different way, from downsizing to upgrading the state, from more to less market, and from conservative to liberal and Marxist.

5. "Good Government . . . is a metaphor for the democratic search to put public order in the service of addressing the problems of the majority. . . . The existence of a political democracy does not guarantee good government, but good government, in the present context of Latin America, is only viable within

a political democracy. . . . In societies in crisis good government also concerns itself with how decisions are put into practice and, above all, for whose benefit. The practice of good government can transform political democracy into social democracy" (see Torres-Rivas 1995, 46–47).

6. It must be said that in Venezuela the need for constitutional reform through the procedure of the amendment that was established in the Constitution of 1961 had been considered by parliamentary commisions since the end of the 1980s but never seriously undertaken until 1999.

7. The index of civil society organizations in the political database of the Americas gives a general perspective of the impressive variety of organizations. See <http://www.georgetown.edu/LatAmerPolitical/MISC/Groups/groups.html>.

8. Corruption, abusive use of public resources by government officials, and weakening of civilian control over the military are examples that, though in different specific ways, apply for both countries.

BIBLIOGRAPHY

Achard, Diego, and Manuel Flores. 1997. *Gobernabilidad: un reportaje de América Latina.* Mexico City: Fondo de Cultura Económica.

Agüero, Felipe, and Jeffrey Stark. 1998. *Fault Lines of Democracy in Post-Transition Latin America.* Miami: North South Center Press.

Arbós, Xavier, and Salvador Giner. 1996. *La gobernabilidad. Ciudadanía y democracia en la encrucijada mundial* (2d ed.). Madrid: Siglo XXI Editores.

Banco Interamericano de Desarrollo (BID). 1997. *América Latina tras una década de reformas, Informe sobre el progreso económico y social en América Latina.* Washington, D.C.: BID.

———. 1998. *Informe sobre el progreso económico y social en América Latina. América Latina frente a la desigualdad.* Washington, D.C.: BID.

———. 1999. *Desarrollo más allá de la economía, Informe sobre el progreso económico y social en América Latina.* Washington, D.C.: BID.

Barragán, Julia. 1990. "El poder normativo de las autoexcepciones." *Revista Relea* (no. 0). Caracas: Cipost–UCV.

Cardozo Da Silva, Elsa. 1995. *Latinoamérica en transición. En busca del Aleph.* Caracas: Panapo.

———. 1998. "Gobernabilidad como Negociabilidad." *Revista Ciencias de Gobierno* (no. 4). Maracaibo: Izepes.

———. 2000. "Desafiando la tempestad. La política exterior de Venezuela 1999–2000." Paper presented to the twenty-third Latin American Studies Association Meeting, Miami, March.

Carmona Estanga, Pedro. 1997. "Comercio e integración." In *Venezuela y Colombia en el nuevo milenio,* compiled by Fundación Pensamiento y Acción, Fundación Rómulo Betancourt, IESA, CAF, and Fundación Banco Mercantil. Caracas: Láser Gráfica.

Coppedge, Michael. 1996. "Venezuela: The Rise and Fall of Partyarchy." In *Constructing Democratic Governance: Latin America and the Caribbean in the 1990s,* edited by Jorge Domínguez and Abraham Lowenthal. Baltimore: Johns Hopkins University Press.

Dahl, Robert A. 1989. *Democracy and Its Critics.* New Haven, Conn.: Yale University Press.

——. 1998. *On Democracy.* New Haven, Conn.: Yale University Press.

Diamond, Larry. 1994. "Introduction: Political Culture and Democracy." In *Political Culture and Democracy in Developing Countries,* edited by Larry Diamond. Boulder, Colo.: Lynne Rienner.

Domínguez, Jorge, and Abraham Lowenthal, eds. 1996. *Constructing Democratic Governance: Latin America and the Caribbean in the 1990s.* Baltimore: Johns Hopkins University Press.

Freedom House. 2000. *Annual Survey of Freedom Country Ratings 1972–73 to 1999–2000.* Available at <http://www.freedomhouse.org/survey/2000/>.

Fundación Estudios de Derecho Administrativo (FUNEDA). 1999. *Compliación de constituciones políticas.* Caracas: Editorial Torino.

Hadenius, Axel, ed. 1997. *Democracy's Victory and Crisis.* Cambridge: Cambridge University Press.

Hakim, Peter. 2000. "Is Latin America Doomed to Failure?" *Foreign Policy* (Winter): 104–119.

Held, David. 1997. *La democracia y el órden global. Del Estado moderno al gobierno Cosmopólita* (trans. Sebastián Mazzuca). Barcelona: Paidós.

Hillman, Richard S. 1994. *Democracy for the Privileged: Crisis and Transition in Venezuela.* Boulder, Colo.: Lynne Rienner.

——. 1997. "Trends and Prospects." In *Understanding Latin America,* edited by Richard S. Hillman. Boulder, Colo.: Lynne Rienner.

Hillman, Richard S., and Elsa Cardozo Da Silva, eds. 1997. *De una a otra gobernabilidad. El desbordamiento de la democracia venezolana.* Caracas: UCV.

Jácome, Francine. 1997. "Las crisis del sistema político venezolano: ¿Ruptura con el modelo statista y la democracia delegativa?" In *Las crisis políticas en Colombia y Venezuela: un estudio comparado (1982–1997),* edited by Francine Jácome. Cuadernos del Invesp no. 3. Caracas: Invesp.

——. 2000. "Venezuela: Old Successes, New Constraints in Learning." In *Political Learning and Redemocratization in Latin America: Do Politicians Learn from Political Crises?* edited by Jennifer L. McCoy. Miami: North South Center at the University of Miami.

Kline, Harvey F. 1996. "Colombia: Building Democracy in the Midst of Violence and Drugs." In *Constructing Democratic Governance: Latin America and the Caribbean in the 1990s,* edited by Jorge Domínguez and Abraham Lowenthal. Baltimore: Johns Hopkins University Press.

Latinobarómetro. 1998. *Informe Metodológico.* Santiago: Corporación Latinobarómetro.

Martz, John, and David Myers. 1971. *Venezuela: The Democratic Experience.* New York: Praeger.

McCoy, Jennifer L. 2000a. "Comparative Lessons." In *Political Learning and Redemocratization in Latin America: Do Politicians Learn from Political Crises?* edited by Jennifer L. McCoy. Miami: North South Center at the University of Miami.

——. 2000b. "Demystifying Venezuela's Hugo Chávez." *Current History* 99, no. 634 (February): 66–71.

Mires, Fernando. 1997. "El comienzo de la historia." In *Democracia para una nueva sociedad (Modelo para armar)*, edited by Helena González and Heidulf Schmidt. Caracas: Nueva Sociedad.

Naím, Moisés. 1995. "New Competitive Tigers or Old Populist Nationalisms?" In *The Consolidation of Democracy in Latin America*, edited by Joseph Tulchin and Bernice Romero. Boulder, Colo.: Lynne Rienner.

O'Donnell, Guillermo. 1994. "Delegative Democracy." *Journal of Democracy* 5, no. 1 (January): 55–69.

Peceny, Mark. 1999. "The Social Construction of Democracy." *International Studies Quarterly* 43, (4): 95–102.

Peeler, John A. 1985. *Latin American Democracies: Colombia, Costa Rica, Venezuela*. Chapel Hill: University of North Carolina Press.

Political Database of the Americas. 2000. *Civil Society*. Available at <http://www.georgetown.edu/LatAmerPolitical/MISC/Groups/groups.html>.

Ramírez, Socorro. 1999. "Colombia a finales del siglo XX." In *Colombia Venezuela. Agenda común para el siglo XXI*, edited by Socorro Ramírez and José María Cadenas. Colombia: TM Editores.

Rey, Juan Carlos. 1989. *El Futuro de la Democracia en Venezuela*. Caracas: IDEA.

Robinson, William I. 1999. "Latin America in the Age of Inequality: Confronting the New 'Utopia.'" *International Studies Quarterly* 43 (4): 41–67.

Sánchez, D., Rubén, and Luis Javier Orjuela. 1997. "Crisis de gobernabilidad y reforma del Estado en Colombia." In *Las crisis políticas en Colombia y Venezuela: un estudio comparado (1982–1997)*, edited by Francine Jácome. Cuadernos del Invesp no. 3. Caracas: Invesp.

Serbín, Andrés. 1997. "El entorno internacional y la estabilidad democrática en Colombia y Venezuela: un análisis desde la perspectiva de la teoría del two-level-game." In *Las crisis políticas en Colombia y Venezuela: un estudio comparado (1982–1997)*, edited by Francine Jácome. Cuadernos del Invesp no. 3. Caracas: Invesp.

Smith, Peter. 2000. *Talons of the Eagle: Dynamics of U.S.–Latin American Relations*. New York: Oxford University Press.

Sørensen, Georg. 1993. *Democracy and Democratization*. Boulder, Colo.: Westview Press.

Stokes, Susan. 1995. "Democracy and the Limits of Popular Sovereignty in Latin America." In *The Consolidation of Democracy in Latin America*, edited by Joseph Tulchin and Bernice Romero. Boulder, Colo.: Lynne Rienner.

Torres-Rivas, Edelberto. 1995. "Democracy and the Metaphor of Good Government." In *The Consolidation of Democracy in Latin America*, edited by Joseph Tulchin and Bernice Romero. Boulder, Colo.: Lynne Rienner.

United Nations Development Program (UNDP). 2000. *Human Development Report*. Available at <http:www//.Undp.org/hdr2000/english/HDR 2000.html>.

Urbaneja, Diego Bautista. 1992. *Pueblo petróleo y democracia en la Venezuela del siglo XX*. Caracas: CEPET.

Welch, Friedrich, and José V. Carrasquero. 1998. "Actitudes hacia la democracia y reforma económica en América Latina." *Revista Venezolana de Ciencia Política* 13: 45–54.

Wendt, Alexander. 1999. "Anarchy Is What States Make of It: The Social Construction of Power Politics." In *International Relations Theory: Realism, Pluralism, Globalism and Beyond*, edited by Paul R. Viotti and Mark Kauppi. Boston: Allyn and Bacon.

Wiarda, Howard J. 1990. *The Democratic Revolution in Latin America: History, Politics and US Policy*. New York: Holmes and Meier.

———. 1995. *Democracy and Its Discontents*. New York: Rowan and Littlefield.

Wilde, Alexander W. 1978. "Conversations among Gentlemen: Oligarchical Democracy in Colombia." In *The Breakdown of Democratic Regimes: Latin America*, edited by Juan J. Linz and Alfred Stephan. Baltimore: Johns Hopkins University Press.

CHAPTER 4

Citizenship and Human Rights Policy in Brazil

Isabel Ribeiro de Oliveira

Similar to the Venezuelan and Colombian cases discussed in Chapter 3, consolidation of Brazilian democracy is still in process. A major concern from a long-term perspective is the way political or civic culture that legitimates this process is patterned. Political culture is the set of conceptions and images that citizens have about power, rulers, the value of voting, media, and other political variables. Therefore, understanding political culture and the attendant symbolic processes and representations of political power is of utmost importance in recognizing its impact on political decisions, and thus, democratic dynamics. There are good reasons for such a concern, since the (not so extensive) available information tends to show that politics in Brazil has a strong elitist and authoritarian bias that is accepted by the majority of Brazilian citizens.

In the Brazilian context, linkages between citizenship and political culture have been examined from several perspectives. The analysis of Reis and Lamounier (1981) in the late 1970s is representative. Recent concern about these themes has stimulated some other studies. Research has focused on high levels of political illiteracy, very low levels of political information, and the significant prevalence of authoritarian values.

I will explain several indications of Brazilian authoritarianism that are easily detected within the symbolic culture of the popular sectors. These indications are clearly related to citizenship practice. The first one concerns the normal understanding of the meaning of the "state." Far from representing a pluralistic political arena, the state is normally understood as something standing "above" private interests and committed to promoting the "common good" over private interests (see Lopes 1971; Pereira 1979; Caldeira 1984; Oliveira 1988). This notion coexists, certainly in a strained way, with the conviction that power is concentrated in the hands of the rich. The tension results from the fact that there is no immediate identification between rulers and the rich, even though some politicians are clearly pictured as representative of the economically privileged segments of the population. Thus, the expectation is that the government's duty is to invest public resources to ensure the common good, even if a sense of frustration is clearly felt.

As a complement to this idea of the state, the notion of political satisfaction of private interests is spurious, since the "general interest" cannot be whatever this or that group believes it to be. Only someone who is "above" such "particularities" can really perceive what is good for the whole society. Thus, regular political activities, like meetings, group deliberations, campaigns, protests, or even the performance of functions pertaining to some appointed office end up by being seen as politically irrelevant. Political apathy imposes itself, since few believe they have enough power to influence government. There are, obviously, organized minorities, such as political parties, nongovernmental organizations, churches, unions, and various associations, that act in a more stable and consistent way. All available information, however, points to the conclusion that for the great majority of the Brazilian population politics is seen as a dirty, dangerous, and complicated game. Political success requires the ability to decode a significant amount of information, a propitious financial position, and a willingness to take risks, conditions that are enjoyed by few Brazilians.

If the state is seen as an entity above organized interests, and citizenship as remarkably "passive," the third feature of our authoritarianism lies within the very precarious knowledge of the language of citizen's rights. If the Brazilian "culture of rights" is compared with the European or North American ones, it is clear that "social rights" are the only familiar rights to Brazilians.[1] As there is not much understanding of what political rights really mean, the obvious result is that government is expected to comply with its duty without much political support.[2] Such rights, therefore, do not constitute a mechanism to be used for decreasing this kind of authoritarianism.

Research efforts aimed at assessing the impact of government policies over this symbolic space are scarce, notwithstanding the fact that the practice of citizenship, as well as the universe of political images that shapes this practice, are both influenced, among other factors, by state deeds. If any political culture is rooted in preserved tradition and bred by ideas concerning power, politics, and images of a "good society," it is actual social interaction that reproduces (or remodels) its main traits. In everyday political life, interaction patterns involving state and society have their course, strengthening or reshaping civic culture, although we may suspect that most of the time nobody is really concerned with more pervasive consequences of political deeds. Nonetheless, deliberate action to shape this pattern of relations is also present in the political arena, mostly within activist groups and specific government policies.

As the contemporary exercise of citizenship rights presupposes the existence or the construction of a reasonably democratic political culture, it is worth examining governmental policies specifically oriented toward the shaping of this way of thinking and acting politically. That is my main present concern, based on research results on human rights policies in Brazil (Oliveira 1998). My analysis is oriented toward detecting the meaning that the government intends to impress upon the practice of citizenship through the exercise of state power.

Human rights constitute a new set of values, concepts, and strategies in the Brazilian language of rights. It has been growing steadily since the late 1970s, and a few analytical efforts have already been made to associate it with the more conventional grammar of individual and social rights of citizenship.[3] If my concern with human rights can be taken in this connection, my focus is oriented to the way public policies are shaped with the intention of molding the symbolic domain. Since the politics of human rights is quite elusive, expressed in messy language, and pervades an enormous field of political action, it is important to sharpen the focus. In order to achieve some accuracy, I will deal exclusively with one policy, which is a good way to explore this rather broad human rights political field.

Before proceeding, I want to stress that I do not take human rights policies as ideologically neutral instruments (with varying degrees of efficacy), oriented to the protection of supposedly universal rights. My point is precisely to bring forth the specifically political dimension of that public policy, enhancing its normative domain where ideals, wishes, and ideologies are expressed and, somehow, disseminated among society at large.[4] What kind of citizen is the ideal bearer of those rights? Which human rights are chosen as more relevant, and why? Is there an ideology converting ideas into a set of policies, or is the choice of a more pragmatic nature? Are there unusual or unexpected interests expressed in human rights language? These are some of the questions that push me further in this research.

This chapter is thus oriented to the analysis of a federal government plan, the Human Rights National Plan (Plano Nacional de Direitos Humanos; PNDH). The focus is oriented to its normative dimension, reconstructed through observation of the expressed values and style of its formulation, as much as in some aspects of its implementation. My analytical effort is thus an evaluative description of the set of ideals that shape state intervention in society through explicit dissemination of political values, concepts, images, and practices related to the language of rights. Selecting the major conceptions concerning democracy and human rights from official public reports, I hope to present a suggestive appraisal of one of the current efforts to mold Brazilian political culture.

In order to gauge the way this conceptual realm is being activated, I will follow two tracks. The first one, more conventional, is concerned with contrasting projected and achieved targets, according to official data.[5] The second track, much more nebulous, aims to identify the "will to power" expressed in the ideational configuration that pervades the plan formulation and implementation. With such an evaluation, it becomes possible to consider the probable impact of this specific exercise of power on the authoritarian traits of Brazilian political culture. The relevance of this type of reflection derives from the fact that this mechanism of political socialization is more manageable than institutions like the media, the family, or the school system.

THE HUMAN RIGHTS NATIONAL PLAN

Brief Review of Human Rights Policies in Brazil

Government action oriented to human rights policies is something quite recent in Brazilian politics. It is only in the present administration (more precisely, from 1996 onward) that a state agency is organized to take care of human rights, and a formal plan established for dealing with this matter.[6] These initiatives can be taken as originating in two independent processes.[7]

The first was initiated in the 1970s by a political movement to mold public opinion in order to influence the military regime to stop torture and extermination of political militants. Resulting from the activities of several groups, the dynamics of such a process changed a lot with return to civilian rule, although it did not lose its focus. Under a human rights banner, so appropriate for authoritarian times, some groups stuck to the question of violence, although defining it in new terms. Many other organizations already concerned with human rights for their specific reasons will cooperate in this process. Therefore, there is a diversification of issues, although violence has always been a dominant theme of human rights language in Brazil.

Let us now consider the second process. As Alves (1994) tells us, at least since 1974 there has been a discussion going on in the U.N. Human Rights Commission concerning a "confidential procedure of investigation" in Brazil, due to denunciation of serious human rights violations from 1968 to 1972.[8] Nevertheless, by 1976 the Brazilian government was able to dismiss such a procedure, supported by the then Yugoslavia and Uruguay (also under a military regime). Azeredo da Silveira, then foreign minister, made an important speech in the opening of the thirty-second session of the General Assembly in 1977, in which he stated that Brazil would comply with U.N. international agreements on human rights. Brazil's determination to follow the international code had as an internal complement the "slow, gradual and steady" return to a democratic regime, initiated by Geisel.[9] From this point onward, a new phase in human rights policy started. Called by Alves the "conservative but not obstructive" phase, it lasted from 1978 to 1984.

With the civilian regime beginning in 1985, pressures from civil society and from the United Nations were more strongly felt, and Brazil adhered to major international conventions, since there were no longer reasons for not doing so. However, it was only in the early 1990s that internal government action for securing human rights really started. Lafer, then foreign minister, expressed the new tone of public policy in the field when he stated that human rights violations in the 1990s had nothing to do with arbitrary power of authoritarian regimes. It had to do "with the difficulties of securing, in a continental country and in an heterogeneous society, permeated by so many inequalities, real respect for human rights" (Alves 1994, 35).[10]

In fact, Itamaraty (the Ministry of Foreign Relations) has a clear saying concerning the main rationale for public policy formulation. Insisting on the relevance of securing "development rights," Alves (1994) argues that absolute priority should be granted, by government and society, to policies oriented to the elimination of hunger and misery. According to him, "Nothing can justify to the eyes of the world the persistence of 32 millions of indigents in the breast of the ninth world economy" (p. 72). Freedom alone, he insists, is not enough to secure in Brazil the full functioning of a state of right. Resolution of those difficulties becomes quite clear in the following: "If, on the one hand, structural conditions have obvious reflection in the state of economic and social rights, affecting also civil rights . . . and Brazil is such an eloquent tragic case—on the other, the absence of satisfactory levels of economic and social development is no longer excusable for not respecting rights" (p. 45).

This concern with social and economic rights took a long time to begin to be considered as a topic for specific policies, as I will show later on. For the time being, it is only important to stress that if violence is clearly linked to "social violence," it should not be taken as a "manifestation of class war" (since the poor are the ones who suffer the most from it). With such a view, Itamaraty also considered that policies oriented to minimize violent behavior had to be formulated.

The Plan's Main Features

Regarding its style, the resulting plan is quite a heterogeneous piece of literature. Some targets are clearly defined, including resources and measures to be taken, while others are just loosely designed and expressed in more exhortative language. There is no clear internal logic that one might detach from it, since it includes a quite variegated set of policies, programs, conferences, pieces of legislation, emergency action, and so on.[11] This can be taken as the result of putting together variegated social interests with differing degrees of organization, as available evidence tends to show.[12] A complementary hypothesis concerns conciliation of the given preferences of two very important actors in the plan formulation; namely, Núcleo de Estudos da Violência (social science research institute on violence at the State University of São Paulo) and Itamaraty. If the process of policy formulation had a clear impact in the heterogeneous character of the plan, it is also true that it follows very closely the recommendation of the World Conference of Human Rights, as stated in the 1993 Declaration of Vienna.

From official data (Programa Nacional de Direitos Humanos [PNDH]: Um Ano de Balanço; Boletim da Secretaria Nacional de Direitos Humanos, Ministerio da Justiça, 1997), we can detach five major plan objectives: protection of the right to life, freedom, equal treatment under the law, education, and international upgrading. Violence is " the major problem selected for Plan intervention," as is made explicit not only in its introduction, but also in the targets pursued and obtained, as I will show later on. This is not altogether surprising if we take into consideration the recent history of human rights in Brazil. In fact, the movement for the defense of human rights, in Brazil as well as in several Latin America countries, was chiefly directed toward criticism of authoritarian rule and ill treatment of political prisoners. It was more of a political movement, using human rights as a means of demanding the establishment of the state of law. Nowadays, violence seems to be specifically connected to police violence and crime, something identified as a big problem already in the mid-1980s. This kind of violence has quite a different nature than torture of political prisoners. Moreover, political rhetoric in the 1960s focused on violence as pertaining to social structure itself, while now it is dealt with by an individualistic approach. It is taken as an individual act (by a police officer) perpetrated against the inviolability of a human person. In fact, social violence is not contemplated in the plan, as we will see later. Emphasis is clearly given to civil rights, mostly to those closer to the "guarantees of physical integrity" of each person (PNDH 1997, pp. 7, 8, 11).

Thus, most of the targets defined within the plan's first goal—"the right to life"—are aimed at the reorganization of the police apparatus.[13] Specification of this major objective seems to result from a diagnosis that violence in Brazilian society is mostly an effect of police force inadequacy (abusive, inefficient, and materially defective). After three years, one can claim that this objective was pursued tenaciously, and with reasonable success. Indeed, after the first year, 25 percent of the targets had been reached, such as those concerning armament control and training of the police force, production of maps of urban violence, legislation development for combating crime and impunity, and traffic control. At the end of 1999, thirty-nine of forty-nine proposed targets were already being implemented, some of them entirely achieved. The goal was slightly modified, a first initiative being made toward the formulation of policies for the reduction of social, economical, and cultural inequalities. Aside from that, some measures were taken aimed at media campaigns for disseminating an awareness of human rights.

Let us now consider the plan's second objective. The "right to freedom" encompasses twenty-six targets, all of them still under implementation in 1999. They can be sorted into three areas: attention to the imprisoned population (mostly aimed at reducing its size), banning of forced work through closer inspection of suspect enterprises, and revaluation of censorship criteria (mainly in mass media). Actions taken with the intention of influencing the judiciary to use "alternative punishment" for nonviolent crimes should be mentioned for their novelty.

The third goal—"equal treatment before the law"—comprehends the greatest number of targets, totaling 105, almost 50 percent of the plan's targets. These targets, mostly oriented to protecting minorities, describe the rights of children and teenagers, the aged, women, blacks, indigenous populations, foreigners, refugees, migrants, people with HIV, drug addicts, homosexuals, and the physically handicapped. Symbolic violence is the major reference of those measures oriented to protect minorities, which include "positive" discrimination.

After its first year, only 17 percent of the targets had been achieved. However, by the end of 1999 most of them were already under a process of implementation. One initiative that deserves mention, under the responsibility of the Ministério de Educação e Cultura, is the inclusion of gender and race as a reference for the basic curriculum of elementary education. The Secretaria de Comunicação Social, on the other hand, is making it possible for "ethnical groups" to be represented in advertisements of the government and public enterprises.

The school scholarship program, under the responsibility of the Ministério de Seguridade Social, by which parents are paid for keeping their children at school, has already shown positive results since 1998. Finally, "citizenship counters" were established in some metropolitan areas, through which law students and lawyers give free advice to underprivileged populations. These counters help in resolving small neighborhood conflicts and in obtaining basic civil records. Besides that, they help to spread information concerning citizens' rights. It would seem that this is the accomplishment of what would be, classically, the first step for ensuring equality before the law, since without documents, an individual cannot exercise his or her citizen's rights. As the status of citizenship is not a metaphysical one, meaning a real chance to autonomously interact with the state bureaucracy, the citizenship counter renders an invaluable service. It helps to universalize this status, acknowledging the immense difficulty that a poor and semi-illiterate population has to understand and take advantage of the bureaucracy that it helps to maintain through taxes.

The dissemination of human rights, the chief content of the fourth goal, encompassed thirteen targets, but not a single one obtained during the program's first year. At the end of the second year, the *Human Rights Manual for Everyday Life* (1997) was released to the public to be used for training "human rights agents." A second manual, a translation of a U.N. text, was published, aimed at disseminating the nature and relevance of the voting process. Furthermore, the Voluntary Civil Service, still in an experimental phase, started to include courses on human rights. To these achievements one should add, by the end of 1999, the institution of a National Award for Human Rights, the sponsoring of an extension course on human rights and citizenship at the University of Brasília, and the formulation and dissemination of curricular parameters for elementary education, to be adopted by the official education network.

Last but not least comes "international action," oriented to grant a "politically correct" image of the Brazilian political system. This goal comprises twenty-six targets, mostly ratification and implementation of U.N. conventions. According to a self-evaluation document, this has been the most successful goal, Brazil being the third country to elaborate a human rights plan.

Before closing this section, it is worth noticing that the plan's first paragraph states that policies must be devised to reduce great economic, social, and cultural inequalities still existing in Brazil. This would take care of the "right to development." However, there is not a single target directly oriented to lessen these very high levels of inequality.

Appraisal of the efforts made by the Human Rights Watch World Report in 1999 was quite critical.[14] Failure to reduce police violence, as well as the increase in the repression of the "landless" movement, the MST (Movimento Social do Trabalhadores, a peaceful social movement that became organized in the early 1980s, spread throughout the country, and struggled for land reform through methods such as land occupation support among landless laborers), constitutes their main criticism of government efforts. Furthermore, this NGO remarks that treatment of prisoners continues to violate international standards. Reduction of forced labor is the only acknowledged positive result of the plan implementation.

Evaluation of the Human Rights National Plan should not be restricted to contrasting proposed and accomplished targets. The very kind of rights that are chosen for special attention indicates main values in policy formulation. Protection of those rights in Brazil grants special attention to the human body as a sacred space, suggesting that human rights should not be read as a legal code but as the expression of the intrinsic and inalienable value of every human being, which is his or her dignity. To ensure that value, the first task is to eliminate violence without purpose. The second major value informing the choice made is expressed in the proposition that human dignity becomes endangered whenever people are living within contexts marked by extreme poverty. Nonetheless, no clear definition is given of the measures that should be taken for altering such a context, even while mentioning the importance of protecting social, economic, and cultural rights. The third important value concerns respect for differences, emphasizing the protection of "minority groups." In this version, the dignity of any human being would be endangered in societies marked by spurious social differentiation. This being the case, human rights policies should turn toward the elimination of prejudice and the protection of legitimated differences.

Based on those values, a definite set of goals was devised for policy implementation. If it is true that we cannot evaluate something that was never intended to be done, we can, on the other hand, evaluate the choice itself, when, as in this case, there exists an obvious reference for defining a human rights policy. If we take the 1947 declaration as a parameter, there are a few usual typologies that might be helpful for defining the choice made, from which I will take the one proposed by Donnelly (cf. Alves 1994, 46).

Viewed within this typology, it is possible to identify objectives 1 to 3 as aimed at the protection of personal rights (art. 2–6, 15), even though some targets pertaining to the first objective could also be taken as having in mind the protection of legal rights (art. 8–12). Objective 4, in turn, considers an aspect that might express cultural and social rights (art. 27–28). Rights to civil freedom (art. 13, 18–20) and to subsistence, as well as economic and political rights (art. 21–26) are absent in the plan.

The examination of those targets that were accomplished revealed the weakness of the efforts to achieve objective 4, compared to the others. Thus, I would suggest that the Human Rights National Plan granted priority to the legal code for protection of personal rights; that is, it assumed a clearly liberal defense of the State of Right. Itamaraty's interpretation did not have enough influence, except for the signing of U.N. conventions. Previously organized interest groups concerned with the issue of violence and the defense of minorities are the ones that obtain public resources for implementing those measures they advocate. Now it is time to consider the way in which this choice may affect the dynamics of Brazilian political culture.

HUMAN RIGHTS POLICY AND CIVIC CULTURE: A CONTRIBUTION TO DEMOCRACY

One can distinguish two main paths on the road of public education directly affecting the culture of rights. The first one derives from institutional and political practice itself, in the sense that the way governors deal with existing institutions can strengthen or weaken the value of human and constitutional rights. Literature on the topic confirms that political action is directly associated with the belief in its effectiveness (Pateman 1970). If the citizen believes that his or her political action can somehow alter his or her life's context, the citizen will be more prone to activate his or her rights than if he or she is convinced that such an investment would be irrelevant. A major factor ensuring this effectiveness is, of course, the real functioning of the democratic system. If governments themselves do not respect democratic institutions, using them to manipulate public opinion or for their own benefits, the results can easily be deduced.

The second path can be better controlled by the government proper, being made up of policies clearly oriented to changing political conceptions. Those policies are supposed to strengthen or introduce into the collective mentality notions of political rights and duties. Here we enter into the area of civic education.

The vastness and complexity of these paths require a precise analytical focus. In regard to the first path, I would like to call attention to the relationship between the state and NGOs, due to their important role in the area of human rights governmental policies, and not just in Brazil (Beetham 1995, 7; Brett 1995; Oliveira 1997). Delivering free public services, their resources come from foundations interested in the running of those services, so NGOs are responsive to those foundations, not to the society in which they work. This is an important distinction with regard to governments that, sustained by taxes collected from society, must publicly justify the allocation of those funds. Partnership between governments and NGOs tends to obscure this point, freeing the government from its responsibility when it delegates to those organizations the power to shape the public sphere. This type of institutional connection is similar to the one established all over the governmental web, through the consulting system. The difference, however, is that consultants do not have the power to manage public policies.

In what concerns the plan under evaluation, there is even a clear denial that it is a deliberate exercise of power. On the contrary, it is presumed that human rights are above political parties, corporations, and ideologies (*Boletim* 1998). And since this is also the presumption on which NGOs act, partnership here functions quite smoothly. If the activation of political rights, crucial for the consolidation of democracy, implies differentiation and possibly a resulting ideological conflict, the unanimity around that specific public policy could be a factor for weakening the incipient Brazilian democratic culture.[15]

Brett (1995) raises a similar problem while studying this issue at the international level. These human rights interest and pressure groups, according to Brett, could have inscribed in their doorways, "Governments lie." With this saying, Brett is calling attention to the fact that only active NGO control can force government to implement human rights policies, since "even the most democratic and law abiding governments do not publicize their human rights violations" (p. 101). Brett then asserts that full acceptance by the international setting of NGO cooperation reduced the "confrontational element inherent in NGO–Government relations . . . with NGO (and governmental) experts together endeavoring to bring about changes in governmental attitudes and actions" (p. 102).

Whenever NGOs and government experts work together, technical gains can be achieved, but, politically, the result will be a reduction of governmental responsibility and contraction of alternative sources of interpretation, conflict, and controversy. Accepting that the relationship between NGOs and government is "perforce a delicate one," Brett (1995) concludes her analysis with the following question: "Are [governments] more likely to act if approached privately or if there is a public campaign?" Her answer is clear: "If the relationship with government . . . becomes too close, the NGOs will in fact become part of the establishment, with a vested interest in it, preserving their status, rights and privileges . . . rather than being prepared to challenge the entire direction" (pp. 107–108).

We recognize the same criticism, already made of the workers' and opposition parties, of social movements or any political association that accepts being co-opted. The main supposition behind this criticism is that only open conflict allows for a clear argumentative confrontation, and it is precisely this confrontation that may bring forth a pluralistic and consensual value domain, the main characteristic of a culture of rights. Brett's (1995) description fits Brazilian policy for human rights quite well. I did not find any organization for human rights that would keep a position, either external or critical, towards the plan. Moreover, preliminary analysis of state and municipal programs for the protection of human rights reveals that the adopted format obeys the pattern established by the federal government.

In the second area of intervention, the core feature derives from the failure in implementing the plan's fourth objective. This objective must be put in the highly controversial context of the adequacy of this kind of education by the state. If we take the English experience, we see that "education for citizenship" does not have any importance at all, because education and politics in that society are viewed as clearly different domains. Politics are fundamentally the province of parties, while education is done by institutions specifically designed for the transmission of knowledge. Political education, for the English, is something viewed with suspicion, because it sounds like political indoctrination. Most of the people are politically socialized by their families, by the media, or by the "implicit curriculum." During the 1980s there were movements toward a "political alphabetization," but it seems that they ended up by provoking a return to "teaching whatever is basic" (Hahn 1998, 6). The North American contrast is significant: Since Jefferson's day, scholars, political leaders, and public opinion held that the future of democracy depends on the education of its citizens. So, under the name of "social studies," democracy was to be taught in schools, and Hahn assures us that every American high school student is introduced to the basic principles of the Bill of Rights and the Constitution in courses on government organization.

Regarding Brazilian tradition, civic education was taken as a state function during the authoritarian period. Initiatives through the plan under analysis require more careful research, but one can suppose that the failing in the achievement of objective 4 can be an indication of the difficulty felt by state agents in assuming that function in a democratic regime. Nonetheless, the plan targets implemented so far account for a significant increase in civic education. If we compare the last four years with the last thirty, for instance, governments have never been so active in disseminating human rights within society. Available data, however, is insufficient for evaluating the impact of this formal teaching in the universe of symbolic representation of power and politics. Further research is needed to grasp what police officers, social movement leaders, or students, to mention a few, are learning in those courses and seminars directed toward the dissemination of the human rights code. In addition, special programs must be devised if one really wants to determine the impact of this learning on actual behavior.

One major obstacle is the very low level of formal education. If, for instance, one takes into consideration the U.N. Manual of Political Rights, it becomes quite clear that the language in which it is written in not understood by the majority of Brazilian adults. Recent data show that 66 percent of Brazilian citizens have less than four years in school (*Jornal do Brasil* 2000), insufficient for understanding the language of official documents. This means that a language compatible with ordinary grammar and vocabulary must somehow be developed for efficient transmission of knowledge. Cabral (1999) has pointed to the consequences of this "communication deficit," in the sense that those who do not understand what goes on in the political world are also less prone to exercise their political rights.

A second important problem has to do with the kind of knowledge that is transmitted. The Human Rights Plan is more concerned with civil rights than with political and social rights. The main question then is whether it is possible to secure human rights without activating the language of political and social rights. In what concerns education, political rights should get priority, since it is through exercising those rights that people may come to understand the very idea of having a right. However, except for the translation of this U.N. Manual of Humans Rights and Elections, political rights are not mentioned in the plan.

But education is not just the ordered and systematic transmission of particular content. It also includes an "implicit curriculum." In other words, measures taken for assuring other plan objectives carry along with them a set of values that disseminate a certain representation of citizenship rights. Whenever the public hears repeatedly that this or that crime, or this or that way of combating it, is against human rights, an association is in process, giving a specific meaning to those rights and favoring adherence or rejection to the very idea of rights. Whenever discrimination based on race, gender, sexual preference, age, and other qualifications is cited for hurting equality, an idea of what it means to respect the rights of citizenship is also being transmitted.

In this sense, education done through the Human Rights National Plan disseminates a concept of rights that is quite akin to liberal democracy. This hypothesis is congenial to the evidence obtained by Duarte, Barsted, Taulois, and Garcia (1993) in their research designed to capture the effect of policies for the dissemination of human rights in an urban outskirts neighborhood. A particularly interesting aspect of this research is the fact that the authors did not stick to the explicit intention of the project, of "converting" the people to the rationality appropriate to the logic of citizenship. "Disciplining" and "macro-institutionalization" hypotheses were also considered. To put into practice liberal–individualistic ideals constitutes a problem for the authors, who leave open the meaning to be conferred on civic education. Hence, it is seen as imposing one's own values on the process of constituting citizenship (p. 9). Those values are identified as "individualization," "rationalization," and "responsabilization." The first has to do with the significance conferred to the individual person above society; the second contrasts with mythical thinking. The moral relationship between them, in its turn, establishes the area of responsibility.

Although I fully agree with the "disciplining" hypothesis, I would like to draw attention to the identification proposed by Duarte and colleagues (1993) of the process of building citizenship with liberal democratic ideals. Recent theoretical developments have questioned the straight association between the language of rights, as it is normally treated, and the concept of citizenship. From this perspective, one may say that citizenship is not necessary and exclusively the status conferred to an individual through which he or she adheres to a chart of rights and duties. Citizenship can come into effect and be represented by other patterns.

Van Gusteren (1998), for instance, reminds us that we could think about the citizen as "a responsible person, who chooses whatever he wants among several possibilities that are offered to him in the market, and accepts the consequences of his choice; or as a person linked to another in a chain of mutual help; or as a proud member of a 'public community', for which he would be ready to sacrifice himself" (p. 14). Here, we find the liberal democratic, the communitarian, and the republican versions of democracy, each one having a specific potential for ordering political society. Pocock's (1975) description of republican politics give us a hint of what could be a democratic polity based on the understanding of the human person as a *zoon politikon*. Apart from the evaluation one could make of these different representations, their very nomination produces a wider dimension for interpreting the strict process of civic education that was weakly achieved via the Human Rights National Plan.

CONCLUSION

If Brazilian culture is in fact clearly marked by authoritarianism, the emphasis conferred by the Human Rights National Plan on individual and minorities rights can be taken as a positive contribution, in the sense that it strengthens a more democratic perspective. The mere consciousness of the citizen of his or her rights, besides the obligation of being subjected to government decisions, constitutes an important source of power for the exercise of resistance to authoritarian decisions. Moreover, the targets are designed to ensure a level of equality that stimulates respect for social differences. Such respect would contribute to legitimacy in their public manifestation. If transformed into everyday practice, this respect will favor an advantageous posture toward a more competent dialogue in dealing with conflicts and deliberating about appropriate public policies.

Conformance or nonconformance with the value configuration of the European political tradition is strongly imbedded in Brazilian culture. Within that tradition, the political system is hierarchically ordained. This means society's governing elite is responsible for political trends. The right to protest is granted to the people whenever they disagree with the direction chosen by the elite, but there is no idea that popular initiative in the sense of proposing an itinerary or programs for action, or, even less, to interfere in state affairs, are rights or duties.

It is in this sense that egalitarianism, typical of the liberal version of democracy, can function as a sledgehammer that demolishes such a traditional representation of the exercise of power. This "negative freedom," defended by that ideology and expressed by policies designed to ensure minority rights, suggests that each member of society has the right to live the way he or she wants, with due respect for the ways of others. The state's duty is to guarantee that right in practice. In this perspective, however, popular claims concerning governmental obligations to guarantee the "common good" become delegitimized, because when freedom is guaranteed to a person, he or she must bear the responsibility of providing for his or her own well-being. This idea, once assimilated, contributes to weakening or even demolishing traditional expectations related to state functions. This can be taken as the first potential consequence of plan implementation for reshaping Brazilian political culture.

However, if the dissemination of positive political rights that grant popular control over the governing elite is not a goal, then the more complete effect of bringing about this model of citizenship is doubtful. Developed as a solution for political crisis involving ample popular mobilization, even its pluralist reformulation according to Schumpeter or Dahl doesn't leave out of consideration the presupposition of ample knowledge of political rights. I refer here not to the right to protest, but to the right to actively influence public affairs. If it is true that Brazilian popular culture is strongly marked by this representation of power as an "emanation" from the top of the social pyramid, egalitarianism can foster anomy before a democratic order would come into force.

It must also be noted that there are requirements to the proper functioning of the liberal democratic model that make its adequacy to Brazilian conditions questionable. One can state that reduction of socioeconomic differences and dissemination of political information would be the primary provisions of plan implementation. As there is no interest within the determination of this plan's goals in attending to these primary conditions, the impact of the Human Rights National Plan for democratic consolidation is put into question.

Finally, I would like to consider some possible consequences of disseminating this language of rights in the modeling of Brazilian popular culture. I believe that it is possible to distinguish three results from this dynamic. The first, which seems highly probable to me if we take into consideration the way knowledge is scattered in our society, would be an increase in the general confusion already in existence. If we admit that political illiteracy and the very low level of information of the great majority of Brazilian citizens hinders the transparency of a language about rights, it is possible that the association of human rights with safety would even strengthen the revulsion for the "rights of bandits," already detected by Caldeira (1991). But putting this vocabulary into action can also lead to an appropriation of new words for solving the question of power and, if it is so, one can consider that even presenting a considerable series of problems that policy would favor the strengthening of a democratic ethos.

Even though the conclusion stated here is tentative, I hope to bring to collective reflection problems that deserve more cautious attention apart from any evaluation of the more canonic discourse about human rights. The domain of the language of rights, beyond the ideals that have a tendency to be associated with that discourse, is crucial for the complete exercise of citizenship. I believe there is a strong consensus regarding this issue and much remains to be done in our society.

NOTES

1. Cf. Lacey and Haakonssen (1992): "Nothing is more deeply rooted in the American political tradition than the vocabulary of rights. . . . The American institutional setup . . . strongly encourages the persistence of ideas or rights" (pp. 1–3). They go on to argue for the importance of the foundational myth that brings with it "self-conscious design" as the chief determinant of political society (pp. 6–7). Social rights are understood, basically, as the rights to health, social security, and education. The right to work, which has had so much significance in the constitution of a Brazilian way of forming a concept of citizenship, is, apparently, out of fashion (Oliveira 1991; Carvalho 1997; Vidal 1998).

2. There are many explanations for this situation. Carvalho (1996), for instance, asserts that political rights in Brazil are traditionally associated with a social function that must be performed only by the more suitable citizens, something that reflects the positivist root in our republican ideas.

3. In the social sciences literature, Caldeira (1991), Pinheiro (1994), Benevides (1994), and Oliveira (1997) are expressive of this kind of concern.

4. About the specificity of the focus of political science on the subject, see Beetham (1995, 6g).

5. The main sources are Federal Government, Brasilia (1996), Department of Justice (http://www.mj.gov.br), and *Boletim da Secretaria Nacional de Direitos Humanos* (1998).

6. The Secretaria Nacional de Direitos Humanos is located in the Ministry of Justice, which recently acquired the status of Secretaria de Estado.

7. For further analysis on Brasilian human rights, see Alves (1994), Lafer (1991, 1995), Fester (1994), and Oliveira (1998).

8. This was an interesting moment in Brazilian politics of the 1960s, because at that point in time guerrilla warfare started. Many militants decided to follow the legal path instead, and pressures in the U.N. Human Rights Commission grew considerably.

9. Carter's human rights policies should also be taken into consideration in understanding this move.

10. Lafer (1991) expressed in the classical conciliatory tone of Brazilian politics what he thought was proper to Brazilian diplomacy: to use a traditional repertoire in order to bring about innovation: "The 'new' emerges from the existent" (cf. Alves 1994, XXXVI).

11. In this last case, it seems that the government reacted as quickly as it could to human rights violations that got a lot of publicity at the time, such as the burning of an Indian or the killing of old people in an asylum.

12. One evidence concerns the kind of space granted in the structure of the Secretaria de Direitos Humanos to two long-standing interest groups (children and teenagers, and the handicapped). The other concerns those groups that were successfully organized during the constituent assembly (Oliveira 1991), whose demands obtained significant attention in the plan itself.

13. Even though reduction of traffic violence appeals to disarmament of society, and some concerns over impunity may also be present.

14. The same thing applies to the yearly report from the U.S. State Department in 2000.

15. For a review of the literature about the relationship between the state and NGOs in Brazil, see Candler (2000, esp. pp. 47–48).

BIBLIOGRAPHY

Alves, J. L. 1994. *Os Direitos Humanos como Tema Global*. São Paulo: Educação Perpetiva.

Beetham, D., ed. 1995. *Politics and Human Rights*. Oxford: PSA/Blackwell.

Benevides, M. V. 1994. "Cidadania e Democracia." *Lua Nova* 33: 35.

Boletim da Secretaria Nacional de Direitos Humanos: OPNDH em Movimento, n.1, n. 2, n.3, n.4 (March/April 1998), n.5 (May/June 1998).

Brett, R. 1995. "The Role and Limits of Human Rights NGOs at the United Nations." In *Politics and Human Rights*, edited by D. Beetham. Oxford: PSA/Blackwell.

Cabral, M. V. 1999. "O Exercício da Cidadania Política em Portugal." Mimeographed.

Caldeira, T. 1984. *A Política dos Outros*. São Paulo: Brasiliense.

———. 1991. "Direitos Humanos ou Privilégio de Bandidos." Novos Estudos, Cebrap.

Candler, G. 2000. "The Professions and Public Policy: Expanding the Third Sector." *International Political Science Review* 21: 23–42.

Carvalho, J. M. 1996. *A Construção da Ordem*. Rio de Janeiro: UFRJ/Relume Dumará.

———. 1997. "Lei, Justiça, Cidadania." Relatório de pesquisa, CPDOC/FGV/ISER.

Donnelly, Jack. 1986. "International Human Rights: A Regime Analysis." *International Organization* 40 (3): 599–642.

Duarte, L. F., L. Barsted, M. R. Taulois, and H. M. Garcia. 1993. "Vicissitudes e Limites da Conversçãoà Cidadania nas Classes Populares Brasileiras." *RBCS* 22: 5–19.

Fester, Antônio C. R. 1994. "Direitos Humanos: um Debate necessário." Instituto Interamericano de Direitos Humanos, São Paulo, Brasiliense.

Hahn, Carole L. 1998. *Becoming Political: Comparative Perspectives on Citizenship Education*. New York: State University of New York Press.

Human Rights Watch World Report. 1999. New York: Human Rights Watch.

Jornal do Brasil. 2000. February 14, p. 5.

Lacey, M., and K. Haakonssen. 1992. *A Culture of Rights: The Bill of Rights in Philosophy, Politics and Law, 1971–1991*. New York: Cambridge University Press.

Lafer, Celso. 1991. *A Reconstrução dos Direitos Humanos—Um diálogo com o pensamento de Hannah Arendt*. São Paulo: Cia. Das Letras.

———. 1995. "A Soberania e os Direitos Humanos." *Lua Nova* 35: 37.

Lamounier, B. 1982. "Formação de um pensamento político autoritário na primeira República." In *O Brasil Republicano*. Vol. 2: *História Geral da Civilização Brasileira*. São Paulo: Difel/Difusão Editorial, S.A.

Lopes, J. B. 1971. *Sociedade Industrial no Brasil, Difusão Européia do Livro*. Rio de Janeiro.

Newman, S. 2000. "Universalism/Particularism: Towards a Poststructuralist Politics of Universality." Paper presented at IPSA 2000. Mimeographed.

Oliveira, I. R. 1988. *Trabalho e Política*. Petropolis: Vozes.

———. 1991. "Direitos Sociais no Debate Constitucional." Relatório de Pesquisa: FORD/ANPOCS.

———. 1997. "Princípios de Justiça e Legitimação do Estado Contemporâneo." Sociedade e Estado, UnB.

———. 1998. "A Política dos Direitos Humanos do Governo Fernando Henrique Cardozo." *Comunicação e Política* 5 (2): 87–102.

Pateman, C. 1970. "Political Culture, Political Structure and Political Change." *British Journal of Political Science* 1: 291–305.

Pereira, V. 1979. *O Coração da Fábrica*. São Paulo: Campus

Pinheiro, P. S. 1994. "Pobreza, Violência e Direitos Humanos." In *Novos Estudos*, Cebrap.

Pocock, J.G.A. 1975. *The Machiavellian Moment: Florentine Political Thought and the Atlantic Republican Tradition*. Princeton, N.J.: Princeton University Press.

Programa Nacional de Direitos Humanos: Um Ano de Balanço. Boletim da Secretaria Nacional de Direitos Humanos, Ministerio da Justiça, 1997.

Reis, F. W., and B. Lamounier. 1981. *Direito, Cidadania e Participação*. São Paulo: Tao Ed.

Van Gusteren, H. R. 1998. *A Theory of Citizenship: Organizing Plurality in Contemporary Democracies*. Oxford: Westview Press.

Vidal, Dominique. 1998. *La Politique au quartier*. Paris: Fondation Maison des Sciences de l'Homme.

PART II

THE UNITED STATES AND THE INTERNATIONAL PROMOTION OF DEMOCRACY

CHAPTER 5

Plowing the Sea?
International Defense of
Democracy in the
Age of Illiberal Democracy

Christopher Sabatini

The expansion of democratic government in Latin America in the 1980s brought with it a growing consensus on the importance of protecting democratic governments through collective action. In the 1990s a web of agreements emerged, individually or inscribed in trade and other international pacts, that threaten expulsion, or, in the case of the Organization of American States (OAS), sanctions where democracy is overturned or interrupted. The high point of this emerging international consensus around democracy came in 1991, when the Organization of American States Permanent Council approved Resolution 1080, and then in less than two years successfully acted to condemn the overthrow of democratic governments in Haiti, Peru, and Guatemala. Yet as Elsa Cardozo Da Silva shows in Chapter 3 and Isabel Ribeiro de Oliveira discusses in Chapter 4, at the advent of the twenty-first century, democracy in the region appears to have stagnated and in some cases reversed. The most overt and obvious cases of authoritarian reversion that agreements such as Resolution 1080 were intended to prevent for now seem to be a thing of the past. Increasingly, the trend appears to be one of elected leaders who, with the legitimacy of the popular vote and often public opinion, bend and trample on many of the basic institutional checks and balances essential to democratic governance. The phenomenon has several names: delegative democracy, plebiscitary democracy, and illiberal democracy. The general concept is the same: the erosion or even violation of democratic norms and institutions by elected officials, often with the support of a public that is increasingly unsatisfied with democracy. Events in countries like Venezuela, Peru, and Ecuador require us to reexamine the existing mechanisms for defending democratic governance. Specifically, how effective have the OAS democratic defense measures been in addressing the deterioration of democracy in some countries? Do these new threats to long-term democratic stability require new measures, and can international consensus around collective defense of democracy support such reforms?

THE OAS AND THE DEFENSE OF DEMOCRACY

In the Western Hemisphere, rhetorical commitment to democracy as the preferred form of government enjoys a long pedigree. As early as 1936, signatories to the multilateral Declaration of Principles of Inter-American Solidarity and Cooperation recognized the need for "a common democracy throughout America."[1] Signed more than a decade later, the OAS Charter established democracy as the only form of government that can realize the goals of the OAS, and to this end committed the organization to defend it. The Charter's preamble declared that "representative democracy is an indispensable condition for the stability, peace and development of the region." Article 2 in the body of the Charter sets out as one of the central aims of the organization "to promote and consolidate representative democracy, with due respect for the principle of non-intervention."[2]

But it is the principle of nonintervention that is most emphasized in the Charter and until the last decade most characterized the OAS's policy in regard to democratic defense. Article 12 of the Charter severely restricts the organization's power to enforce its rhetorical commitment to democracy, stating that the organization "has no powers other than those expressly conferred upon it by the Charter and none of whose provisions authorizes it to intervene in matters that are within the internal jurisdiction of Member States." For Latin American states who feared that defense of democracy would be used as a cover for U.S. unilateral intervention in domestic affairs, these principles of state sovereignty and noninterventionism took precedence over the hemisphere's goals of creating a common democracy. During the Cold War, the United States for its part made selective and instrumental reference to the OAS's democratic mission when it fit with its larger foreign policy objectives of preventing Communist incursion in the hemisphere. In the cases where the OAS did draw on its original charter to denounce violations (Nicaragua in 1979 and Panama in 1989), it stopped short of recommending actions, and, particularly in the case of Panama, the denunciations were inconsistent and contradictory. Thus, for the better part of the OAS's existence, military coups and nondemocratic governments were allowed to persist despite the organization's stated commitment to democratic norms and government.

Not until 1991, after all member states boasted elected governments, did the OAS adopt a series of measures that would bring the collective weight of the institution to defend democracy. In 1991, in a General Assembly meeting in Santiago, the OAS adopted the Santiago Commitment to Democracy, and later the OAS approved Resolution 1080. While the Santiago Commitment reaffirmed and strengthened the organization's "inescapable commitment to democracy," Resolution 1080 established steps that would allow the OAS to respond quickly to any immediate interruption of democratic government in the region.[3] According to the groundbreaking resolution, "Any occurrences giving rise to the sudden or irregular interruption of the democratic political institutional process or of the legitimate exercise of power by the democratically elected government in any of the Organization's member states" requires the OAS General Secretary to convene a meeting of the Permanent Council to analyze the situation and decide whether to call an ad hoc meeting of foreign ministers or a special meeting of the General Assembly.[4] The emergency session is "to look into events collectively and adopt any decisions deemed appropriate, in accordance with the Charter and international law."[5] While the adoption of diplomatic, political, or economic sanctions by member states is to be voluntary, by setting out a series of procedures the resolution established steps that would allow the OAS to respond quickly to an interruption of democratic government in the region. Within those procedures the resolution provides the opportunity for member states to decide whether or not to apply measures to punish the offending party.

In 1992 the OAS added the Washington Protocol to the possible threat of economic and political sanctions. Fully ratified in 1997, the document amended the OAS Charter to allow the suspension of member-state representatives from the OAS by a two-thirds vote in the General Assembly if the member's "democratically constituted government has been overthrown by force."[6] In effect, the measure established the OAS as a hemispheric association of democracies, which reserved the right to determine membership based on the democratic credentials of the governments.

In 1993 the OAS General Assembly reaffirmed and—at least in principle— expanded its commitment to its collective support of democracy in the Declaration of Managua. The Declaration states the organization's awareness of the need to expand its mandate from seeking solutions to crises "towards preventing such crises." Through the declaration, the OAS recognizes that "the ongoing threats to the stability of the democratic systems in the Hemisphere call for a new, dynamic and comprehensive look at the role of the organization."[7] Unfortunately, as a declaration, the document has no formal bearing on the operations of the OAS, and offers little in the way of concrete initiatives. What exactly is to be done as a multilateral diplomatic effort by the regional body remained unstated.

The existing OAS measures (Resolution 1080 and the Washington Protocol) to defend democracy rest primarily on their deterrent effect. The primary aim of Resolution 1080 and the Washington Protocol is to deter coup plotters and, once a violation has taken place, to punish the offending regime through economic and diplomatic sanctions. The central assumption behind the deterrent effect of these agreements is that those tempted to seize power by force will take into their calculations the threat of diplomatic, political, and economic sanctions that their act will trigger and determine them to be too costly. For these measures to effectively deter potential aggressors, however, the threat of punishment has to be credible and the threatened sanctions need to be sufficiently strong to genuinely promise a cost to the offending regime or actors. This is as true of political denunciations and diplomatic isolation as it is of economic sanctions.[8]

The key difficulty with Resolution 1080 and the Washington Protocol is that they are aimed at an overt crisis. The event or act that triggers collective action is clear: the "interruption of the democratic political institutional process." Since its adoption, Resolution 1080 has been invoked four times—Haiti, Peru, Guatemala, and Paraguay—each time in situations where democratic government had been interrupted, either through a coup or through the dissolution of democratic government. Increasingly, however, the overt cases of authoritarian reversion seem to be a thing of the past. A series of events in Ecuador (in 1997) and in Paraguay (in 1999) served as a sharp reminder that long-term democratic stability can be shaped more by domestic political processes outside the authority of Resolution 1080 and the Washington Protocol.

In recognition of this, following the assassination of Paraguayan vice president Luis Maria Argaña, the U.S. mission to the OAS put forward an initiative at the 1999 General Assembly to strengthen the role of the OAS in mediating domestic political crises. The U.S. initiative outlined a series of measures intended to expand the legal authority and capacity of the thirty-four-member OAS to offer its good offices to situations of domestic turmoil before they reach regime-threatening crises. Coming from the United States, however, the proposal was promptly voted down by the General Assembly. Another proposal emerged as a compromise that granted the OAS secretary general broader powers to act to prevent a crisis. Nevertheless, the proposal left a number of important points open for debate, including the steps that would trigger the secretary general's action and the latitude of the secretary general to act on behalf of the larger body.

The 1999 proposed reforms to the secretary general's office did little to address the weaknesses of the OAS's capacity to respond collectively in a way that would deter more subtle violations of democratic stability beyond the gross "interruption of the democratic political institutional processes" envisioned in Resolution 1080. The OAS collective defense of democracy remained wedded to deterring a more traditional style coup d'etat. At the same time, however, ambiguous but equally serious cases of disruption of democratic institutions and rights between 1997 and 2000 did not meet with collective reproach or action by the OAS. Attempts by the OAS to respond to several of these cases (as in Ecuador) and its failure to respond in others (as in Haiti, Peru, and arguably Venezuela) highlighted the deficiencies of Resolution 1080 and the Washington Protocol. The net effect of the OAS's inaction was to weaken the intended deterrent effect of these democratic defense measures. The following sections examine cases of democratic erosion and the international response (or lack thereof) in three countries: Peru, Ecuador (in 1997 and 2000), and Venezuela.

DEMOCRATIC EROSION AND
THE INTERNATIONAL RESPONSE

Three separate case studies in democratic crisis and erosion analyze a narrow period of time during which a series of events arguably signaled looming democratic challenges. The OAS's scope for action at these particular moments was severely limited by the existing regime governing collective defense of democracy, which bound the organization to an anachronistic definition of the threats to democratic stability. By failing to assume a stronger role in the events, the OAS weakened the internal cohesion of the body to act in the future at crucial turning points and diminished its moral and collective weight in the hemisphere in issues of democracy.

In 1992 the OAS invoked for a second time its powers under Resolution 1080 when Peruvian president Fujimori closed down Congress, suspended the constitution, and detained political opponents. While not a traditional military-style coup, the president's *autogolpe* set in motion the steps outlined in Resolution 1080: a snap meeting of the Permanent Council, a meeting of the foreign ministers, collective denunciation of the act by the ministers, and a demand to restore democracy. While the response helped to pressure the government into holding constituent assembly elections to draft a new constitution and restore elected government one year later, OAS member states were reluctant to take a more active oppositionist stance toward the government. Only the United States, Japan, and a handful of other countries imposed sanctions unilaterally.

OAS collective pressure in Peru only lasted as long as the crisis. In essence, as David Scott Palmer argues, "The OAS accepted the official Peruvian position that the measures suspending democracy reflected the special circumstances then present in the country and that they were temporary."[9] Under the siege of a bloody civil war and faced with an economic crisis, the government's claims of necessity and the support of Peruvian popular opinion appeared to influence the actions of the OAS.[10] Only eight months after Fujimori's coup, on December 14, 1992, the OAS "closed its consideration of the Peruvian case" after the Peruvian foreign minister agreed to submit a plan for the restoration of democracy within a year.[11]

The threat to democracy, however, did not end with the implementation of the plan, which eventually involved the election of a constituent assembly to draft a new constitution and new presidential elections, which Fujimori won handily. Unfortunately, after its brief denunciation of the coup, the OAS stepped back during the period of constitutional revision and approval that followed. The 1993 constitution and the institutions it created established several idiosyncrasies that permitted Fujimori to consolidate his power at the expense of political parties and state institutions. The constitution established a single chamber of Congress elected in a national, at-large district, the result of which was to further fragment and marginalize political parties. The constitution also included provisions that gave the executive broad powers to dissolve Congress and govern by decree and debilitated the supposedly independent electoral commission by dividing its functions into three different institutions.

After his reelection in 1995, the Fujimori government continued to demonstrate its authoritarian affinities, with little OAS response. Rather than dissolve government in one fell swoop and risk provoking an international response, the administration incrementally disassembled democratic institutions and selectively limited democratic rights and protections, all under the patina of legitimacy provided by the fact that the president and the progovernment Congress had been elected and enjoyed a certain degree of popular support. The clearest indication of the government's intention to impose its will was the controversy concerning Fujimori's desire to run for a third consecutive term in the 2000 elections. Under the 1993 constitution a president is banned from serving three consecutive terms, but in a bit of legalistic sophistry the president and his supporters in Congress argued that since Fujimori had served his first term under the earlier constitution, his 1995 to 2000 term was only his first under the existing constitution. In April 1997 the progovernment majority in Congress removed three justices of the constitutional court who had declared "inadmissible" under the constitution a law passed by the Congress that would allow the president to run for a third consecutive term. Later the government again violated the constitution when electoral authorities refused to recognize a petition with the constitutionally required number of signatures calling for a referendum on Fujimori's third term. The government's efforts to quash any challenge to Fujimori's constitutionally questionable third term were successful, and despite opposition, the president won the 2000 elections.

During the same time, the government embarked on a series of incremental policies intended to weaken the judiciary and bring it under the control of the executive. The list of policies and actions is dizzying: expansion of the supreme court and the appointment of new progovernment justices, reorganization of the judicial system and the public ministry under executive-appointed councils, the appointment of temporary justices favorable to the administration, and the gradual curtailment of the judiciary council's powers to promote and appoint justices. All of these measures came from the pro-Fujimori Congress and the executive through a series of laws and decrees that individually made it difficult to point to one specific act, but the net effect was to undermine judicial independence. The incremental nature of these laws also made it difficult to mobilize domestic popular opposition. While civil society may be able to stage a demonstration over a large event like the dissolution of the Supreme Court, people are unlikely to take to the streets because some arcane law on judicial appointments has been overturned.

Between 1997 and 2000 an alarming pattern of violations also emerged against freedoms of expression and the press that ranged from outright repression to intimidation from tabloids directed by the government. In 1997 the owner of a television station and a journalist were forced into exile after running a series of reports critical of the government. The reports included allegations that the government had wiretapped the phones of political opponents and that state security had tortured a former security agent who had leaked information to the press, and evidence of the illegal enrichment of the head of the state security agency, Vladimiro Montesinos. A host of other reporters also suffered similar intimidation and was forced to flee. This was accompanied by another more subtle strategy by the government that used progovernment tabloids (called the *prensa chincha*) to launch attacks against journalists who had been critical of the regime and against opponents. In all, according to a Peruvian civil society organization, the International Press and Society Institute, there were over 130 attacks against journalists and the media between November 1998 and June 2000. The overwhelming majority of these came from the state or actors believed to be working on behalf of the government.[12]

Yet while this pattern of abuse prompted a series of individual reactions by the OAS Inter-American Commission for Human Rights, it failed to provoke a collective response by the larger OAS body in the name of democratic defense. Coincidentally, the OAS General Assembly was meeting in Lima in 1997 when the government dismissed the three Constitutional Court justices. The OAS Secretary General, César Gaviria, refused to take a stand, calling it a domestic matter. The only official OAS response came from the Inter-American Commission of Human Rights. In a press release, the Commission denounced the removal of the justices and "warned of the negative effect this will have for democracy and the rule of law and, especially, for the independence and impartiality of the judges, which is a fundamental factor for the protection of human rights."[13] In November 1998 the Inter-American Human Rights Commission traveled to Peru at the request of the government to study the human rights situation. The Commission's trip report cited specific concerns about political intervention in the judicial system, the expansion of military trials of civilians, attacks against freedom of expression, and the dismissal by the electoral authorities of the petition requesting a referendum on a third term for Fujimori.[14] The spate of attacks on the press was treated in the same way. The Human Rights Commission accepted the cases of the television owner and journalist and of the three dismissed constitutional court justices, and the OAS's Special Rapporteur for Freedom of Expression issued a report on media in Peru in 1999.

By treating the issues through the Commission, however, the OAS gave the impression that the situation was a human rights concern, rather than a democracy issue that warranted collective reproach by the OAS and possible sanctioning. Despite these mounting incidences and the request by the three dismissed constitutional court judges for OAS action, no member government attempted to invoke Resolution 1080 or force a collective discussion of Peru on these issues. In isolation these do, of course, qualify as human rights cases. The question was if this pattern of abuses against basic democratic institutions and rights constituted a larger democratic issue that merited attention by the larger body.

The problem of treating each human rights case individually was brought home in 1999 when the Peruvian government withdrew from the obligatory jurisdiction of the Inter-American Court of Human

Rights. Under the OAS Charter, all member states are subject to the jurisdiction of the Inter-American Commission and the provisions of the American Declaration of the Rights and Duties of Man. Obligation to adhere to the decisions of the Inter-American Court, however, depends on a country's acceptance of the Inter-American Court's jurisdiction. In 1999, in reaction to a ruling concerning Chileans convicted of terrorism in Peru, the Fujimori government announced that it no longer accepted the jurisdiction of the Inter-American Court. Many suspected that the decision was aimed not at the case of the Chileans but at two upcoming cases: the case of television owner Baruch Ivcher that was next on the court's docket for Peru and the case of the three dismissed constitutional court justices. Both of the cases had turned into public-relations disasters for the government. The Inter-American Court declared the government's decision "inadmissible," but there was little it could do to actually force the government to accept its jurisdiction.[15] In the absence of a more active position on the part of the collective body of the OAS to examine the case of Peru, by publicly renouncing the Inter-American Court's jurisdiction the government reduced the scope of the hemispheric community's influence over Peru in matters of democracy.

The OAS's role in the 2000 elections was also less than effective as a collective body, a position that reflected a number of competing institutional interests and demands. Early in the process leading up to the 2000 presidential elections, a number of independent international groups openly criticized preelectoral conditions, citing the lack of objectivity of the media, physical attacks against candidates, smear campaigns organized by the government-supported *prensa chincha*, and the use of public funds for electoral purposes.[16] In March 2000 the OAS sent a delegation mission to Peru, at the request of the Peruvian government, to monitor the preelectoral and election-day processes. The hope of the Peruvian government was that the OAS delegation, led by former foreign minister of Guatemala Eduardo Stein, would prove less critical of a member state than independent groups such as the National Democratic Institute and the Carter Center. Instead, as part of the agreement for the funding of the OAS delegation, the OAS had to agree to let Ambassador Stein operate semiautonomously from the OAS Permanent Council; the stipulation allowed Stein to make declarations and determine the mission's position without consulting the larger body. Much to the Peruvian government's frustration, the OAS Electoral Mission to Peru turned into one of the government's staunchest critics.

In the first round of elections, on April 9, 2000, opposition candidate Alejandro Toledo, a Stanford-trained economist, surprised observers by receiving 40 percent of the vote and forcing a second-round

election between Fujimori and Toledo. Nevertheless, the first round
had been marred by irregularities in the voting process and unex-
plained delays in the tabulation of votes, large portions of which observers had not been allowed to witness. By the time of the second
round of the elections, on May 28, the OAS observer mission concluded
that little had been done to correct the serious deficiencies it had noted
in the first round. The conditions were made worse by an inexplicable
eleventh-hour decision by the Peruvian electoral authorities to institute a new computerized voter-tabulation system. In the highly charged
political atmosphere, the opposition candidate, Toledo, refused to participate in the second-round elections unless they were postponed and
these concerns were addressed. Shortly afterward, Ambassador Stein
and the OAS mission officially declared that they would not observe
the second-round elections. In an official statement, the mission denounced the "persistence of a pattern of insufficiencies, irregularities,
inconsistencies, and inequalities in the second round of the presidential elections."[17] In conclusion, the mission determined that "in accordance to international standards, the Peruvian electoral process is far
from being considered free and fair."[18] Despite the absence of international observers and a competitor, the government refused to change
the date, and held the election. It was not surprising that Fujimori
won, but only with just over 50 percent of the total vote. Despite pulling out of the race, Toledo received over 16 percent of the vote, and
over 30 percent of the ballots were spoilt, a number that obviously
was in part a response to Toledo's call to voters to file spoilt ballots in
protest. Given the results, the legitimacy of the elections was in doubt.

The Peruvian opposition, human rights groups, and some members
of the U.S. Congress clamored for an immediate invocation of Resolution
1080. Instead, the OAS decided to wait until the regular General Assembly meeting to be held less than a week later, on June 3–5 in Canada,
to discuss the Peruvian case and possible actions. At the assembly the
gathering of foreign ministers listened to reports by Ambassador Stein
and by the Peruvian government. Immediately afterward, the U.S.
delegation to the OAS, led by U.S. Ambassador Luis Lauredo, put forward a call to debate the case under Resolution 1080, which would
carry with it a possible collective denunciation of the regime and sanctions. However, the proposal had little broad backing from the member
states, and the representatives from Brazil and Mexico led a successful
charge to vote it down. Many of the states argued that in the end elections were an internal affair, and that proposing international sanctions amounted to international meddling in domestic issues.

As a result of a compromise among the member states, the General
Assembly issued a resolution without invoking Resolution 1080 or any

formal mechanism of democratic defense. The resolution only noted concern about the "credibility of the process and the outcome of the elections," and that reports of irregularities had not been "satisfactorily addressed." In a nod to ongoing and mounting worries about the state of democracy generally in Peru, the report noted the need to strengthen democratic institutions and rights, such as the judicial branch, the Constitutional Tribunal, and freedom of the press. The report proposed to send a high-level delegation to Peru, comprising the Secretary General of the OAS and the chair of the General Assembly, Canadian Foreign Minister Lloyd Axworthy, to explore with the government and opposition groups "options and recommendations aimed at further strengthening democracy in that country."[19]

In the end, many observers and even member representatives of the OAS felt that the issue had been inadequately addressed. The Peruvian government disingenuously claimed that a collective denunciation or action based on concerns about the freeness and fairness of the electoral process was unwarranted. However, the very basis of the democratic process that Resolution 1080 seeks to uphold is popularly elected government. The normative and legal claim upon which collective defense of democracy is based is that the right of popular sovereignty, manifested by the right of citizens to choose their own leaders, is greater than national sovereignty. In these cases, elections constitute the sine qua non of democratic governance and thus the basis of democracy contained in democratic defense documents. This position is strengthened by the condemnation of the election by a mission of the OAS. Unfortunately, the inability of the resolution to detail the application of democratic defense, and what specific rights and institutions that implied, weakened the resolution.

To be sure, there were general and specific conditions that made the Peru case more complicated. First, because the opposition candidate refused to participate in the second round, it appeared as if the international community was taking his side and supporting his decision and candidacy. In the weeks leading up to the second-round election and immediately afterward, Toledo had demonstrated himself to be both erratic and inexperienced. It became difficult to separate support for a free and fair electoral process from an opposition candidate who had been victimized by the process and who was clumsily trying to present himself as the legitimate alternative to Fujimori. Second, both Venezuela and Mexico were facing elections after the General Assembly and wanted to avoid setting a precedent that could come back to haunt them. Third, the fact that the United States launched the initiative with little consultation with member states beforehand generated a knee-jerk opposition among member states against U.S. unilateralism. Further, the Peruvian election debate came at a time when Brazil was attempting to assert its regional leadership. The complexity of the issue and the U.S. attempt to trigger Resolution 1080 allowed the Brazilian government to present itself as a moderate alternative to interventionism.

The Gaviria and Axworthy mission to Peru produced a twenty-nine-point proposal for strengthening democracy that covered the independence of the judiciary, the protection of basic rights and security, freedom of expression and the media, electoral reform, balance of powers, and reform of the intelligence services. The plan served as a working document that would bring together the government and the opposition. Nevertheless, while the OAS was successful in heading off a full-blown domestic crisis and breakdown in Peru, the question remained if it had done so too late. Given the reluctance of the OAS to condemn the Fujimori government after it flagrantly violated electoral norms and the conclusions of the OAS Electoral Mission, there was little faith among the opposition that the thirty-four-member OAS had the political will to enforce a vague plan against the government that many already considered illegitimate. The events after the elections demonstrated that short of a full-blown coup there was little that Resolution 1080 and the Washington Protocol could do to prod the body to action.

If the case of Peru represents difficulties in mustering the collective weight of the OAS to address and admonish violations of democratic institutions and rules, recent events in Ecuador represent a different set of obstacles for collective defense of democracy. The OAS's clumsy attempts to play a role during the 1997 removal of Ecuadorian President Abdalá Bucaram and the 2000 coup d'état that removed Jamil Mahuad highlighted the difficulties of defending democracy in cases where the solutions (not to mention the enemies) are not so clear-cut.

Elected president of Ecuador in 1996, Abdalá Bucaram had proudly referred to himself during his campaign as "El Loco" because of his outlandish antics. As the nickname suggests, Bucaram ran as an outside candidate to a political system and a political class that many Ecuadorians saw as corrupt and discredited. In the election campaign, Bucaram promised in bold and at times vulgar rhetoric to clean up the political system. The strategy worked, and Bucaram was elected with the overwhelming support of the poor, not only in the coastal region where he was from, but also in Ecuador's indigenous highlands. Once in office, however, President Bucaram's popularity quickly evaporated as the economy worsened and credible charges of corruption mounted against his administration, including against his own son. These allegations, along with efforts to implement austerity measures, sparked massive public protests, with citizens and groups taking to the streets demanding Bucaram's removal.

In response to public outcry, in February 1997 the Ecuadorian Congress attempted to remove the President under a constitutionally required two-thirds vote. When it failed to achieve that, it relied on a dubious provision in the constitution that permitted the removal of the President on grounds of mental incompetence. The vote succeeded in stripping Bucaram of his power, despite the fact that there had been no medical proof of his mental incompetence other than his now infelicitous nickname, "El Loco." But congressional intervention did not stop there. So as not to permit the Vice President to assume power, as required by the constitution, Congress appointed the President of the Senate to the presidency. Through all of this the Ecuadorian military remained in the background as the critical arbiter. After several days of uncertainty, the military finally threw its weight behind the Congress's solution and their new president.

In the midst of this, OAS Secretary General César Gaviria traveled to Ecuador in an attempt to mediate the dispute. By that time, however, things had progressed to a point at which there was little the Secretary General could do. His actions were perceived by some Ecuadorians as an attempt to negotiate a solution for Bucaram that would allow him to remain in power, and OAS member states bristled at what appeared to be OAS intervention in Ecuadorian internal politics. As a result, the OAS quickly backtracked and allowed the matter to be settled internally. Nevertheless, as distasteful as people may have found "El Loco" and as much as public opinion supported, even demanded, his removal, the fact remained that there had occurred an "irregular interruption of the democratic political institutional processes," albeit orchestrated by an elected body. The events risked setting a dangerous precedent that constitutionally elected leaders could be removed when voters and elected institutions supported it.

The events repeated themselves on January 21, 2000, only this time the military came to the foreground. Under a newly drafted constitution and a newly elected president, Ecuador again underwent an unconstitutional change of leadership when indigenous groups led by the Confederation of Indigenous Nationalities in Ecuador (CONAIE), with the support of lower-level officers in the armed forces, seized the National Congress. For the weeks preceding the seizure of the Congress, the country had been paralyzed by a series of strikes and public marches protesting the decision by President Jamil Mahuad to dollarize the Ecuadorian economy. More generally, however, the protests also marked the growing frustration and anger among the Ecuadorian poor and the indigenous that make up the overwhelming majority of the poor over their political and economic marginalization. According to a public-opinion survey conducted eight months earlier, 65 percent of the Ecuadorians trusted the armed forces, more than any other public institution, while only 6 percent trusted politicians. The alliance of indigenous groups and the military rode this wave of popular dissatisfaction with President Mahuad. In control of the Congress, with a junta comprising a junior military officer, Colonel Lucio Gutiérrez, the leader of CONAIE, Antonio Vargas, and a former head of the Supreme Court, Carlos Solórzano, the indigenous and the military removed Mahuad from power.

In the early hours of the crisis in Ecuador, when the groups seized the Congress, Secretary General Gaviria condemned the action and assured his support for the elected government. As the events dragged on and the junta requested that Mahuad step down, the Ecuadorian Ambassador to the OAS, Patricio Vivanco, requested an emergency meeting of the OAS Permanent Council. The Council strongly condemned the action, and in conjunction with several governments warned the triumvirate that replaced Mahuad that it would face international isolation if it did not seek a constitutional solution to the crisis. The threat forced the dissolution of the triumvirate which resolved the leadership crisis by appointing the elected Vice President, Gustavo Noboa, to the presidency. The act restored a constitutional government, but unconstitutionally.

After the crisis, the OAS Permanent Council repeated its condemnation of the events that led to Mahuad's ouster but reaffirmed its support for the Noboa government. Throughout the crisis the OAS had not formally invoked Resolution 1080, although the steps that it followed and the threat against the junta of international isolation clearly followed its pattern and authority. Nevertheless, the outcome, while it may have averted a seizure of power by a nondemocratic junta, had violated constitutional processes and the rule of law. The January 21 events had again unseated an unpopular president in response to a popular uprising. There could be little doubt that like the 1997 ouster of Bucaram an interruption in the democratic process had occurred. The implicit message was that the OAS could accept a coup as long as a man in uniform did not assume the reins of power. Several diplomats and policy makers worried openly about the implications of the incomplete enforcement of the OAS's commitment to democracy for the rest of the hemisphere and Ecuador's future. Chilean Ambassador to the OAS, Carlos Portales, stated shortly after the January 21 events and their resolution, "The abrupt interruption of the presidential mandate in Ecuador constitutes an act of utmost gravity for the democratic development of the region."[20] Statements by other ambassadors, privately and publicly, voiced a mounting concern that the ability of the OAS to deter the overthrow of democratic governments had been weakened as a result of the events in Ecuador.[21]

In Venezuela, the case for OAS action is less clear, but events since the 1998 election of one-time coup leader Hugo Chávez to the presidency again point to definitional difficulties for collective defense of democracy, particularly at a time of dramatic and uncertain political change. Only six years before his election to the presidency, then Lieutenant Colonel Chávez headed a failed military insurrection to overthrow elected President Carlos Andrés Pérez. The coup attempt catapulted Chávez to the status of a popular hero, and during the 1998 presidential campaign the ex-paratrooper promised, in rhetoric heavily tinged with authoritarian overtones, to clean up the government, overturn the party-dominated political system, and write a new constitution. The message tapped the growing frustration of Venezuelans with their political system and the dire economic situation. Two political parties, COPEI (Independent Electoral Political Organizing Committee [*Comité politica electoral independiente*]) and *Acción Democrática* (AD), who had virtually shared power and built a huge welfare state based on the country's petroleum profits, dominated Venezuelan politics for thirty years, but by 1998, nearly twenty years after the halcyon days of Venezuela's oil boom, close to 80 percent of Venezuelans lived in poverty and unemployment hovered at just under 16 percent. For many voters the blame for Venezuela's economic troubles lay at the feet of the political and economic elite whom they believed had robbed citizens of their individual entitlement and the country of its potential. Chávez's populist, antielite campaign tapped into the country's profound anger, and he was elected with 56 percent of the vote.

Less than seven months after being sworn in, President Chávez held an election to select a constituent assembly that would draft the new constitution. As expected, the pro-Chávez coalition *Polo Patriótico* swept the July 1999 constituent assembly elections, winning 94 percent of the elected seats. (Three of the seats were reserved for indigenous representatives.) With a popular approval rating between 60 and 70 percent, President Chávez's National Constituent Assembly (ANC) set out not only to rewrite the constitution but also to take over the functions of the now discredited and lame-duck Congress and judiciary. Shortly after being seated, the ANC attempted to close down the Venezuelan Congress, and in effect remove any vestiges of COPEI and AD power over the government. The ANC's efforts provoked a violent public confrontation between the Constituent Assembly and the Congress before the Catholic Church mediated a compromise that allowed the Congress to remain open but stripped of its powers.

After the new constitution was drafted and approved by referendum in December 1999, the ANC dissolved the Congress, arguing that the national legislative body no longer had any constitutional authority. In its place, the ANC created a twenty-one-member assembly, made up, not surprisingly, of Chávez supporters, and charged it with the legislative functions of the country, including appointing judicial officials and proposing and approving legislation. The twenty-one-member minicongress (*Congresillo*) in effect governed from January until August 2000 until the new pro-Chávez Congress was elected on July 30.

The judiciary also came under increasing control by the government and its supporters in the time between the ANC elections and the July 30 elections were held under the new constitution. In August 1999 the ANC declared a judicial emergency and established the Commission for the Judicial Emergency. The Commission subsequently suspended or removed over 300 judges on allegations of corruption. While many agreed that widespread corruption and inefficiency had hobbled the judicial system, critics argued that the shakeup was an attempt to unilaterally remake a judicial system that would be more favorable to the government. Shortly after the December 1999 referendum, the ANC conducted a dramatic housecleaning, single-handedly replacing the public prosecutor and the National Electoral Council (CNE) with allies of the government. The latter change was particularly strategic, since the electoral council was to have overseen the original planned May 2000 "mega-elections" that would elect officials under the new constitution.[22]

Despite the absence of a Congress from December to July, the government plowed ahead with appointing judicial officials and overseeing the reorganization of the court system envisioned under the constitution. The controller general, the public defender (ombudsman), and the new general prosecutor, who formed the new "moral" branch of the judiciary, were all unilaterally appointed by the ANC. While the chief justice of the Supreme Court, Iván Rincón (who was also designated by the ANC), conceded that the new appointments were temporary, he argued that the ANC had the authority to make these appointments based on the legitimacy derived from the character of the ANC as a collective body that represented popular sovereignty. Nevertheless, many critics saw the nominations as an attempt to impose the government's imprint on the judiciary before a new, more politically balanced Congress could assume its constitutional responsibilities of approving judicial appointments.

In effect, in less than two years, Chávez had replaced Venezuela's almost forty-year-old constitution with what he called a new Bolivarian Constitution, reorganized the judiciary, and buried Venezuela's traditional two-party system. While the constitution did little to dramatically remake the Venezuelan state, both formally and informally, it bore the stamp of the Chavista political project. The previous bicameral legislature was reduced to one chamber, the Congress's role over the promotion of military officers was reduced, the presidential term was extended to six years with the possibility of a one-term reelection, and a new moral branch of the judiciary was created that included the public defender, the comptroller general, and the general prosecutor. Generally, in terms of the formal division of powers between the branches of government and between the federal and state governments and protection over basic rights, little had changed from the old constitution of 1961. The real changes occurred at the level of politics and the party system.

The July 30 elections reelected President Chávez to a six-year term, but while the Chavista *Polo Patriótico* coalition won a majority in the National Assembly, it failed to get the two-thirds necessary to pass constitutional legislation. The question after July 30 was if the government would abide by constitutional processes and rules of its own making or would continue to override legal and political limits on its power.

From January 1998 until August 2000 the OAS did not initiate any actions to denounce the Chávez government's actions or initiate a process to discuss the matter, despite several requests by the opposition. While arguably there was little cause under Resolution 1080 to justify collective action, President Chávez's actions between his election in 1998 and the seating of the new government pushed the limits of constitutionality. At the same time, Chávez's rhetoric against his opponents, both political and civil, tended to polarize political discourse and verge on the antidemocratic. The President openly threatened journalists and on several occasions attempted to dissolve the powerful Venezuelan trade union, the Venezuelan Confederation of Workers (CTV). Overall, the pattern demonstrated little respect for the give and take of democratic politics and the constraints on power in a democratic system. Yet the actions were always justified by the popular will, justification that signaled a belief that popularity can trump democratic norms and the rule of law. While the Chávez government may have avoided flagrantly violating the constitution, the actions raised a larger question of the importance of supporting democratic norms and processes. By flouting democratic rules and overriding extant institutions, even with the legitimacy of popular support, political leaders corrode the normative and consensual foundations of a democracy.

Venezuela and to a certain extent the cases of Peru and Ecuador demonstrate the difficulties confronting democratic stability in the region today. What does it mean for the future of democracy in Latin America when political leaders use the legitimacy of popular opinion and stoke public distrust and alienation to aggrandize power at the expense of institutions? Democratic stability depends not just on the survival of an elected regime, but on the respect and strength of a set of rules and institutions. Future democratic reversals in Latin America may not come with a single swoop, but instead through the gradual erosion of democratic norms and rights over time until all that remains are hollow, meaningless institutions. The issue then turns to what multilateral organizations such as the OAS can do. When illiberal leaders and their actions enjoy the support of their citizens, and the changes come in increments rather than dramatic authoritarian acts, the timing and political will for multilateral action become more problematic.

CAN THE OAS ADAPT TO NEW DEMOCRATIC CHALLENGES?

The overall result of the OAS's inability to react to these situations has been to weaken the effectiveness and moral power of the OAS's once-lauded democracy defense clauses. In cases such as Peru, Ecuador, and Venezuela the OAS has proven unable to address or prevent crises or the erosion of democratic institutions by elected governments. In the future the OAS will need to develop a set of mechanisms and policy responses that do two things: (1) permit the OAS to play a more proactive role in mediating political crises and threatened democratic breakdown and (2) recognize and, if necessary, approve overt but subtle efforts by elected governments to abuse power and subvert democratic rights.

Regarding the first of these, the OAS, if it is to serve as an effective agent in promoting democratic stability, will need to develop the flexibility and authority to respond to moments of impending crisis. At the 2000 General Assembly the OAS approved a resolution that established a Special Fund for Strengthening Democracy, supported by voluntary contributions and under the control of the secretary general, that could support short-term missions to mediate disputes and support democracy in moments of crisis. Under the resolution, a member state can appeal to the secretary general for assistance in moments when the state is "affected by situations that, in the view of the state involved, affect the development of democratic process or the exercise of power by the democratically elected government."[23] Unfortunately, the resolution did little to address the broader definitional and organizational problems surrounding the OAS's collective defense of democracy. The declaration indicated a general conceptual lack of clarity with the regard to the secretary general's role; namely, on whose behalf was he or she to mediate or intervene. The stipulation that the request must come from a member state, while politically wise, raised questions about the autonomy of the mission, its responsibility, and its role. As the situation in Ecuador demonstrated in 1997, the OAS may have a reluctance to intervene on behalf of an embattled and unpopular government. In this case, when there was no single actor that threatened democracy, it remained unclear what was to be the preferred outcome. Moreover, the resolution, by tying the secretary general's action to a consideration by the Permanent Council, threatened to undermine the secretary's capacity to act. In the past, the thirty-four-member Permanent Council, in which all members have an equal vote, has proven a political challenge to spur action. The resolution did little to address that problem. For such a resolution to work—indeed, as a general principle in improving the OAS's capacity to act along the lines of the recommendations suggested here—will require a broader reform of the OAS decision-making structure. Such a reform could include the creation of a smaller, rotating council of members for limited decision making.

Second, improving the OAS's role in defending democracy will require developing mechanisms that can allow it to punish and thereby deter democratic transgressions less overt than outright military coups. As argued earlier, the effectiveness of democratic defense mechanisms rests on their deterrent capacity. Improving the OAS's capacity to deter democratic violations to address the problems of illiberal democracy requires several steps: improved and regular monitoring of democratic conditions in the hemisphere, a consensus within the OAS on how collective discussion for action will be triggered, and a set of policy responses that are finer grained than those outlined in Resolution 1080. The first step in such a reform would involve the creation of a permanent, independent body in the OAS, charged with monitoring democratic stability in member countries. The body could comprise individuals nominated by member states and approved by the Permanent Council, who would be separate from the Permanent Council's authority but would report to both it and the secretary general's office. A potential model for such a body could be the existing Inter-American Commission for Human Rights.

The event or act that would trigger collective discussion and consideration of action is admittedly more difficult in a context of democratic erosion. Under Resolution 1080, the act that provoked the convening of a broader body in the OAS was relatively clear, although conceptually fuzzy in the recent context. It would be difficult to establish a similarly clear link in a reformed system. Some possibilities, however, should involve a variety of processes, such as a request for consideration by the democracy monitoring commission, a request for assistance from one or a predetermined number of member states, and a request by opposition and civic leaders in the affected country. Admittedly, the last is the most radical, and for this reason an OAS reform plan could involve several means that would allow it to respond in a number of ways to moments of democratic erosion.

A reform of the OAS's defense of democracy procedures will also require a refinement of the tools available to both the OAS and individual countries to respond. Such a series of measures could combine the responses contained in Resolution 1080 with the monitoring and human rights activities of an independent commission like the Inter-American Commission on Human Rights. Should the OAS (either in the form of the democracy commission or a larger body such as the Permanent Council or the General Assembly) decide to respond, responses could range from dispatching a fact-finding team, to establishing a temporary in-country mission, to collective denouncement, to voluntary sanctions. Even the act of sending a fact-finding mission to investigate charges of executive aggrandizement of power, the subversion of judicial independence, or systematic violation of political rights can serve to elevate these cases internationally and deter such acts. Countries can also include punishment in regional bodies (Mercosur, Andean Pact, Summit of the Americas), such as expulsion or even removal from free-trade negotiations.

One of the last areas of reform that the OAS will need to consider is improving its technical capacity in the area of democracy, and with it the collective will to ensure that the technical decisions and actions of the democracy monitoring commission are followed. The OAS and other regional bodies should be prepared to serve the role of technical advisor in times of institutional design or crisis. Under its current reactive mechanism, the OAS has failed in the past to become more engaged in terms of institutional crafting or constitution drafting. As mentioned, in Peru, the OAS's role remained one of condemning the coup, but then disengaging during the process of constitutional revision. In this case, the result, whether intentional or unintentional, was a document that has served to weaken political parties and the autonomy of countervailing state institutions. Closer monitoring of these moments is crucial. The point should not be to support any election or any institution that is produced during a moment of transition or post crisis. The rules of the game do matter in the strength and survival of democracy. Simply put, some norms and designs can better serve democratic consolidation than others. The OAS should not shy away from vesting a semiautonomous democracy monitoring group with the capacity to point out the deficiencies or consequences of institutions, laws, or poorly administered elections, similar to the role of election monitoring groups in individual electoral processes.

Establishing the basis and framework for a more proactive OAS in matters of collective democratic defense requires a new democratic bargain among the member states. When the threats to democracy are subtle and stem from elected governments themselves, they blur the boundaries between domestic affairs and the right of international intervention. A collective consensus around measures that protect against and punish an overt and clear transgression of democracy (primarily threatened by the military) was much easier to achieve in the 1990s when for the signatories themselves it represented a guarantee of their survival. Any effort to inscribe in a formal document anything more, particularly measures that would affect elected and sitting governments, would touch on the frailties and failures of the governments that would negotiate and approve such a resolution. Such a process would by implication mean circumscribing future actions and opening oneself up to the scrutiny of fellow states.

This new democratic bargain must begin from a shared vision and definition of democracy. A debate has traditionally existed within the region about the meaning of democracy, with a greater emphasis given by Latin American governments to social justice and equity in addition to democratic norms and institutions. This debate has assumed greater force as leaders such as Fujimori and Chávez have claimed that they are seeking a more Latin American variant of democracy. This may or may not be the case (it is certainly arguable), but it highlights the philosophical and practical tensions of defending democracy in the hemisphere. Precisely what kind of democracy are the OAS and other regional bodies seeking to defend? The issue was raised at the 1999 OAS General Assembly, not coincidentally, by the Venezuelan mission, which expressed a wish to have a broad discussion on the meaning of "participatory democracy," which President Chávez contrasted with "representative democracy."

The first step in establishing a new democratic bargain within the OAS will entail an open and frank discussion among member states of the meaning of democracy, one that may involve a possibly painful process of self-examination. But the discussion could begin a broader process of appraisal and exploration that may begin to lay the basis for a consensus within the body.

The 1993 OAS Managua Declaration has already set the tone and direction for this path of future reform. The Managua Declaration began to move the OAS from its more reactive position to a more proactive stance in the protection of democracy, and in doing so provides a conceptual starting point for a collective policy to prevent crises and protect democratic norms and institutions. In an implicit recognition of the limits of Resolution 1080 and the existing mechanisms to defend democracy, the document urges the OAS toward adopting the means to "preventing [democratic] crises" and recognizes that "the ongoing threats to the stability of the democratic systems in the Hemisphere call for a new, dynamic and comprehensive look at the role of the organization."[24] In this vein, the declaration calls for a renewed emphasis on the "promotion of civil, political and eco-

nomic rights" in the context of democracy, draws the connection between the strengthening of a democratic system and the "balance and
independence of the branches of government" and respect for the "role
and responsibility of minorities and of all political groups," and stresses
the importance of cooperation between governments and opposition
and citizen participation in governance.[25]

Unfortunately, as a declaration, the document has no formal bearing
on the operations of the OAS and offers little in the way of concrete
initiatives. What exactly was to be done as a multilateral diplomatic
effort by the regional body remained unstated. But in articulating the
declaration, member states have begun to outline, by agreement, a set
of principles necessary for the survival of democratic regimes, and set
out a series of areas that the OAS can begin to explore as the conceptual basis for a new posture to defend democracy in the hemisphere.

Are all of these measures possible? Certainly, given the historical
sensitivities within the region to anything that smacks of intervention, reform of the OAS represents a giant step. Nevertheless, despite
a weakening consensus among member states concerning the OAS's
role in democracy, when looked at over the long term there has been a
remarkable evolution toward international monitoring of and activity
in internal domestic processes. Fifteen years ago the idea that countries would allow international and OAS teams to observe and pass
judgment on elections was fiercely debated, yet by the late 1990s international scrutiny of national electoral processes was a commonly
accepted practice. Even despite President Fujimori's attempts to discredit the OAS electoral mission in Peru in 2000, no country disputed
the right of the OAS to monitor the elections. (The ability to hold them
to that standard, however, was another problem.)

As described, a basis for launching such an initiative is embodied in
the OAS Declaration of Managua. There are international precedents
as well. The Conference on Security and Cooperation in Europe (OSCE)
has taken measures to increase the monitoring capacity and scope of
its agencies to protect democracy and prevent democratic erosion.
Under the Copenhagen Document and the Paris Charter, the Conference on Security and Cooperation in Europe established clear links
between the protection of political and civil rights, the rule of law,
pluralism, and democracy. By establishing these links, the Copenhagen
Document and the later Paris Charter set out a clear right of member
states to monitor and evaluate one another on the basis of democratic
practice. As one participant in the Copenhagen meeting stated, "Once
the rule of law, human rights and democratic pluralism are made the
subject of international commitments, there is little left in terms of
governmental institutions that is domestic."[26]

CONCLUSION

Defending democracy in the Latin American region (and in the world) in the future will mean more than elections and preventing the interruption of elected governments. Institutional weakness, corruption, the increasing violation of political and human rights in the region, and the growth of personalistic governments threaten to undermine democracy in Latin America. Effectively supporting and defending democracy in the region will increasingly demand addressing these issues.

Establishing greater collective consensus around norms and practice of democracy and measures to enforce them will also lend greater legitimacy to democratic rights and bolster the groups and individuals in civil society inside of countries struggling for democracy. To be sure, the strength and survival of democracy in Latin America ultimately rests on internal factors, but multilateral organizations like the OAS can have a role in deterring autocratic leaders from violating democratic norms and in responding to democratic crises in country. Deterrence is only effective when multilateral institutions work collectively to condemn acts and policies that violate the principles they have committed themselves to defend. When the OAS fails to act in the defense of democracy in cases such as Peru and Ecuador, it sends the message that presidents can do anything short of suspending elections and openly allowing men in uniform to assume the presidency. Reforming the OAS to better defend democracy today against the many challenges it faces holds the promise of realizing the original goals of the OAS Charter "to promote and consolidate democracy in the region."

NOTES

The views expressed in this chapter are the author's and do not represent the views of the National Endowment for Democracy.

1. Inter-American Conference for Maintenance of Peace, *The International Conferences of American States*, Res/27 Supp. I (Buenos Aires: IACMP, 1933–1940).

2. Cited in Domingo Acevedo and Claudio Grossman, "The Organization of American States and the Protection of Democracy," in *Beyond Sovereignty: Collectively Defending Democracy in the Americas*, ed. Tom Farer (Baltimore: Johns Hopkins University Press, 1996), 135.

3. OAS, "The Santiago Commitment to Democracy and the Renewal of the Inter-American System," OEA/Ser. P/XXI.0.2, adopted at the Third Plenary Session, 4 June 1991.

4. OAS, "Representative Democracy," AG/RES. 1080 (XXI-O/91), adopted at the Fifth Plenary Session, 5 June 1991, sec. 1.

5. Ibid., sec. 2.

6. The amendment only applies to members who signed the original protocol, and thus excludes Mexico (who voted against it) and Trinidad and Tobago (who abstained).

7. OAS, "Declaration of Managua for the Promotion of Democracy and Development," Ag/Dec. 4 (XXIII-O/93), adopted at the Fourth Plenary Session, 8 June 1993.

8. Admittedly, the effectiveness of the measures in reversing a coup or a democratic reversal once it has occurred is less clear, and is even more problematic in cases of democratic erosion. The record behind the efficacy of international sanctions in forcing the removal of a regime and restoring democratic government is hotly debated. Indeed, in the cases where sanctions have been applied—primarily Haiti and to a lesser extent Peru—the results have been mixed. At worst, international sanctions proved a clumsy, imprecise mechanism. The link between economic pain—often inflicted more on the general population than on the regime—and diplomatic isolation and the political decision to step aside and restore democracy is unclear in theory and practice.

9. David Scott Palmer, "Peru: Collectively Defending Democracy in the Western Hemisphere." In *Beyond Sovereignty: Collectively Defending Democracy in the Americas*, ed. Tom Farer (Baltimore: Johns Hopkins University Press, 1996), 274.

10. According to one poll conducted five days after the dissolution of Congress, 91 percent of the respondents were in full or partial agreement with Fujimori's actions. Eduardo Ferrero Costa, "Peru's Presidential Coup," *Journal of Democracy* 4 (1993): 28–40.

11. Viron Vaky and Heraldo Muñoz, *The Future of the Organization of American States* (New York: Twentieth Century Fund Press, 1993), 26.

12. *Inter-Prensa Edicion Especial.* Annual report on press and democracy, Instituto de Prensa y Sociedad, Lima, Peru, 1998 and 1999.

13. OAS, "Press Communiqué no. 9/97," Lima, 5 June 1997.

14. OAS, "Press Communiqué no. 20/98," Lima, 13 November 1998.

15. OAS, "Court Rules on Peruvian Decision," November–December 1999, Washington, D.C.

16. National Democratic Institute and Carter Center, "Statement of the First NDI/Carter Center Pre-Election Delegation to Peru," Lima, 3 December 1999.

17. "Misión de Observación Electoral: Elecciones Generales República del Peru Año 2000, Boletin No. 12," Lima, 25 May 2000.

18. Ibid.

19. OAS, "OAS to Lead High-Level Mission to Peru," OAS news release, 15 June 2000.

20. OAS, "OAS Reacts to Crisis in Ecuador," OAS news release, March–April 2000.

21. Ibid. and author's private interview with OAS ambassadors, April–June 2000.

22. The handpicked CNE, however, proved unable, technically and managerially, to prepare for the elections. Three days before the May 28 elections, the Supreme Court, citing mounting evidence that the CNE was not ready, postponed the elections. As a result, the CNE was removed and replaced with a new group appointed through a broader process of consultation and negotiation. The elections were eventually split up, with the balloting for all but local offices being held on July 30.

23. OAS, "Resolution Strengthening Democracy: Special Fund," Ag/Res 1724 (XXX-0/00), adopted at the First Plenary Session, 5 June 2000.
24. OAS, "Declaration of Managua."
25. AG/Dec. 4, "Declaration of Managua."
26. Thomas Franck, "The Emerging Right to Democratic Governance," *American Journal of International Law* 86 (1992): 68.

BIBLIOGRAPHY

"Advancing Democracy and Human Rights in the Americas: What Role for the OAS?" 1994. In *An Inter-American Dialogue Conference Report*. Washington, D.C.: Inter-American Dialogue.

Farer, Tom, ed. 1996. *Beyond Sovereignty: Collectively Defending Democracy in the Americas*. Baltimore: Johns Hopkins University Press.

Ferrero Costa, Eduardo. 1993. "Peru's Presidential Coup." *Journal of Democracy* 4: 28–40.

Franck, Thomas M. 1992. "The Emerging Right to Democratic Governance." *American Journal of International Law* 86: 46–91.

Freedom House. 1987. *Freedom in the World, 1986–1987*. New York: Freedom House.

———. 1996. *Freedom in the World, 1995–1996*. New York: Freedom House.

Hakim, Peter. 1993. "The OAS: Putting Principles into Practice." *Journal of Democracy* 4: 39–49.

Halperin, Morton H. 1991. "Guaranteeing Democracy." *Foreign Policy* 91: 105–122.

Organization of American States (OAS). 1991. AG/Resolution 1080. Adopted at the Fifth Plenary Session, 5 June 1991.

———. 1993. "The Declaration of Managua for the Promotion of Democracy and Development." AG/Dec. 4 (XXIII-O/93). Adopted at the Fourth Plenary Session, 8 June 1993.

———. 1997. "Press Communiqué no. 9/97," Lima, 5 June.

———. 1998. "Press Communiqué no. 20/98," Lima, 13 November.

"The Organization of American States: Advancing Democracy, Human Rights and the Rule of Law in the Americas." 1994. In *A Report of the Inter-American Dialogue Commission on the OAS*. Washington, D.C.: Inter-American Dialogue.

Palmer, David Scott. 1996. "Peru: Collectively Defending Democracy in the Americas." In *Beyond Sovereignty: Collectively Defending Democracy in the Americas*, ed. Tom Farer. Baltimore: Johns Hopkins University Press.

Reding, Andrew. 1996. "Exorcising Haiti's Ghosts." *World Policy Journal* 22: 15–26.

Shifter, Michael. 1997. "Tensions and Tradeoffs in Latin America." *Journal of Democracy* 8: 114–128.

Vaky, Viron, and Heraldo Muñoz. 1993. *The Future of the Organization of American States*. New York: Twentieth Century Fund Press.

Valenzuela, Arturo. 1997. "Paraguay: The Coup That Didn't Happen." *Journal of Democracy* 8: 43–55.

CHAPTER 6

U.S. Policy for the Promotion of Democracy: The Venezuelan Case

María Teresa Romero

During the twentieth century, many things were said, debated, and written about U.S. policy on defense and promotion of democracy around the world. Christopher Sabatini's excellent chapter in this book (Chapter 5) is a case in point. It can be observed that a kind of literary "boom" on this issue appeared during the 1990s, when the Cold War came to an end and brought what Huntington (1991) called "the third wave of democratization" in the history of the modern world.

The Bush and Clinton administrations established the policy of promotion of democracy as a key issue of the new international role of the United States in the world. Many studies and analyses, as well as academic and journalistic reflections, have been published on this matter, but specific works on the promotion of democratic mechanisms in Venezuela are practically nonexistent.[1] Furthermore, Venezuelan academia agrees that U.S.–Venezuelan relations do not have enough contemporary bibliographic coverage (C. Romero 2000, 7).

A specific study of U.S. promotion and defense of democracy in Venezuela is especially important today, when a process of "decomposition" of democracy is taking place. This is particularly true when considering that Venezuela until recently was the model of representative democracy in the region and a principal ally of the United States in oil and strategic matters in Latin America.

Since the 1980s, but mostly in the 1990s, Venezuela went through a considerably serious political and economic crisis, which led to the election of a revolutionary government (with authoritarian and military undertones) in December 1998. Moreover, a new constitution was approved that intends to rebuild the republic, replacing the *puntofijista* model established in 1958, which prevailed in Venezuela for forty years but disintegrated in the 1980s and 1990s.[2]

The purpose of this chapter, therefore, is to deal with the following questions: How has the United States defended and promoted democracy in Venezuela during a time of crisis and rupture of its traditional democratic model? Does the United States have a clear strategy on this matter? What are the mechanisms and tools used for the defense and promotion of democracy? In spite of the rhetoric on this matter, it is essential to find out if the North American policy or role in Venezuela has had any impact or influence on the evolution (or devolution) of Venezuelan democracy.

It is to be noted that this chapter contains only a preliminary approach. As such, and as a starting point, an analytical method that separates two levels in political inquiry is used: First, the state–macro level or high political level, and second, a microlevel or low political level proposed by Thomas Carothers (1991, 1993, 1999) about decision making and actions in support of democracy.

The general behavior of the American government toward Venezuela will be studied with emphasis on the more significant diplomatic efforts and democratic help during the period between 1990 and 1999. This is not a detailed analysis of the numerous declarations and economic and military agreements carried out by the American government, nor it is an exhaustive revision of the multiple programs to strengthen democracy in the long run. This study rather intends to identify the principal lines of American action at the two levels of analysis, and thus to contribute to forming a basis for more specific studies.

THE PROMOTION OF DEMOCRACY AS A FUNDAMENTAL ISSUE OF AMERICAN FOREIGN POLICY IN THE 1990s

The defense and promotion of democracy has been a fundamental part of U.S. foreign policy since the beginning of its history and especially during the twentieth century. Greater emphasis on the matter appeared after the end of the Cold War. In fact, it became apparent at the end of the 1980s with the emergence of a new "unimultipolar" international order dominated by the United States. George Bush as well as Bill Clinton established the promotion of democracy as a key issue within their country's new international role in the world, and therefore as an important part of their agendas.

In 1995, and due to the "third wave of democratization" that was already becoming global, an optimistic President Clinton said that "the best strategy to insure security and to build a lasting world peace was to support the advancement of democracy all around the world" (Carothers 1999, 5). Two years before, his national security advisor, Anthony Lake, had announced that the United States would continue with an enlargement and engagement policy toward the market democracies. The central goal was to increase the number of countries and persons that enjoyed a democratic government and civil and political rights guaranteed by their constitutions.

This enlargement strategy of the United States included democratic initiatives within the United Nations and especially within the OAS, such as Resolution 1080, the Washington Protocol, and the creation of Unity for the Promotion of Democracy. The strategy is also reflected in its active participation in the Summit of the Americas (in Chile in 1998 and in Miami in 1994).[3] Unilaterally, the United States used an integrated approach for the promotion of democracy, which included a series of tools at both levels of government policy. Diplomatic instruments of pressure, dissuasion, and applause were preferred to confrontation and the use of force.

It also used international cooperation as an instrument, especially "democratic assistance," which refers to all those aid programs designed to strengthen democratic institutions, principles, and processes in countries with nondemocratic or semidemocratic governments. This form of promoting democracy is used in institutions and government agencies like the U.S. Information Agency (USIS) and the U.S. Agency for International Development (USAID), the state and justice departments, and through government organizations such as the National Fund for Democracy (NED) and private institutions of different kinds. During the 1990s U.S. annual expenditures for this kind of help came to around $600 million, and at the end of 1998 the democratic programs carried out by government and private organizations covered more than 100 countries (Carothers 1999, 7). Just in 1994, USAID spent around $23 million on civic education (Finkel, Sabatini, and Bevis 1999, 1).

As expected, this new drive toward liberal democracy created enormous expectations in U.S. elites and leaders, who thought that this new approach to promoting democracy from "above" as well as from "below" would give a stronger impulse to these countries without their being perceived as interventionists. In practice, however, these expectations have been more or less frustrated, because, in spite of the considerable expansion of the democratic system, there are still many antidemocratic regimes, processes, values, and attitudes. In Latin America, for example, there are still "fragile" democracies (Hakim and Lowenthal 1996) or semidemocratic systems (Diamond, Hartlyn, Linz, and Lipset 1999) with evident limitations. The twentieth century in general closed with the presence in Latin America and other nations in the world of populist and authoritarian democracies, with fragile institutions, centralized and corrupt political processes, problems of democratic governance, and strong state capitalism. Moreover, people's attitudes, values, and beliefs do not appear to be sufficiently supportive of democratic government.

There are other problems in American policy for the promotion and defense of democracy. One of the most important is a rhetoric that does not reconcile with practice. This can be explained, in part at least, because along with the goal of promotion of democracy the United States has other goals and strategies that have become priorities. In Latin America, for example, as Ambassador Jeffrey Davidow declared in 1996, "There are three principal goals in the hemispheric policy of the United States: the creation of a free market zone, the strengthening of democracy and the war against drug traffic and international crime, illegal aliens, and terrorism." But, in fact, the war against drug traffic in the Americas has become the central goal of American policy in the hemisphere, and today it receives most of the help from the American government. For the year 2000 only, the White House asked for $1.6 billion for the war against drugs in Colombia, and $300 million more for the rest of the "high-risk zone" (which includes Ecuador, Peru, Bolivia, and Venezuela).[4] Washington and the South Command considers drug trafficking a problem that threatens U.S. security and the region's democracy.

Nevertheless, there is no doubt that the promotion and defense of democracy in the continent and the rest of the world remains a fundamental goal of U.S. foreign relations policy. This obliges its revision and permanent analysis, especially in specific cases such as Venezuela.

VENEZUELA AND ITS SYSTEMIC EVOLUTION (OR DEVOLUTION): EXHAUSTION, CRISIS, AND RUPTURE OF THE VENEZUELAN DEMOCRATIC SYSTEM

For almost thirty years, Venezuela was a model of stability and democratic governance. This model, however, began evidencing a critical stage during the "lost decade," and in the 1980s entered an "overflowing period" (Hillman and Cardozo Da Silva 1997) that culminated with the 1992 coup d'état attempts. This stage of accelerated institutional decay ended in 1999 with the arrival of a new revolutionary government and a new constitution that set forth new democratic guidelines and a new basis for the political system. The *"puntofijista* model," as it is colloquially called today in Venezuela, was a populist model based on the power of the principal political parties that monopolized the political process. It functioned as a complex negotiation and interest accommodation scheme agreed to by the country's elite (Rey 1989; Hillman 1994). The latter eroded insofar as the economic model based on oil rent felt the weight of the oil price crisis (Guerón 1992; McCoy and Smith 1995). Also, the clientelelistic model between the political powers and the masses adopted by the political parties caused frustration when the system did not live up to the people's expectations (M. T. Romero 1997).

We can identify three periods within the overflowing stage of the systemic crisis (1989–1999). The first corresponds to the Carlos A. Pérez and Ramón Velásquez administrations (1989–1994) during which the crisis became evident. The second period coincides with Rafael Caldera's administration (1994–1998), when the crisis deepened. The third period is the present period, the government of Hugo Chávez (1999–), where the rupture of the political model is established.

The Pérez–Velásquez period was characterized by a series of unexpected political tensions. The first happened just after the first month of the Pérez administration. It was called the "Caracazo," took place in February 1989, and was caused by economic adjustment measures (the rise of fuel prices and therefore of public transportation) initiated by the new government. It was also a consequence of people's frustration. These emotions accumulated over the two former administrations (Lusinchi and Herrera). The new economic policy, called *El Gran Viraje* ("The Great Turning Point"), put into practice by Carlos Andrés Pérez, also served as a detonator. Pérez was thrown out of office in May 1993. After a transition period, Rafael Caldera was elected in 1993, but his programs did nothing but increase the institutional decay within the state, political parties, and society, and the situation degenerated into the people's rejection and political frustration toward government and democratic institutions.

For the first time since 1958 a candidate not belonging to a traditional political party won the election with 30 percent of the votes. Even if AD and COPEI continued to be the dominant parties in the political process, they could not control power within the executive or Congress. This new composition of power, where traditional parties lost 29 percent of their influence in the senate and 32 percent of the house of representatives, affected relations between the presidency and Congress. President Caldera began his mandate without a party majority or permanent allies in Congress. Also, even if there was not a rupture of the constitutional thread, the tension between political actors became so strong that in December 1998 every antistatus, antiparty proposal won against a liberal democracy and led to the disintegration of the traditional political system; in other words, to the end of the *puntofijista* democratic system.

President Hugo Chávez's first year in office served to dismantle what remained of the system agreed to in 1958. His task was to build the basis for a new political system. However, it is not clear if the new system is truly democratic. According to Luis Vicente León, director of the private polling company Datanalisis, in his first year, "Chávez succeeded in establishing what he calls a pacific revolution. With the support of the majority of the people, he succeeded in winning their approval in the most important of his political offers: the installation of a Constitutional Assembly, the selection of its 131 members, and the approval of a new Constitution in 1999."[5] According to the second article of the new constitution, "Venezuela is a social, democratic State which advocates the right to live in liberty, justice, equality, democracy, social responsibility and the defense of human rights, ethics and political pluralism." However, in practice and according to many political analysts opposed to the regime as well as international observers, the democratic system currently being developed in Venezuela evidences strong signs of authoritarianism, militarism, and centralizing forces, along with a populist model against a market economy. From another perspective a critical point of view emerged, especially within the *chavistas* and present government representatives: Rather than constituting a true democracy, it is a continuance of the *puntofijista* model and they hope that a real revolutionary change will take place, one that would include greater participation of the military because, if not, "the *soberano* could consider a coup d'état."[6] Beyond the different opinions and views regarding this new Venezuelan democratic model, it is necessary to raise questions about its efficacy as a liberal democratic model.

The three periods described serve as a basis for the analysis of the policies of Presidents Bush and Clinton on promotion and defense of democracy.

THE UNITED STATES AND VENEZUELA

One must recognize that, in spite of certain particular disagreements, the relationship between the United States and Venezuela during the 1990s was one of mutual friendship and cooperation. It is in this context that we can understand U.S. foreign policy on the promotion of democracy in Venezuela.

In fact, since the end of the 1950s both the United States and Venezuela have been important oil and commercial partners, and also strategic allies in the Latin American region. Venezuela, for example, has been the primary oil supplier to the United States, and has always been a reliable and sure ally on this matter (Ewell 1996; C. Romero 2000; Cardozo Da Silva 1992). Also, the United States is the most important importer of Venezuelan goods, as well as an exporter to Venezuela. Moreover, at least until 1998 both countries agreed on which kind of democratic system had to prevail in Venezuela and in the Caribbean. It is not strange that Luigi Einaudi (1992), permanent U.S. representative to the OAS (in Washington), insistently declared that "Venezuela is the banner-bearer of democracy in Latin America and that an interruption of its system would have significant consequences for the rest of the hemisphere." He affirmed that "that country has been a key factor in helping American decision makers base their work on the proposal which considers that democracy is vital for the evolution of modern stability" (p. 12). According to Einaudi, therefore, "the continuance of Venezuelan democracy is essential for the US and the hemisphere."

In sum, as Carlos Romero (2000) has asserted, there were four premises on which bilateral relations were based in the last forty years: first, the Venezuelan governments' thesis about its strategic importance within a hemispheric context (reliable partner); second, the idea of historic exceptionality of the Venezuelan case relative to other countries of the zone (a politically and economically stable partner); third, the predominance of cooperation over conflict in both countries (no preoccupations about partners); and fourth, the predominance of bilateral issues partly free from their regional and global agenda (known partner). These four premises show two historic tendencies: In the last forty years, Venezuela received no political, military, or economic sanctions from the United States, and "it has been able to mark the boundaries between its bilateral commitments and a more independent international performance" (C. Romero 1998, 142).

The First Phase: 1989–1993

This period of U.S.–Venezuelan relations had more political and economic relevance than previous ones. Carlos A. Pérez and George Bush maintained close communication and coincidental views about Latin American politics. The critical economic situation and possible help from Washington in restructuring external debt and external financing meant that, more than ever, Venezuela needed help from the "colossus of the north." In fact, Venezuela had to be more flexible and open to possibilities, and had to make concessions and political alliances. Venezuela, therefore, supported U.S. antidrug policies as well as the Initiative for the Americas and the Bush policy toward the Persian Gulf.

In 1989 the following contacts and actions between the countries stand out: the visit of Senator Richard Lugar and David Mulford, undersecretary of the treasury, to talk about external debt; signing a tourism cooperation agreement; agreeing to a 172-percent increase of steel exports to the United States; and the meeting between the two presidents in Atlanta to examine the Venezuelan debt problem.

Pérez's April 1990 visit to the United States and Bush's visit to Venezuela in December strengthened the "special" relations between both countries and led to the signing of further agreements (scientific cooperation and intellectual property). During the first of these meetings, Bush declared his satisfaction in "receiving the leader of one of the most solid democracies in Latin America and one of the most respected statesmen of the continent (Cardozo Da Silva and M. T. Romero 1991).

In 1991 Dan Quayle, vice president of the United States, visited Caracas. During this time the Council of Commerce and Investment of Venezuela and the United States of America were created. In 1992 Venezuela supported the United States in its antidrug policy conference in Texas, the goal of which was the development of a global strategy to confront the drug problem on the continent.

There is no doubt that during those years, and especially because of Venezuelan support for U.S. actions in the Persian Gulf War, along with PDVSA's (Petróleos de Venezuela Sociedad Anónima [Venezuela State Petroleum Company]) entering the American oil market, the United States strategically revalued Venezuela as its stable and sure oil supplier. At the same time, the economic program initiated by Pérez emphasized the economic aspects of the relations between both countries. An increase in commercial exchange of nontraditional products was on the way, even though the agreement discussed within the Uruguay Round was never signed (Cardozo Da Silva and M. T. Romero 1991).

In spite of these political coincidences and its economic viability, Venezuela was never part of a special strategy for the promotion of democracy, as were some other Latin American countries. The only manifestation of this policy toward Venezuela was a result of the coup d'etat attempts in 1992, when the Bush administration strongly supported the Venezuelan government, condemning the "unworthy" attempt of elements of the Venezuelan military to oust the Venezuelan president. Also, President Bush personally called Pérez to guarantee U.S. support for democracy. Similarly, American ambassador Michael Skol warned against any extraconstitutional action that would be unacceptable to the United States.[7] Furthermore, the United States signed an OAS resolution condemning the November attempt, giving all its support to the Venezuelan government and its democratic institutions. Bush called Pérez again to offer his support, while the White House staff issued a declaration that "the basis of U.S. policy in the region was the support of democracy, and even if we understand that Venezuela, among other nations, is going through a difficult period, authoritarianism is not the solution."

When Bill Clinton came to power in 1993, relations between both countries remained the same: Friendship, cooperation, and support of Venezuelan democracy was the basis of policy, as well as rejection of military coups. In fact, this position was made clear in a letter written by Clinton to Pérez insisting that "a democratic and peaceful Venezuela was essential for the well being of the Venezuelan people but also for the community of democratic nations of the western hemisphere." Albert Coll, undersecretary of defense for special affairs and low intensity conflicts, ratified this decision in March 1993. Representatives of the State Department again ratified this position after the Venezuelan Congress ousted Pérez in August 1993. When Venezuelan Foreign Relations Minister Fernando Ochoa visited Washington shortly afterward, Christopher Warren, the new secretary of state, declared that "we are prepared to work with president Velásquez until December elections, and also with any other candidate who is elected on that occasion" (C. Romero 1998, 147). During Undersecretary for Inter-American Affairs Alexander Watson's visit, he said, "Maintaining its brilliant traditional democracy is an indispensable requirement for normal relations between US and Venezuela" (C. Romero 1998, 147).

Phase Two: 1993–1994

The December 1993 elections kept the thread of constitutional continuity in Venezuela. Rafael Caldera won the presidency and this calmed the U.S. government, but only partially, because at that time it became quite clear that the Venezuelan economic and political crisis was deepening and the traditional model was decaying. At the same time, bilateral relations started to manifest tensions and conflicts in spite of the optimistic declarations of American ambassador Skol regarding an expectancy of very good relations with President Caldera.[8]

Relations between the United States and Venezuela showed evident points of friction. For example, the embargo of Venezuelan tuna, discrimination regarding Venezuelan fuel (in this case Venezuela appealed to the Organización mundial del Comercio [OWC], also known as the WTO), difficulty in the introduction of Orimulsion in the North American market, disagreement on investment and the double tax system, and the unwillingness of president Caldera to continue the Pérez economic reform and adjustment program.

The disagreements were fundamentally a product of political considerations. The United States supported Cesar Gaviria (former president of Colombia) for secretary general of the OAS instead of a Venezuelan candidate (former foreign minister Miguel Burelli). Venezuela rejected the U.S. embargo against Cuba, and in particular the

Helms–Burton law. The United States criticized Caldera's treatment of human rights matters (a human rights report from the State Department to Congress in 1996 provoked an irate protest from Caldera's government). Although in general Caldera supported U.S. policy on the war against drugs, he would not approve flights over Venezuelan airspace in order to combat drug traffic. This decision was the object of strong disagreement. Protest notes from the Venezuelan government were issued against the Casablanca Operation (money laundering), and John Maisto, the American ambassador, declared, "Venezuela is not prepared to handle organized crime and drug traffic problems."[9] These assertions urged an answer from Foreign Relations Minister Burelli, who said, "The golden rule of diplomacy is to maintain discretion about local issues in the country where one is working."[10]

For some analysts and observers of U.S.–Venezuelan relations in this period, these disagreements partly explain the delay of President Clinton in naming a new ambassador to Venezuela. In fact, almost a year passed before the new ambassador was named. John Keane was in charge until Maisto was named. The disagreements also explain why President Clinton excluded Venezuela from his visit to Latin American countries in 1997. Finally, after diplomatic movement by Venezuelan diplomats, Venezuela was included in Clinton's second Latin American tour (C. Romero 1998, 2000), though this visit did not fulfill Venezuelan government expectations that included the signing of two important agreements: double tax payment and investment promotion. Instead, a document was signed promoting a strategic alliance against drugs that was very important to Clinton's administration.

In spite of these tensions and disagreements, and because bilateral relations were not as "special" as in 1989–1993, U.S.–Venezuelan relations developed normally and in some aspects were positive. A confluence of interests and points of view, for example, can be observed in relation to the struggle against corruption. Both countries' battles against corruption were essential instruments in support of local and external democracy. President Clinton took into account this issue without forgetting others, such as antidrug policies, collective defense of democracy (through the OAS), expansion of free commerce, and democratic financial assistance.[11]

In Venezuela's case, from 1994 to 1998 foreign policy pointed to a war against corruption (M. T. Romero 1998, 2000). Venezuela promoted this goal, as President Caldera declared, considering it a key element for the preservation of democracy in the region.[12] In his first trip abroad he said, "Corruption is deteriorating the image of the democratic system in our countries, therefore, this problem demands an international commitment. We all should agree not to help, support nor give refuge to those who are responsible for serious crimes, such as corruption."[13]

This initiative began a week later with the Declaration of Belem (Brazil), which was the principal document produced by the OAS General Assembly in June 1994. The document stresses the need to fight corruption and think about civic ethics and administrative probity. In the same way, and as a proposal without precedent in all twenty-four former Assemblies, it recommended the study of measures within the laws of each country oriented to combat corruption, which is considered a problem in most of the region's countries.[14] This proposal demonstrates a regional concern in the matter, even before the Venezuelan initiative. President Caldera, however, was one of the most committed and at various opportunities presented a project to fight international corruption (at the OAS, the Rio Group, the United Nations, the Ibero–American Summits, and the Summit of the Americas in Miami in 1994), and sought the establishment of an international convention on the matter (M. T. Romero 2000).

This Venezuelan project was well received by Latin American governments and particularly by the United States, which openly supported the motion presented by Venezuela at the Summit of the Americas. Just before that conference, Michael Skol, undersecretary for inter-American affairs of the state department, declared when visiting Venezuela that his government would support the Venezuelan initiative for the creation of a legal international instrument against corruption. He added that President Caldera "is the unquestionable leader in this matter which is very strongly felt in the hemisphere."[15] Afterward, during the same meeting in Miami, Jeffrey Davidow, the American ambassador at that time, ratified his government's support of the Venezuelan proposal (in order to extradite corrupt persons and repatriation of capital), and added that his government would make efforts in the OAS so that this plan could be put into practice.[16] As a consequence, the United States and Venezuela signed a mutual legal assistance agreement in March 1995 for the administration of justice in relation to banks and financial institutions. This support from the Americans led to the adoption of the Inter-American Convention Against Corruption on March 29, 1996 (twenty-one countries out of twenty-nine signed the agreement). Soon afterward, in May of the same year, and during the visit to Caracas of Strobe Talbot, undersecretary of state, an agreement on cooperation and technical assistance to the Public Ministry of Venezuela was signed in order to improve administration of justice and reinforcing capacity in the fight against corruption.

At the same time, during Caldera's administration, Clinton's government showed signs of concern due to the political situation and support of Venezuelan democracy. For example, on June 3, 1994, Strobe Talbott affirmed American support for Venezuelan democracy and its role in promotion of democracy in the region, and especially in the

Caribbean Basin.[17] Later on, President Clinton assured that "Venezuela is a banner of Latin American democracy; and it is also our first oil supplier and one of our partners in the hemisphere."[18] This support was even more forceful after Caldera's government started making changes in the economic policy during March 1996. Strobe Talbot declared that "support of the US in general, and of President Bill Clinton in particular, to President Caldera and his government in the Venezuelan Agenda is strong because they consider that it is a healthy initiative with good economic ideas." He added, "We would like to use our position in the multinational forums like IMF, World Bank and IDB to support Venezuela and insure the success of its economic plan."[19]

In 1998, during a difficult elections campaign, the American government showed more concern and support for Venezuelan democracy, even though a visa for presidential candidate Hugo Chávez was rejected (because of his participation in an attempted coup d'état). President Clinton made it clear that his administration would remain neutral in the process and that it would recognize the winner, whoever he was. Ambassador Maisto repeatedly ratified these sentiments. Also, the secretary of defense declared, "The United States will respect the Venezuelan people's decision. We hope the elections are democratic."[20] As I demonstrate in the following pages, during the first year of President Chávez's administration the American policy was one of "let's wait and see" (C. Romero 1998) combined with a policy of appeasement.

In sum, the U.S. policy of defense and promotion of democracy toward Venezuela during the period from 1994 to 1998 was more active and concrete than the one pursued between 1990 and 1993. Within the level of high politics, it went from a diplomacy of praise, which dominated during the Pérez administration, to a more critical one, even if the American government sought not to be perceived as "interventionist." At the level of low politics, a closer cooperation can be observed as well as more dynamic behavior from U.S. government and quasi-government agencies like USIS and NED. In fact, during 1993–1994, NED, after a controversial argument between its members who didn't think it necessary to waste money in a democratic oil country, started to work for the first time in Venezuela through the CIPE (International Center for Private Enterprise), which financed a *Consecomercio* project for economic reform. Moreover, the Republican Institute also financed projects of the Thought and Action Foundation (Fundación Pensamiento y Acción). From that moment, NED and the American Center for Labor Solidarity started to increase aid in the country and to work more closely with other nongovernmental organizations and government projects in areas of civic education, democratic formation, and enforcement of judicial and technical formation. The help from NED to Venezuela through its institutes developed as follows: 1995, $362,603; 1996, $485,882; 1997, $167,725; and 1998, $534,770 (National Endowment for Democracy, http://www.ned.org). Although the amounts are small with respect to Venezuelan necessities, they show at least an increasing concern on the part of the United States.

The promotion carried out by USIS, and especially through the cultural department of the U.S. Embassy in Venezuela, was of special relevance. Although specific numbers are unavailable, sources from the embassy assured me that the programs had increased since 1994. Among them are the creation of a program for education for democracy, CIVITAS, which involved civil society and prestigious institutions.[21] There was also the affiliation program between teachers and students of the Central University of Venezuela and St. John Fisher College in Rochester, New York, sponsored by the U.S. Department of State. This exchange program included the creation of the Institute for the Study of Democracy and Human Rights.[22]

U.S. government and other nongovernmental institutions showed special interest in the Venezuelan elections of 1998, sending a group of observers led by former president Jimmy Carter, who declared that "a real electoral revolution had happened."[23]

Phase Three: 1999–2000

Despite the denial of both governments, tension and disagreements increased in the relations between the United States and Venezuela during the first year of the Chávez administration. Employing a "participative and revolutionary" concept of democracy that has produced strong doubts in the international community about the nature of the new Venezuelan model, President Chávez and Foreign Minister Rangel have begun an autonomous and independent line of action that seems (as some analysts think) to have a purpose: to drift away from and provoke conflict with the U.S. government.[24] Some analysists, for example, see the Chávez government as "a sort of exhibitionism and provoking factor against Washington."[25] Former foreign minister Ochoa Antich declared that this attitude of constant provocation and confrontation is part of a new ideological project, continentally searching for a geopolitical "revolutionary Latin American Great Colombia." To this effect he adds, "This desire of the President to separate from the US and OAS [Venezuela, for example, didn't sign the OAS resolution against insurgent movements in Ecuador], to approach Cuba in its support for these Latin American movements, and also create a Latin American Army" is revealing.[26]

To the main provocations and tensions of the Chávez government toward the United States can be added the following: criticism of NATO for its attacks on Yugoslavia (Kosovo); the Venezuelan vote in the United Nations in favor of Cuba, Iraq, and China in the U.N. Human Rights Commission; denouncing alleged pressures from the American ambassador in Venezuela in order to avoid Venezuela's vote; public declarations relating Venezuelan concern about installations of antidrug bases in Aruba and Curaçao; direct petition to Clinton to cease the Cuban embargo; proposing a Commonwealth of Latin American Nation, excluding the United States; support of the Ibero–American Summit in Havana, Cuba; denouncing the possible internationalization of the Colombian conflict and a unilateral American intervention; Chávez's conversations with leftist Colombian guerrillas and his disposition to personally speak with the leader of a guerrilla group considered by Washington to be a menace to hemispheric security; declarations regarding the maintenance of a neutral attitude toward the Colombian conflict, perceived by the United States and Colombia as an unnecessary support for these guerrilla groups; the approach to Iran, a country Washington considers a promoter of international terrorism; the Venezuelan decision to reject U.S. military aid (engineers and machinery) after the disastrous floods last December; the repeated rejection of the U.S. petition to fly over Venezuelan territory (in its struggle against drug traffic); and Chávez's visit to Bagdad in order to invite Saddam Hussein to the Caracas OPEC meeting in September 2000. Each of these matters has brought numerous impasses between Miraflores and the White House.

In the face of all this provocation, the U.S. government has responded with an appeasement and nonaggression policy in an attempt to minimize conflict and avoid confrontation. The United States has been very "patient" indeed, as a desperate Secretary for Hemispheric Affairs Peter Romero declared to the Spanish newspaper *ABC* on January 30, 2000. Venezuelan Foreign Minister José Vicente Rangel responded, "Venezuela does not accept counsel nor warning from the United States."[27] This reaction provoked an immediate visit to Rangel by American ambassador John Maisto. Maisto delivered an official communication from the State Department explaining the scope of Romero's declarations.[28] This conciliatory line from the U.S. government has been accompanied by a diplomatic initiative and political support as well as a moderate economic support.

The U.S. approach began soon after Hugo Chávez was elected president in December 1998. American Ambassador Maisto visited him in order to personally deliver a congratulatory message from President Clinton: "In the name of the United States of America and in my own name, please accept my congratulations for your election as President of Venezuela. The high number of ballots and your impressive margin of victory is a testimony of a long and strong democratic conviction and of the desire of positive change Venezuela desires."[29] A second visit by Maisto, along with the first by Romero, served to ratify American policy and financial support for the new government.[30] This was soon demonstrated, when President Chávez received his U.S. visa. The United States sent many other messages of goodwill during 1999. The visit of Charles Wilheim, chief commander for the South, offered U.S. army cooperation for Venezuelan development and also an enormous amount of humanitarian assistance, given as a consequence of the national disaster caused by the December floods and mud slides.[31]

Chávez has visited the United Sates three times since he was elected. The first time was in January 1999. The second visit was to New York and Houston in search of investors. The third was to New York and Washington in order to take part in the annual U.N. assembly (and to continue searching for new investments). In fact, even if this visit to Washington was not official, President Clinton received him, and some sources say even helped him to get in touch with American investors and multilateral organizations such as the International Monetary Fund (IMF), the World Bank (WB), and the International Development Bank (IDB), which was hard work, because in Venezuela the absence of a clear ruling on economic and legal matters caused a paralysis of investments and multilateral credit.[32]

Regarding democratic assistance, the Clinton administration continued the same policy of moderate assistance as during Caldera's administration. Accordingly, NED made a disbursement of $698,659 and USAID started working informally in Venezuela, giving approximately $1 million for antidrug, military training, and human rights programs. Afterward, as a consequence of the December floods, USAID gave $3 million in humanitarian aid. The U.S. Embassy maintained its programs in support of democracy and cultural and academic exchange, even if its budget was lowered, since USIS became part of the State Department.

U.S. government policy (and its criticisms and pressures) toward Venezuela has been timid and perfunctory. It has been directed against the Venezuelan government's lack of cooperation in the hemispheric struggle against drug trafficking and its weak policies of economic adjustment and reform. Critics have not emphasized, as would be expected, the model of democracy that is being established in Venezuela. The only significant critic of the Venezuelan government has been Undersecretary Peter Romero, who said, "We will support Chávez as long as he operates within the constitutional parameters to reform the country."[33] Also, when asked by the Spanish newspaper *ABC* about his opinion of the Chávez government, he answered,

Uncertainty. . . . We have extended our hand since the beginning; I went to Caracas to offer assistance, unfortunately what one sees is a press conference. But we are still keeping our hands extended and hoping that he uses the $15 billion oil revenue surplus in diversifying the economy, generating jobs, reforming institutions. . . . But there is no government administration that can be seen, instead, one only sees referendums, plebiscites and more elections, and we only hear "we have to wait", but we "gringos" are not known for our patience.[34]

Nevertheless, Clinton avoided questioning Chávez. According to Thomas Pickering, undersecretary of political affairs, the United States supported the form "in which the Venezuelan National Assembly and Congress have consulted the people all along the process of greater political reforms," recognizing that Venezuela "is in the most important crossroads of its history," and therefore offered his best wishes for the success of the process.[35]

I believe the American position marks a departure from its traditional strategy of promoting and defending Latin American democracy. First, President Chávez has threatened neither the security nor the national interests of the United States. Had he done so, the U.S. attitude would have changed. Although Venezuela is in danger of losing its place as primary oil supplier to the United States and the oil program started in the last administration fell apart, Venezuela is still a reliable supplier. Also, if Chávez's rhetoric is strongly anti–United States and politically flamboyant, it has threatened neither American companies, property, nor people in Venezuelan territory. Nor has Chávez stopped the government's cooperation with the United States in the antidrug struggle (despite the denial of American surveillance flights over Venezuela). In fact, there may be secret assistance, which has gained the country a renewal of U.S. certification.

In the case of economic policy, even if Venezuela has not yet carried out any economic reforms, and on the contrary it maintains a populist and state-centered program, Chávez has announced certain modern fiscal and tax measures. In sum, even if the relations between the two countries are characterized more by discrepancies than coincidences, these conflicts are not serious. Washington, therefore, prefers to "wait and see."

Some agree that Clinton, due to the already strong resentment against the United States in Latin America and because the Venezuelan president is indeed a charismatic and popular leader, did not want to turn Chávez into a martyr. In other words, the United States avoided a "second Fidel Castro." Well-known and respected analysts such as Andrés Oppenheimer have expressed that this position dominated the State Department, although it is not exempt from strong criticism. Ambassador Maisto has maintained the position, hence, Foreign Minister Rangel's declaration that "my relation with Maisto is excellent . . . he has helped us a lot."[36] Some American businessmen share this position. For example, George Landau, president of the U.S. Council of International Relations for Latin America, said, "We have to help him [Chávez] succeed; if he doesn't, Venezuela collapses."[37]

However, for other groups of politicians and American and Venezuelan analysts, Washington's policy toward Chávez is a result of plain negligence, indifference, and even boredom with the reiterative populism of Latin American governments. Along these lines, political scientist Anibal Romero maintains,

Washington has decided that what is important is that Chávez takes part in the elections and wins them, the rest: how he wins them, which limitations he imposes on his adversaries, what are the controls and clamps he applies to his adversaries, which is the real quality of his revolutionary democracy, is not very important to a State Department probably annoyed and exhausted by the never ending comings and goings of Latin American politics. Besides, if there is a democratic façade, and the oil continues to flow into New England and Texas, then Washington is happy and the rest is music. (A. Romero 2000)

Of course, the Venezuelan case is not unique. The U.S. position is the same toward other Latin American governments with visible anti-democratic behavior when there is legitimation through elections, maintenance of acceptable economic modernization, and cooperation with Washington's antidrug policy. The case of Fujimori in Peru is an example (authoritarianism with a democratic façade). In that country, the Clinton administration felt inclined toward neutrality and appeasement policies in spite of the existence of a very restricted concept of democracy that reduced it to the fact that elections had been realized.

The George W. Bush, Jr. administration has continued essentially the same policies. President Bush's appointment of Otto Reich, former ambassador to Venezuela, as Undersecretary of State for Hemispheric Affairs, and Donna Hrinak as ambassador to Venezuela, however, signal a potentially hard-line approach to Chávez.

CONCLUSION

During the acute period of the Venezuelan democratic crisis in the 1990s, the U.S. government did not put forward a "special" policy of defense and promotion of democracy. The first time Venezuela became an object of concern for Washington, economic help slightly increased and a closer diplomatic approach was taken. But it has not translated into a clear, active, or coherent strategy. On the contrary, an absence of strategy may be observed along with a reactive policy (considering that the action is decided according to Venezuelan political actions) in the face of the rapid and unexpected political changes of this Latin American oil supplier. It has also been more a rhetorical than an active policy, subordinated to American security and national interests such as antidrug programs, the oil market, and expansion of market economies. Even if there is insufficient evidence to support this, the mechanism for democratic assistance is not a priority. Venezuela, in spite of its profound economic recession, is still perceived within the Third World context as a prosperous oil-exporting country. It is not a coincidence that the Agency for International Development has not opened an office in Caracas.

U.S. policy during the Pérez administration changed from one of praise to a diplomacy of pressure, especially during Rafael Caldera's administration. However, during the first year of Chávez, the line of political pressure not only decreased, but accompanied appeasement and political support. The way the U.S. government responded to the crisis of the Venezuelan democratic model does not appear to have helped enforce or maintain a representative and modern democracy in the country. Obviously, it did not prevent the victory of a "revolutionary democracy." Consequently, there is little doubt that the Venezuelan case means (and presents today) a complex challenge for the United States and for its traditional conception and form of defense and promotion of democracy.

It is not only Venezuela that challenges American policy on democracy in Latin America. Peru, Paraguay, Haiti, Colombia, and Ecuador are also cause for concern and stirring up doubts about the democratization wave in the region (Hakim 2000).[38] As Alvaro Tirado said in 2000,

Today, every active government in the OAS has elections; however, many doubts emerge about the reality of our democracies and about the dangers they face. There is not only one model of democracy, but in a representative democracy there are elements that when absent, become suspicious. Among those, insufficient participation in the elections and the possibility of alternate government, the lack of an independent and impartial justice administration, the absence of guarantees for the exercise of fundamental liberties, separation of powers and legal control over the rulers. There is a conspiracy against democracy in our region because of the tremendous social inequalities, corruption, drug traffic and terrorism as well as the disrepute of political parties and people's apathy in favor of participation, political assassinations, Constitutional organization's dissolution or the annulment of its actions, prolongation of mandates without a judicial defined base, electoral fraud, and the fact of not letting a legally elected government exercise its authority. It seems that the attacks against democracy come more from some of the elected rulers than those who come from military coups.

In the face of such challenges, there are some questions that deserve more than rhetorical answers. How should the United States proceed against typical military threats, or prevent them? How is it possible to reconcile the traditional principle of defense of democracy with the non-intervention principle? As Robert Pastor has affirmed, "The United States is not developing an active strategy to enforce democracy in the hemisphere. I don't know why, if it is because of fatigue, indifference or lack or imagination, but what we have today is a reactive strategy."[39]

In the specific case of Venezuela, and due to the potential decomposition of its democratic process, there is an urgent need for answers. The purpose of this analysis is to emphasize this urgency and importance. Although the problems of Venezuela are essentially Venezuela's and Venezuelans must solve them, the United States in its powerful role as a pillar of hemispheric democracy has a responsibility to influence the Venezuelan process without intervening in such a way as to violate Venezuelan sovereignty.

NOTES

1. An exception is found in Konrad Adenaur Stiftung, Fundación Rómulo Betancourt, and Fundación Pensamiento y Acción (1996).

2. See Rey (1989), A. Romero (1986), and Kornblith (1998) for discussions of the Venezuelan party system.

3. See Farer (1996) for analysis of the collective defense of democracy in the Western Hemisphere.

4. *El Nacional*, 27 February 2000, p. A-2.

5. *El Nacional*, 03 February 2000. pp. 1–16.

6. Declaraciones del general Francisco Visconti, lider de la intentona golpista del 27 de noviembre de 1992 (Declarations of General Francisco Visconti, leader of the attempted coup on November 27, 1992), *El Universal*, 27 February 2000, pp. 1–10. *Soberano* refers to the masses of Chávez supporters.

7. *El Universal*, 05 February 1992, pp. 1–2.

8. *El Diario de Caracas*, 04 January 1994, p. 25.

9. *El Nacional*, 26 November 1998, p. A-2.

10. *El Nacional*, 21 November 1998, p. A-2.

11. *El Nacional*, 11 December 1996, p. A-2.

12. "Balance del primer mes del presidente Caldera," *El Nacional*, 3 March 1994, p. D-1.

13. "Cartagena encumbrada," *El Nacional*, 16 June 1994, p. A-6.

14. "OEA preocupada por la corrupción en América," *El Nacional*, 7 June 1994, p. A-2.

15. "Skol: USA secundará iniciativa venezolana anticorrupción," *El Diario de Caracas*, 1 November 1994, p. 23.

16. "Apoyo de USA a gobierno venezolano," *El Globo*, 18 January 1995, p. 16.

17. Ministerio de Relaciones Exteriores de Venezuela," *Libro Amarillo*, 1994, p. 181.

18. *El Nacional*, 17 March 1996, p. E-8.

19. *El Nacional*, 1 June 1996, p. D-3.

20. *El Diario de Caracas*, 8 August 1998, p. 23.

21. Among these institutions are CEDICE (Centro para la Divulgación del Conocimiento Científico [Center for the Dissemination of Scientific Knowledge]), Queremos Elegir, la Fundación Pensamiento y Acción, and Dividendo para la Comunidad. These have developed workshops, conferences, and other events and national programs on civic education.

22. This program was financed by USIS at a cost of approximately $150,000 between 1997 and 2001.

23. *El Nacional*, 24 January 1999, p. A-6.

24. This new conception of democracy was clearly articulated during the twenty-fourth General Assembly of the OAS in Guatemala in June 1999. José Vicente Rangel presented a project on "Participartory Democracy" that contrasted with the U.S. initiative to fortify "Representative Democracy" in the hemisphere. The sovereign–antonomous foreign policy emphasizes the principles of nonintervention and self-determination.

25. "Diplomacia a plomo parejo," *El Universal*, 13 January 2000, p. 4-2.

26. "Política Exterior a contracorriente amenaza con aislar a Venezuela," *El Nacional*, 3 March 2000, p. A-2.

27. *El Nacional*, 2 February 2000, p. A-2, 1–14.

28. *El Universal*, 4 February 2000, pp. 1–13.

29. *El Nacional*, 10 December 1998, p. D-2.

30. *El Nacional*, 15 December 1998, p. A-2; 31 December 1998, p. A-2.

31. *El Universal*, 15 January 1999, pp. 1–2.

32. According to Superintendencia de Inversiones Extranjeras (SIEX) data, U.S. direct investments in Venezuela rose to $122,151,805.90 in 1998 and dropped to $58,230,485.17 in 1999 (from an unpublished report from the Venezuelan American Chamber of Commerce and Investment).

33. *El Nacional*, 31 December 1998, p. A-2.

34. *ABC*, 30 January 2000, available at <http://www.abs.es>.

35. *El Nacional*, 16 February 2000, p. A-2.

36. *El Nacional*, 7 February 2000, p. A-2.

37. *El Nacional*, 19 June 1999, p. E-1.

38. John Lancaster, "US Sees Democracy Wane in Latin America," *The Washington Post*, 30 January 2000, p. A-21.

39. Cited in Andrés Oppenheimer, "América Latina necesita diplomacia preventiva," *El Universal*, 20 February 2000, pp. 1–6.

BIBLIOGRAPHY

Cardozo Da Silva, Elsa. 1992. *Continuidad y consistencia en quince años de política exterior Venezolana, 1969–1984*. Caracas: UCV.

Cardozo Da Silva, Elsa, and María Teresa Romero. 1991. "Política exterior de Venezuela en 1990: dinamismo y contradicciones en un contexto cambiante." In *Anuario de políticas exteriores latinoamericanas 1990–1991*, ed. Jorge Heine. Caracas: Editorial Nueva Sociedad/Prospel.

Carothers, Thomas. 1991. *In the Name of Democracy: US Policy towards Latin America in the Reagan Years*. Berkeley and Los Angeles: University of California Press.

———. 1993. "El resurgimiento de la ayuda de Estados Unidos para el desarrollo político en América Latina." *Sintesis* 21: 14–19.

———. 1999. *Aiding Democracy Abroad: The Learning Curve*. Washington, D.C.: Carnegie Endowment for International Peace.

Diamond, Larry, Jonathan Hartlyn, Juan Linz, and Seymour Martin Lipset, eds. 1999. *Democracy in Developing Countries: Latin America*. Boulder, Colo.: Lynne Rienner.

Einaudi, Luigi. 1992. *Public Diplomacy Query*. Washington, D.C.: Woodrow Wilson Center Press.

Ewell, Judith. 1996. *Venezuela and the United States: From Monroe's Hemisphere to Petroleum's Empire*. Athens: University of Georgia Press.

Farer, Tom, ed. 1996. *Beyond Sovereignty: Collectively Defending Democracy in the Americas*. Baltimore: Johns Hopkins University Press.

Finkel, S., C. Sabatini, and G. Bevis. 1999. "Civic Education, Civic Society and Political Mistrust in a Developing Democracy: The Case of Domenican Republic." Mimeographed.

Fundación Konrad Adenauer Sliftung (KAS), Fundación Rómulo Betancourt (FRB), and Fundación Pensamiento y Acción (FPA). 1996. *Hacia la promoción de la democracia en Venezuela y América Latina*. Caracas: KAS–FPA–FRB.

Guerón, Eva Josko de. 1992. "Cambio y continuidad en la política exterior de Venezuela: una revisión." In *Reforma y Política Exterior en Venezuela*, compiled by C. Romero. Caracas: Copre–Invesp. Editorial Nueva Sociedad.

Hakim, Peter. 2000. "Is Latin America Doomed to Failure?" *Foreign Policy* (Winter): 104–117.

Hakim, Peter, and A. Lowenthal. 1996. "Las frágiles democracias de América Latina." In *El resurgimiento global de la democracia*, edited by Larry Diamond and Marc F. Plattener. Mexico: UNAM.

Hillman, Richard S. 1994. *Democracy for the Privileged: Crisis and Transition in Venezuela*. Boulder, Colo.: Lynne Rienner.

Hillman, Richard S., and Elsa Cardozo Da Silva, eds. 1997. *De una a otra gobernabilidad: el desbordamiento de la democracia venezolana*. Caracas: Fondo Editorial Tropykos–UCV.

Huntington, Samuel. 1991. *The Third Wave: Democratization in the Late Twentieth Century*. Norman: University of Oklahoma Press.

Kornblith, Miriam. 1998. *Venezuela en los 90: Las crisis de la democracia*. Caracas: UCV–IESA.

McCoy, Jennifer, and William C. Smith. 1995. *From Deconsolidation to Reequilibration? Prospects for Democracy Renewal in Venezuela*. Atlanta: Georgia State University Press.

Rey, Juan Carlos. 1989. *El futuro de la Democracia en Venezuela*. Caracas: IDEA.

Romero, Aníbal. 1986. *La Miseria del Populismo*. Caracas: Editorial Centauro.

———. 2000. "La política de Washington ante Hugo Chávez." *Venezuela Analítica*. Available at <http://www.analitica.com>.

Romero, Carlos. 1998. "Las relaciones entre Venezuela y Estados Unidos durante la presidencia de Clinton: coincidencias estratégicas y diferencias tácticas." In *Estados Unidos y los países Andinos 1993–1997: poder y desintegración,* edited by Andrés Franco. Santa Fe de Bogotá: Universidad Javeriana.

———. 2000. "Las relaciones entre Venezuela y Estados Unidos durante la era Clinton: entre la cooperación y las diferencias." Trabajo de ascenso para la Universidad Central de Venezuela (actualmente en preparación) (Thesis for faculty promotion at the Central University of Venezuela [forthcoming]). Mimeographed.

Romero, María Teresa. 1996. "Comentarios." In *Hacia la promoción de la democracia en Venezuela y América Latina.* Caracas: KAS–FPA–FRB.

———. 1997. "La agudización de la crisis del sistema político venezolano." In *De una a otra gobernabilidad: el desbordamiento de la democracia venezolana,* edited by Richard S. Hillman and Elsa Cardozo Da Silva. Caracas: Fondo Editorial Tropykos–UCV.

———. 1998. "Estrategias de promoción de la democracia en la política exterior de Venezuela." *Política Internacional* 46: 23–28.

———. 2000. "Transición sistémica y promoción de la democracia en la política exterior venezolana de los noventa." Paper presented at the 2000 LASA conference, Miami, Florida.

CHAPTER 7

Democracy and International Military Intervention: The Case of Haiti

Irwin P. Stotzky

In previous chapters, Chris Sabatini and María Teresa Romero raised questions regarding external interventions for the promotion of democracy. This chapter focuses on one case in which, on October 15, 1994, the so-called restoration of democracy took place in Haiti. But the premise that an international military force can simply and magically restore democracy to a nation that has never experienced democracy and that lacks most of the institutional infrastructure, material resources, and an experimental agenda necessary to successfully complete this mission and thus to overcome the almost impenetrable cultural, economic, political, and social barriers of its own history, is seriously flawed, and it has serious consequences for the Haitian people. This flawed idea has created expectations among Haitians and the international community that cannot be met. Moreover, it has caused an outpouring of criticism of the efforts of both Haitians and the international community, particularly in the United States. While the international effort can be criticized on many valid grounds, international aid remains indispensable to Haiti's march—from "misery to poverty with dignity"—toward democracy. In this chapter I wish to look at Haiti and ask what lessons one can learn from the international intervention that will have more general application to the incredible movement—the transition to democracy—that has occurred in the past three decades all over the world.

Indeed, during the closing decades of the twentieth century a wave of democratization spread through most of Latin America, the Soviet Union, and parts of Eastern Europe, Africa, and Asia. This movement from dictatorship to democracy has not, of course, always run smoothly. There have been serious internal threats to fledgling democracies, retrenchments, setbacks, and counterrevolutions leading to new authoritarian regimes. What role has and should the international community play in this democratic drama?

Haiti is, of course, a unique case. It is a small, poor, vastly underdeveloped nation almost abandoned over the years by its neighbors and the world community. But Haiti is nevertheless an important example of a nation undergoing the rigors of the transition from dictatorship to democracy. How the international community handles questions concerning Haiti thus has broader, more general implications. It suggests methods to employ and paths to follow in future crises. It also suggests actions that the international community should avoid taking in future crises. Moreover, looking at Haiti's difficulties and suggested solutions to them also has broader, more general implications for the consolidation of the transition process around the world.

The story of Haiti is, at one level, uncomplicated. In 1990 a vast majority of the Haitian people—67.8 percent—elected Jean-Bertrand Aristide president in the first democratic election to take place in Haiti in its nearly 200-year history as an independent state.[1] Equally impressive was the election process.[2] It represented the culmination of an extraordinary international effort to launch Haiti on the path of democracy. Both the Organization of American States and the United Nations played major roles in helping Haitian officials assure the dignity of the election process.

Within months after his installation as president, Aristide was overthrown in a military coup and forced into exile, first in Venezuela and then in Washington. The OAS and United Nations immediately condemned the coup, speaking out forcefully against the de facto regime and in support of the democratically elected Aristide government. After several years of failed efforts to coax the de facto government to negotiate with Aristide for his return, and ostensibly because of serious human rights abuses resulting in the murders of several thousand people and the economic chaos created and then exacerbated by the embargo, the international community resorted to force. The international community also responded with several other unprecedented actions. Indeed, between 1990 and 1997 the United Nations engaged in an unusually broad range of activities in support of democracy in Haiti, including election monitoring, U.N. Security Counsel–mandated sanctions, two peacekeeping operations, a naval blockade, and U.N. Security Council–authorized use of force against the de facto regime.

The international community's response to the military coup that ousted Aristide is unique in at least three respects. In July 1994 the U.N. Security Council, for the first time in its history, gave approval for a forcible intervention in a member state to change its government—to restore its democratically elected government. This clearly differed from other situations in which the OAS and United Nations had been involved, such as Nicaragua and El Salvador. Unlike those cases, the stated goals of the military intervention were neither to support democratic processes as a means of national reconciliation nor to uphold the integrity of the electoral process as a means of securing the fragile peace accords. Instead, the primary and publicly proclaimed goal was simply and solely the restoration of democratic governance. Stated otherwise, the overriding purpose of intervention was to replace an illegitimate regime (the de facto military government) with the legitimate regime (the democratically elected and internationally sanctioned Aristide government).

This was also the first time that the United States sought Security Council authorization for the use of force within the Western Hemisphere. This is, of course, a sharp contrast from the unilateral interventions by the United States in Latin America during the twentieth century, the most recent examples being Grenada (1983) and Panama (1989). Despite the fact that the Clinton administration viewed the crisis in Haiti with a growing urgency because of the increasingly large refugee migration from Haiti to the shores of Florida between 1991 and 1994, the United States did not take unilateral military action. Rather, the United States used multilateral channels to resolve the crisis. While the use of multilateral avenues was less "efficient" than unilateral methods would have been, the Clinton administration correctly understood that multilateral action offered important advantages, both domestically and internationally.

The Haiti case is unique in one other respect: This was the first test of the June 1991 OAS Santiago Declaration on the protection of democracy.[3] Indeed, this case suggests a growing consensus among OAS member states and internationally that the Western Hemisphere should develop into a democratic zone free from military dictatorship.[4] Moreover, the Haiti case has been used as a precedent for the OAS in its efforts to react to threats to democracy in Peru (1992), Guatemala (1993), and Paraguay (1996).

The international effort continues. The attempt to help Haiti create the necessary infrastructure for democracy to develop economically, politically, and socially, however, has not been as successful as the original military intervention. Unfortunately, the outside world's intervention in Haiti may well prove unsuccessful and impermanent in a way that Graham Greene would have well understood.[5] Nevertheless, the questions that the Haiti case raises are surprisingly numerous and important. For example, is democracy so widely accepted as an international norm, at least in the Western Hemisphere, that the international community has a right, indeed, even a duty, to restore it when it is forcibly overthrown by a military coup whose de facto government has committed gross human rights violations, trampled on the rights of the people, and caused massive refugee flows? If so, what particular bodies can legitimately (and legally) exercise such a right of intervention? Can an outside military intervention and then a peacekeeping mission create the conditions for democracy to develop and help to secure it?

Before analyzing some of these issues, several preliminary observations seem relevant. They color the horizon and add perspective to the analysis. The first is the role of the United States and the decision to use force. The United States took a very long time and a circuitous path to decide to use force. Indeed, it is not the case that the United States was intent on intervening militarily in Haiti from the beginning of the crisis and originally planned on using the OAS and the United Nations as institutional structures in which to implement and legitimize its military plans.

In point of fact, as the Haitian crisis developed, it was not at all clear what the Clinton administration intended to do in Haiti. Clinton appeared first to favor negotiations, then economic sanctions, and later a naval blockade to force the coup leaders out. Mysteriously, Clinton's position vacillated almost daily. It was only after several years of inconsistent approaches and actions by the United States, including the forced repatriation of thousands of Haitian refugees, coupled with severe domestic criticism of his actions by the Congressional Black Caucus, human rights organizations, and other groups, and the skilled work of Aristide in exerting domestic and international pressures on Clinton, that Clinton decided to use force. In retrospect, it now seems self-evident that only the threat or the use of force would dislodge the de facto regime from Haiti. But this was not so obvious to those involved, and there was certainly no strong U.S. interest in taking military action.

It is irrefutable that the decision to use force was reached late and somewhat chaotically, through the vagaries and uncertainties of the American domestic political process. The Clinton administration employed the U.N. framework to legitimize military action only after the United States concluded that force was absolutely necessary to restore the Aristide government to power. Security Council Resolution 940 gave authority for "all necessary means"—meaning the use of military force—to be used.[6] This, of course, helped to legitimize military action in a divided and skeptical United States.

A second, and perhaps contentious observation, is that one of the main catalysts—if not the main catalyst—for U.S. intervention in Haiti was the migration to the shores of South Florida of vast numbers of Haitian refugees who were seeking asylum in the United States. As a result of the 1991 military coup and President Aristide's ouster from power, thousands of Haitians seeking asylum departed Haiti by boat and attempted to reach the United States. Between 1992 and 1994, the U.S. Coast Guard interdicted Haitians bound for the United States on the high seas and returned them directly to Haiti. This action was taken in direct violation of an agreement between the Haitian and U.S. governments and in violation of international law. Many of those returned faced persecution from the de facto government. The inflow of refugees increasingly became a politically sensitive issue, and it was in response to domestic political pressure to take action to stem the tide of boat people that the Clinton administration pushed for an internationally sponsored intervention in Haiti. Clinton feared that the spectacle of thousands of poor, black Haitians washing up on Florida's shores would harm his presidential reelection campaign. He particularly feared that he would lose votes in Florida, a pivotal state in his reelection strategy. Stated otherwise, the major reason for the U.S.–led intervention was the flow of refugees to the United States and Clinton's fear of losing vital votes because of it. Every other issue, including the murders of 5,000 people, takes a backseat to that reason. It is likely that the Clinton administration hoped that if democracy could be "restored" to Haiti, perhaps the flow of refugees would cease. The fear of Haitian boat people continues to be a strong incentive for U.S. aid to Haiti.

A third observation, and quite a troubling one, is also irrefutable. Particular elements of the U.S. government encouraged the intransigence of the military coup leaders and thus needlessly prolonged the crisis, with dire consequences for the Haitian people. Select members of Congress and the defense establishment, most notably officials of the Central Intelligence Agency, the Pentagon, and the State Department, continued to assure the coup leaders, in subtle and not so subtle ways, that the United States actually supported the de facto military government and not the democratically elected Aristide government. The de facto military leaders simply did not believe that the United States and the international community would ever take military action to restore Aristide to power. The coup leaders, therefore, placated the international community by pretending to negotiate with the Aristide government in good faith, all the while hoping to delay the return of Aristide until his official term in office had ended.

In addition to encouraging the coup leaders not to compromise with the Aristide government, the U.S. government officials opposed to Aristide orchestrated a campaign to smear Aristide's public image. Early in Aristide's exile, for example, the CIA distributed a false report that branded Aristide as mentally unstable, claiming that he had spent time in a mental hospital in Canada. The CIA also spread a false rumor that Aristide and his cohorts committed political assassinations. Senator Jesse Helms, who has always had reservations about Aristide and attempted to undermine President Clinton's goal of restoring Aristide to power, basing his conclusions on the CIA report, referred to Aristide as a "psychopath" and a "demonstrable killer."[7] The report was a sham. CNN found no report of Aristide being treated for mental depression or any other problem in Canada, and the report was revealed to be based on unconfirmed information supplied by the very people who overthrew Aristide. The CIA admitted that it had been paying individuals in the Haitian military leadership for this and other kinds of information since the early 1980s.[8] These and other actions taken by those U.S. officials opposed to Aristide's return clearly continue to cause problems for the creation of democracy in Haiti.[9]

A fourth important observation is also a somewhat touchy and speculative one. It is whether there was an implicit or explicit agreement among the five permanent members (the Permanent Five) of the U.N. Security Council.[10] While there is no direct proof of this, there has been a great deal of speculation that horse trading took place to allow the military intervention in Haiti. The speculation suggests that in exchange for a free hand in Haiti, including the use of force, the United States agreed that other members of the Security Council could have a similarly free hand in their areas of influence. For example, Russia wanted autonomy to deal with Georgia and Tajikistan, and believed that France and the United States owed it such a free hand in exchange for its support of French action in Rwanda and U.S. action in Haiti. In reading the discussions of the Security Council during this period, there certainly appears to be an acceptance by the Permanent Five that actions taken in their regions of interest would be tolerated by the other Security Council members. To put it another way, national political concerns rather than deep moral principles seem to have played the most crucial role in the use of force in Haiti.

One final observation. In many parts of the world, particularly in Latin America and the Caribbean, including Haiti itself, there was and remains a deep suspicion of U.S. military intervention, and with good reason. Such intervention in the past invariably had questionable purposes and results. It was almost always used to support rather than to overthrow authoritarian regimes and to support U.S. commercial interests. The 1915–1934 U.S. occupation of Haiti is a prime example.[11]

One result of this history was that the OAS, while struggling valiantly to do the right thing about Haiti, was not able to do everything necessary to restore democracy. The U.N. Security Council was better situated and able to make the difficult decisions than was the OAS, the principal regional body. Employing the U.N. Security Council as authority for the intervention also offered the Clinton administration an important moral force. Most important, the U.N. approval of the use of force limited the international and domestic opposition to the U.S.–led action.

There were other advantages to U.N. approval. The coalition-building role that the United States had to assume to get international support through the Security Council for the intervention in Haiti was critically important. It helped shape U.S. methods and goals in Haiti, and for the better. Moreover, the fact that the United States did put together an internationally accepted policy on Haiti suggests broader consequences for the methods employed to justify the use of force in the future. Unilateral military action by the United States has certainly become more difficult to justify after the internationally sanctioned military intervention in Haiti.

These observations put into context the underlying but perhaps well-hidden reasons for the intervention. They show the role of power in the resolution of international legal issues. They act as filters on the possibilities of future international interventions. On a broader level, they also help keep the focus on the possible transformative resolutions to some of the incredibly difficult problems facing nations undergoing the transition process.

After these preliminary observations, I proceed in the following manner. First, I discuss the international legal implications of the multinational intervention in Haiti, concentrating on the doctrine of humanitarian intervention and the clash between sovereignty and human rights. I conclude with an analysis of the lessons that the Haiti case teaches about U.S. domestic politics and the use of force, and possible future international military interventions in other developing nations. Second, I analyze some of the major problems of the transition process, and conclude that the international community failed to understand those problems in its dealings with Haiti, with disastrous consequences. Third, I analyze the current electoral crisis in Haiti and its implications. Finally, I propose solutions to some of the problems of the transition process through an experimental political economy, using Haiti as the primary example.

A note of caution. The issues involved are highly complex, layered, and ever changing. Every nation has its own peculiar culture, history, social structure, and economy. Thus, every case is, in some sense, sui generis. Nonetheless, broad patterns can be discerned and generalizations can be made that are quite helpful in analyzing the transition process and the possibilities of developing strong democracies in former authoritarian nations.

HUMANITARIAN INTERVENTION

With these observations, I proceed to the next issue: Can the multinational military intervention in Haiti be correctly categorized as a case of legitimate "humanitarian intervention," and therefore be justified under international legal principles? If so, is it a precedent for future multinational military interventions?

Before I analyze these issues, I address a preliminary question: What is meant by the term "humanitarian intervention"? While the term has recently become more acceptable in international law, it is a fuzzy term, and any definition is open to varying interpretations. A number of scholars have crafted their definitions to describe a right of states, inserting conditions into their definitions that make an intervention legal when undertaken consistent with that definition. Antoine Rougier, for example, in the early part of the twentieth century, claimed that "the theory of humanitarian intervention is that which recognizes the right of one state to exercise international control over the acts of another in regard to its internal sovereignty when contrary to the laws of humanity."[12] On the other hand, one who holds a neo-Kantian perspective on international law and therefore sees sovereign rights as derived from the people may define humanitarian intervention as "the proportionate transboundary help, including forcible help, provided by governments to individuals in another state who are being denied basic human rights and who themselves would be rationally willing to revolt against their oppressive government."[13]

For the purposes of this chapter, however, my definition describes a wide range of actions by states. This, I believe, helps avoid some normative ambiguities and better helps to define the permissibility or legality of specific actions by the international community and thus what occurred in Haiti. I use the term in the following way: Humanitarian intervention is the threat or use of force, by a state, group of states, or international organization, primarily for the purpose of protecting the nationals of the invaded state from widespread deprivations of internationally recognized human rights. The very idea of a valid (legitimate) humanitarian intervention, however, raises serious legal problems.[14] It creates a direct clash between two contradictory ideals of international law: sovereignty and human rights.

For more than 300 years, sovereign states have been the most important political units in the international system. During this period, states have claimed a monopoly on the legal use of force within their borders as well as freedom from interference by external forces. Indeed, state sovereignty has long been viewed as a necessary condition of peace.[15]

Moreover, the U.N. Charter strongly supports this vision of sovereignty. The foundation of the U.N. Charter, after all, is the sovereign equality of all U.N. members.[16] Under Article 2(4) of the U.N. Charter, member nations are required to "refrain in their international relations from the threat or use of force against the territorial integrity or political independence of any state."[17] More specifically, the U.N. Charter prohibits interference in a nation's domestic affairs.[18] As Article 2(7) of the U.N. Charter states, "Nothing contained in the present Charter shall authorize the United Nations to intervene in matters which are essentially within the domestic jurisdiction of any state or shall require the Members to submit such matters to settlement under the present Charter."[19]

Chapter VII of the U.N. Charter represents the major limitation to state sovereignty.[20] The Security Council, as authorized by Article 39, is empowered to "determine the existence of any threat to peace, breach of the peace, or act of aggression and shall make recommendations, or decide what measures shall be taken."[21] One of the major difficulties in interpreting Article 39, of course, comes in defining what is meant by the phrase "any threat to peace." Are gross human rights violations, the flow of refugees, or the overthrow of a democratic regime by an authoritarian one "threats to peace" within the definition of Article 39?

The other major limit to state sovereignty is provided in Article 51 as the "inherent right of individual or collective self-defense."[22] Both Article 51 and Article 39 present a similar difficult problem: How are they to be applied? Important terms are left intentionally vague and undefined. For example, self-defense could mean the act of repelling attacking forces or could even include preventive measures to avoid war. Are self-serving motives to protect economic markets a form of self-defense? Is stopping the chaos in a neighboring country? From a purely legal standpoint, the U.N. Charter creates a presumption that a nation's sovereignty is paramount. Only in the most serious cases can Articles 39 or 51 be used as valid authority to breach that sovereignty.[23]

The U.N. Charter, while upholding sovereignty as nearly absolute, also recognizes the significance of human rights.[24] The U.N. Charter's Preamble lists as a goal to "reaffirm faith in fundamental human rights, in the dignity and worth of the human person, in the equal rights of men and women and of nations large and small."[25] This dedication is reaffirmed in the U.N. Charter itself in defining a purpose of the United Nations: to solve "international problems of an economic, social, cultural, or humanitarian character, and [aid] in promoting and encouraging respect for human rights and for fundamental freedoms for all without distinction as to race, sex, language, or religion."[26] This illustrates the importance bestowed on human rights and points out a major goal the United Nations wishes to undertake in solving humanitarian problems. At a legal level, it would be permissible for the United Nations to act for purely humanitarian purposes as long as a nation's sovereignty is not sacrificed.[27]

The dedication to human rights is reaffirmed in Chapter IX, suggesting international cooperation.[28] Moreover, to promote stability and well-being, the U.N. Charter provides in Article 55 that it will promote "universal respect for, and observance of, human rights and fundamental freedoms for all without distinction as to race, sex, language, or religion."[29] In Article 56, members pledge themselves to joint and separate action to achieve these purposes.[30] These two key provisions of the U.N. Charter combine to reaffirm the U.N. commitment to human rights.

The problem for the ideal of human rights is that the U.N. Charter does not provide any affirmative methods for accomplishing its human rights goals. No enforcement mechanism or authority for action is provided within the U.N. Charter to secure human rights. Promoting and encouraging human rights remains an ultimate, but perhaps an uncertain, even illusory goal. The U.N. Charter uses the word "promotes" when referring to human rights. Many actions short of an intervention can be said to promote human rights. For example, is voicing support for human rights or writing a criticism of human rights violations in a nation an undertaking to promote human rights?

Although not legally binding, the United Nations reaffirmed its support and commitment to human rights when it adopted the Universal Declaration of Human Rights.[31] This document sets forth a common standard that all nations should strive to achieve.[32] The rights are quite specific and range from the most fundamental rights, like freedom, dignity, freedom from slavery, and life without torture, to more narrow ones, including the rights to a fair trial, to privacy, to own property, to work, and to education.[33]

Even with all of these provisions, theoretical and practical problems exist between the competing notions of sovereignty and human rights.[34] The difficulty is always one of deciding which ideal should prevail in which circumstance. The lack of clarity in the U.N. Charter coupled with the different natures of state sovereignty and human rights illustrates the problem. Any lack of clarity about when intervention is proper usually results in inaction. The result for state sovereignty is automatic protection until it is found to be clearly improper. A decision to intervene by the Security Council is effectively a decision that sovereignty should no longer be protected in that particular circumstance. The presumption is otherwise. Historically, human rights have come in second to state sovereignty. Increasingly, however, that presumption is being altered.

In resolving the dilemma between sovereignty and human rights, national leaders always seek some sort of balance between the two ideals.[35] If, when, and how to intervene thus becomes a very tricky question and often is resolved by the perceptions of the most powerful nations as to their national interests. Humanitarian concerns usually become after-the-fact justifications.

The right of humanitarian intervention is a doctrine that has been used to legitimate the use of force against the sovereignty of a nation. Until the early 1990s, humanitarian intervention was generally understood to target oppressive governments that were violating the human rights of their populations. For example, humanitarian concerns were said to justify the Indian invasion of East Pakistan (now Bangladesh) in 1971, and the U.S. military operation in Panama in 1989 to arrest General Manuel Noriega. These operations fit the broad Grotian doctrine of humanitarian intervention: the right of states to intervene in order to prevent oppression and maltreatment in other states.[36]

U.N. involvement in northern Iraq in 1991 and in the former Yugoslavia in 1992 can also be seen as cases of humanitarian intervention. But these mandates were concerned with providing relief supplies to civilians adversely affected by civil war, not based on the promotion of human rights or the restoration of democracy.

Haiti is, therefore, an exceptional case. It was the overthrow of a democratic government that put the crisis onto the international agenda. The flood of refugees, particularly to the United States, heightened international interest and focused the attention of the U.S. government. Human rights abuses by the de facto government and its paramilitary supporters certainly added to this crisis, but they were simply not the overriding concern of the international community. Indeed, I sincerely doubt that the military intervention would have occurred simply because of these human rights violations. Unlike Somalia or Iraq, thousands of people were not being murdered in Haiti daily because of the repression of their government. The media was not daily broadcasting the human rights abuses on television. Nevertheless, serious human rights abuses, including arbitrary arrests, abductions, politically motivated rapes, and approximately 5,000 murders certainly added to the urgency of the international campaign.[37]

The two most important Security Council resolutions on the Haitian crisis, Security Council Resolution 841, initiating the Security Council's active involvement on Haiti, and Security Council Resolution 940, which authorized military intervention there, shed some light on the role that human rights abuses played in the justifications for the eventual intervention.[38] In Security Council Resolution 841, a resolution that imposed economic sanctions on Haiti, the Security Council determined that the Haitian situation threatened international peace and security and registered the Council's concern "that the persistence of this situation contributes to a climate of fear of persecution and economic dislocation, which could increase the number of Haitians seeking refuge in neighboring Member States, and *convinced* that a reversal of this situation is needed to prevent its negative repercussions on the region."[39] Thus, at this stage, the Security Council seemed more concerned about refugee flows inconveniencing neighboring countries than over human rights violations.[40]

Security Council Resolution 940 shows greater concern than Security Council Resolution 841 over massive human rights violations.[41] It states, inter alia,

Condemning the continuing disregard of [the agreements to transition back to democracy] by the illegal de facto regime, and the regime's refusal to cooperate with efforts by the United Nations and the Organization of American States (O.A.S.) to bring about their implementation,

Gravely concerned by the significant further deterioration of the humanitarian situation in Haiti, in particular the continuing escalation by the illegal de facto regime of systematic violations of civil liberties, the desperate plight of Haitian refugees and the recent expulsion of the staff of the International Civilian Mission (MICIVIH), which was condemned in its Presidential statement of 12 July 1994, . . .

Taking note of the letter dated 29 July 1994 from the legitimately elected President of Haiti and the letter dated 30 July 1994 from the Permanent Representative of Haiti to the United Nations, . . .

Reaffirming that the goal of the international community remains the restoration of democracy in Haiti and the prompt return of the legitimately elected President, Jean-Bertrand Aristide, within the framework of the Governors Island Agreement, . . .

Determining that the situation in Haiti continues to constitute a threat to peace and security in the region, . . .

4. *Acting* under Chapter VII of the Charter of the United Nations, *authorizes* Member States to form a multinational force under unified command and control and, in this framework, to use all necessary means to facilitate the departure from Haiti of the military leadership, consistent with the Governors Island Agreement, the prompt return of the legitimately elected President and the restoration of the legitimate authorities of the Government of Haiti, and to establish and maintain a secure and stable environment that will permit implementation of the Governors Island Agreement, on the understanding that the cost of implementing this temporary operation will be borne by the participating Member States;

5. *Approves* the establishment, upon adoption of this resolution, of an advance team of UNMIH of not more than sixty personnel, including a group of observers, to establish the appropriate means of coordination with the multinational force, to carry out the monitoring of the operations of the multinational force and other functions described in paragraph 23 of the report of the Secretary-General of 15 July 1994 (S/1994/828), and to assess requirements and to prepare for the deployment of UNMIH upon completion of the mission of the multinational force; . . .

8. *Decides* that the multinational force will terminate its mission and UNMIH will assume the full range of its functions described in paragraph 9 below when a secure and stable environment has been established and UNMIH has adequate force capability and structure to assume the full range of its functions; the determination will be made by the Security Council, taking into account recommendations from the Member States of the multinational force, which are based on the assessment of the commander of the multinational force, and from the Secretary-General;

9. *Decides* to revise and extend the mandate of the United Nations Mission in Haiti (UNMIH) for a period of six months to assist the democratic government of Haiti in fulfilling its responsibilities in connection with:

a. sustaining the secure and stable environment established during the multinational phase and protecting international personnel and key installations; and

b. the professionalization of the Haitian armed forces and the creation of a separate police force;

10. *Requests also* that UNMIH assist the legitimate constitutional authorities of Haiti in establishing an environment conducive to the organization of free and fair legislative elections to be called by those authorities and, when requested by them, monitored by the United Nations, in cooperation with the Organization of American States.[42]

A concern about human rights violations, as well as a concern about refugee flow, thus played a role, but only a secondary one, in the justifications for the use of force by the United Nations in Haiti. The major publicly stated goal of the Security Council was the restoration of the democratically elected government.

Even if restoring democracy was the main publicly proclaimed goal of the intervention, three actions taken by the international community clearly fall within a broad definition of "humanitarian intervention." First, the imposition of comprehensive economic sanctions in Haiti was a highly coercive step that sought to dictate a political result. Second, the naval blockade off the coast of Haiti to enforce those sanctions was a use of force by states against Haiti that would normally implicate Article 2(4) of the U.N. Charter and thus constitutes a form of intervention.[43] Finally, the statements made by Clinton and his representatives from May 1994 through the Carter delegation visit of September 17 and 18, 1994, regarding a military invasion of Haiti, constituted a threat of force by the United States that implicated Article 2(4) of the U.N. Charter.[44]

The reasons stated for the economic sanction, naval blockade, and threat of military intervention by the Security Council members were that these actions were necessary to alleviate the violence taking place in Haiti and to restore Haiti's democratically elected government. The Security Council members believed that Haiti's best chance for future development was a return to democracy. In particular, the United States, the driving force behind the Security Council's resolutions, saw itself as committed to resisting threats to democracy in its own backyard, the Western Hemisphere.[45] Even more important to the United States, specifically to President Clinton, was a parochial concern: the goal of stopping the flood of Haitian refugees to the shores of the United States. Finally, there was considerable domestic pressure on the Clinton administration, particularly by the Congressional Black Caucus, to take action on Haiti as a show of U.S. moral leadership on racial issues.

If the Haiti case can be seen as one of humanitarian intervention, was the intervention justified? The literature suggests that for this to be so several conditions have to be met.[46] A justified humanitarian intervention must (1) be aimed at restoring human rights, (2) necessary, (3) proportionate to the evil that it is designed to suppress, and (4) welcomed by the victims of oppression. While the Haiti intervention generally meets these conditions, a serious problem remains in concluding that the intervention was absolutely justified. The motivations of the key actors in intervening, particularly those of the United States, were not primarily humanitarian. Nor were the motivations of many who supported the resolution in the Security Council. Moreover, the intervention was not principally aimed at restoring human rights. This makes it difficult to place the Haiti case comfortably as one of pure humanitarian intervention.

The Haiti case, however, raises another intriguing issue. Should a justified, legitimate, humanitarian intervention include support for democratic governments imperiled by violent antidemocratic forces? The argument for such a conclusion is straightforward. Popular government is an internationally prescribed human right. Article 21(3) of the Universal Declaration on Human Rights provides, "The will of the people shall be the basis of the authority of government; this will shall be expressed in periodic and genuine elections which shall be by universal and equal suffrage and shall be held by secret vote or by equivalent free voting procedures."[47] It is clear, therefore, that when a democratically elected government is overthrown by force, when the law is blatantly violated, and when terror sets in, all the other human rights that depend on the lawful institutions of government become matters for the dictators and their supporting casts. When that happens, dictators and their supporting casts invariably violate a wide array of human rights. Stated otherwise, military coups can be seen as violations of the political rights of the people that, unfortunately, invariably lead to the violation of other rights. Thus, a violation of the right to create and maintain a democratic government can be seen, in itself, as the most serious human rights violation.

Universal and therefore internationally recognized human rights are matters of international concern. Moreover, violations of popular sovereignty are increasingly subject to international condemnation. Indeed, even in the Western Hemisphere, with its long and sad history of interventions and its acute concern for national sovereignty, the Santiago Declaration of the OAS has committed the members of the OAS to some regional action when a democratically elected government has been overthrown.[48]

It is encouraging that the international community as a whole has also made a stronger commitment to democracy, and that many nations now recognize that democratic government enhances the protection of human rights. Such governments may even reduce the likelihood of aggression. Nevertheless, there are certainly significant dangers to including the restoration of democracy as part of the doctrine of humanitarian intervention. This doctrine will only be applied to smaller and weaker states, and there is a clear danger that the notion of restoring democracy will be used, as in the past, only as a smoke screen for intervention. In addition, restoring democracy is rarely a simple task, as Haiti well illustrates. It is violent, costly, and susceptible to abuse even when the intentions of the intervenors are "relatively pure." For example, it is difficult to determine the right thing to do when a particular government is brought to power through democratic elections but espouses a program intended to violate fundamental human rights.[49] Even when it is clear what the correct action should be, external action may not be feasible. Even when the issues are clear and the mission is feasible, the results may not be stellar.

Suppose the United States decides to use military force to "restore democracy" to Colombia, Ecuador, or Venezuela.[50] Is Haiti a precedent for a future legal and legitimate humanitarian intervention in other states? Indeed, Security Council–mandated use of force in support of democracy in Haiti will surely be cited as a precedent for similar action in some other country. But too much should not be made of the Haiti case, and certainly not a new doctrine. The decision to use force to restore Aristide to power came about only after many other approaches over a three-year period failed, including a series of economic sanctions, attempted negotiations, and a naval blockade, so that its groundbreaking nature is less compelling as a precedent than it might otherwise be. Moreover, the Security Council's decision to use force was driven almost exclusively by the national interests of the United States. Furthermore, the anticipated effective military opposition from Haiti was virtually nonexistent. Even more significant is another unique situation. The democratically elected head of government essentially authorized these steps in exile. In addition, a strong regional interest existed in reversing the coup against Aristide, both because of the refugee flows from Haiti and because of the fear that military forces in other emerging democracies would be encouraged by the intransigence of the Haitian coup leaders. All of these conditions were singular.

Moreover, world events since that time suggest a cautious approach in the use of Haiti as a precedent for the use of multinational military interventions all over the world. For example, the palace coup in Cambodia in which the second prime minister effectively removed the first prime minister in July 1997 provoked no serious talk at the United Nations of military intervention.[51] This is so even though the United Nations had played an instrumental role in the Cambodian elections leading to the creation of the first prime minister's government.[52] Further, the commission of massive human rights abuses in other nations after the Haiti experience simply did not lead to multinational military intervention. For example, human rights abuses in East Timor, Afghanistan, and Algeria have not brought military intervention by the international community for a variety of reasons, including historical and regional factors, economic interests, the causes of the violations, the scale of the problems, and the perceived cost of the remedy.

But the Haiti case is a precedent in several ways. Never before had the Security Council authorized force to remove a de facto government and reinstate a democratic one within a member state. Never before had the international community used force to restore a democratically elected president and replace the very coup leaders who had overthrown him. If the United States wishes to act multilaterally again in the Western Hemisphere, its approach to Haiti will be an important precedent. There is a caveat to offer, however. The circumstances of the Haiti case were unique, particularly in the domestic politics of the United States, and unlikely to be replicated.

There are, nonetheless, some important lessons to be learned from the Haiti crisis and the intervention that may be suggestive for future crises. First, military enforcement of economic sanctions imposed on a state as a means for preventing repression can itself have serious effects on the well-being of the nationals of that country. The sanctions imposed on Haiti created considerable hardships on the very people who were meant to be helped. This resulted in or at least aggravated serious problems of malnutrition, deteriorating health care, and hunger that approached starvation. The sanctions also harmed the ability of hospitals and relief organizations to function because of the lack of fuel. In addition, the de facto leaders withheld supplies to place pressure on the international community. At the same time, Haiti's military leaders and the economic elite avoided economic hardship by smuggling supplies for themselves across the porous border with the Dominican Republic. The de facto military government actually thrived on the embargo and other economic sanctions by taking over the drug trafficking business. Context is crucial. Economic sanctions are effective only if the rational economic maximizer (here the de facto regime) perceives that it will be harmed.

Second, the interplay between the United Nations, the OAS, and the United States was a significant element of the intervention. It led to sanctions, forced negotiations, and, eventually, military intervention. But it was the United States that intended to call the shots, while simultaneously being somewhat constrained by these organizations. While the United States was eager to obtain U.N. approval for military intervention and to develop cooperation with these international organizations and, more particularly, certain nations, in the end it wanted to decide when and how to intervene. The multilateral approach, however, to some extent limited the freedom of the United States to act unilaterally. Horse trading almost certainly took place.

Third, the Security Council resolution contained some important restrictions that affected the development of troops in Haiti. It authorized invasion only by a "multinational force," so the United States had to seek support from other states. Moreover, the resolution authorized using "all necessary means" only to "facilitate the departure from Haiti of the military leadership consistent with the Governors Island Agreement." Furthermore, with respect to a new government, it authorized only the restoration of the Aristide government. This is important because Aristide was viewed negatively by many politicians—mostly very conservative and right-wing politicians—in the United States. The resolution also established a U.N. observer force to monitor the operations of the multinational force and to lay the groundwork for a peacekeeping force.

Fourth, the Haiti case illustrates the inherent tension between seeking all possible nonforcible means for ending a crisis and effectively addressing that crisis. For example, the last-hour success of the Carter delegation in averting a violent military invasion undoubtedly saved lives. Unfortunately, it also resulted in recognition of the "honor" of and a general amnesty for the de facto military leaders, who had frequently been branded by President Clinton as thugs and murderers. One can generalize from these facts as follows: The less force used in the intervention, the greater is the sense that the international community is not intruding too excessively into the sovereignty of a nation. At the same time, however, the less forcible the intervention, the greater must be the compromises made by the international community to accommodate the de facto authorities who necessitated the intervention in the first place. This, of course, may cause problems for the creation of a democracy for years to come.[53]

Fifth, Haiti is an example of a pattern of initial intervention led by a major power to be followed by a U.N.–commanded force charged with assisting in establishing, to some extent, some form of national reconciliation. The United Nations demanded that the initial force disarm the de facto government forces because it feared that a U.N.–commanded force would be unable to do so. The United States, however, refused to engage in a broad disarmament campaign, which resulted in serious security problems for the democratically elected government and the people of Haiti.

Sixth, the Haitian people strongly desired justice and reconciliation, thereby establishing a strong basis for the international community to provide useful assistance and resources to Haiti in helping to create the conditions needed to establish a democracy. But over the years frustration has replaced hope. Unless significant changes occur, increased violence may replace frustration.[54]

Seventh, it is undeniable that Security Council Resolution 940 will be seen in at least two ways.[55] It will be seen as a precedent for a very expansive view of what can constitute a threat to international peace and, therefore, used in support of multinational action through the United Nations to promote the development (or at least the preservation) of democracies. On the other hand, Haiti may also be seen as a singular, unusual case in which the vagaries of domestic U.S. politics are not likely to be repeated.

Finally, the Haiti case illustrates the difficulty the U.S. government faces in using force unilaterally or even with multinational support and, simultaneously, a method for overcoming any domestic roadblocks to the use of force. The difficulty in using force reflects the influence of the doctrine attributed to General Colin Powell when he served as chairman of the Joint Chiefs of Staff.[56] According to this doctrine, U.S. military force should be used abroad only rarely, and then with overwhelming power, in order to avoid debilitating casualties and engagements such as the Vietnam War. This approach caused the Pentagon to oppose most of the military engagements urged on it by others in Washington.[57] As long as Powell remained in power (until September 1993), the use of force in Haiti was unlikely. In addition, Powell's doctrine derived not only from his personal charisma and military credentials, but also from Clinton's weak position vis-à-vis the U.S. military. He was seen as someone who had chosen to avoid serving in Vietnam, and whose earliest policy priorities included the acceptance of gays in the military, which had foundered ignominiously on the Pentagon's opposition.

Precisely because Clinton's military options on Haiti were circumscribed by the Pentagon's reservations and by Congressional skepticism over the use of force in Haiti, a U.N. framework for addressing the crisis was invaluable to Clinton. Thus, as of 1993, the United Nations was at the heart of Clinton's Haiti policy. Once the Clinton administration decided that only the use of force would dislodge the de facto regime in Haiti, it still faced the very tricky problem of lending domestic and international legitimacy to this goal. It used the U.N. Security Council to achieve it. For example, with Security Council authorization in hand, the Clinton administration did not seek Congressional support for the multinational force under the War Powers Resolution, as many of its critics in Congress of both parties then demanded.[58] The timing of the multinational forces landing in Haiti was apparently designed to occur before Congressional opposition overwhelmed the Clinton administration.[59] Thus, one important lesson from the Haiti case is that the multilateral route for the promotion of what is perceived as U.S. national interest and for the use of force can be rewarding. It certainly can help to overcome domestic opposition and perhaps even convince domestic opinion of the legitimacy of the use of force to "restore democracy." It can also be used to defuse any regional opposition to such strategy.

THE PROBLEMS OF THE TRANSITION PROCESS

The Haiti case is suggestive for other significant issues. It teaches important lessons about the difficulties of the transition process and the creation and stabilization of a democratic nation. It demonstrates that if the relevant political actors, both domestic and international, are to be successful in helping to create the conditions for democracy to bloom, they must be highly educated and thoughtful on a number of significant issues. They must be intimately familiar with and understand the history and culture of a nation. They must understand the major problems and complexities inherent in the transition from dictatorship to democracy. And they must have a clear vision of the justificatory theories for democracy. To put it another way, the creative experiments necessary to transform a society will not take place without such knowledge, and the international community's effort to help nations overcome their authoritarian legacies will simply fail. Unfortunately, the international community's recent efforts in Haiti illustrate this failure.

The international community's approach to Haiti has been successful in a very limited way, but the long-term prognosis for creating the conditions for democracy to flower appears uncertain at best. The international community was successful in restoring the Aristide government to power, and political power was transferred from one duly elected government to another—from Aristide to Preval. The army was abolished and a new and relatively well-trained police force has been created, which, for all its limitations, is functioning reasonably well under extremely difficult conditions. Even though political violence, criminal violence, and human rights violations persist, they are not the serious problems they were during the coup period. But abject poverty, disease, unemployment, and an electoral crisis, among other serious problems, persist. Life for the vast majority of Haitians remains frightening.

In spite of their problems, Haitians do not expect or want a return to dictatorship, however benign. When one looks to the future, it is clear that democratization remains at an embryonic stage, and that the democratization process is not irreversible. In point of fact, in 2000 Haiti appeared to be sliding in the wrong direction.

The 1999 U.S. Department of State Reports on Human Rights Practices, for example, summarizes some aspects of the current state of Haitian political society as follows:[60]

Haiti was in a constitutionally irregular situation throughout the year. Prime Minister Jacques Edouard Alexis, appointed in December 1998, completed only the first stage of the required two-part ratification process. The terms of office of the entire 85-seat House of Deputies and all but 9 of the 27 members of the Senate expired on January 11. Before Alexis could submit his Cabinet and plan of government to Parliament for approval as required by the 1987 Constitution, President Rene Preval announced that he would not recognize Parliament's decision to extend its incumbents' mandates until new elections could be held. This effectively dissolved the Parliament on January 11, leaving the country without a functioning legislative branch of government or any duly elected officials apart from President Preval and eight remaining senators.[61] In March, after negotiations with a five-party opposition coalition, Prime Minister Alexis formed a cabinet. However, due to the absence of a parliament, the new ministers took office without being confirmed. At year's end, there were plans to hold a first round of parliamentary elections in March 2000, a second round in April, and presidential elections in December. The judiciary is theoretically independent; however, in practice it remained largely weak and corrupt.

In September 1994, a U.N.–sanctioned multinational force restored the country's democratically elected president. The Armed Forces of Haiti (FAd'H) were subsequently disbanded. At that time, the Government established the Haitian National Police (HNP), which continues to gain experience and to benefit from international training and advisors, although it has severe attrition problems. Moreover, it remains an immature force that is still grappling with problems of corruption and human rights abusers within its ranks. Allegations of corruption, incompetence, and narcotics trafficking target members at all levels of the force. The HNP has a variety of specialized units, including a crisis response unit, a crowd control unit (CIMO) serving Port-au-Prince and the Western department, crowd control units (UDMO's) serving each of the remaining eight departments, a presidential and palace security unit, an 81-officer Coast Guard unit, and a Special Investigative Unit (SIU). The SIU was formed to investigate high-profile political killings but is ill-equipped, inexperienced, and has made limited progress on its cases.[62] Some members of local government councils (CASEC's) exercise arrest authority without legal sanction. Members of the HNP and other security forces committed some serious human rights abuses.

The mandate of the U.N. Police Mission in Haiti (MIPONUH), which advised and trained the HNP, is currently set to expire on March 15, 2000. The United Nations plans to replace that mission with a civilian follow-on technical assistance program.

Haiti is an extremely poor country, with a per capita annual income of around $400. This figure probably does not fully include significant transfers from the over 1 million Haitians living abroad, as well as income from informal sector activities that constitute an estimated 70 percent of actual economic activity. The country has a market-based economy with state enterprises controlling telecommunications and utilities. The Government had proposed a broad plan for privatization of state-owned enterprises. However, aside from the sale of two previously closed enterprises, the process has come to a halt. A small elite controls much of the country's wealth. Accurate employment statistics are unavailable.[63] About two-thirds of the population work in subsistence agriculture, earn less than the average income, and live in extreme poverty. A small part of the urban labor force works in the industrial and assembly sectors, with an equal number in government or service sector employment. Assembled goods, textiles, leather goods, handicrafts, and electronics are a source of limited export revenue and employment. Other important exports are mangoes and coffee.[64] The Government relies heavily on international assistance.[65]

The Government's human rights record was generally poor, and its overall effort to respect the human rights of its citizens was marred by serious abuses and shortcomings in oversight. The HNP's tendency to resort to excessive force resulted in a sharp increase in extrajudicial killings. Police were linked to several disappearances. Police continued to beat, at times torture, and otherwise mistreat detainees. While some HNP members were fired and some were incarcerated for human rights abuses, methodical investigations and prosecutions are rare, and impunity remains a problem.[66] Poor prison conditions, arbitrary arrest and detention, and prolonged pretrial detention also remained problems. However, instances of brutality in prisons decreased during the year. The judiciary remained plagued by understaffing, inadequate resources, and corrupt and untrained judges. Judicial dockets remain clogged, and fair and expeditious trials are the exception rather than the rule. The judiciary is not independent in practice, and in at least 22 cases the executive branch detained persons in defiance of release orders issued by judges. Security forces carried out illegal warrantless searches. Most media practice some self-censorship; however, the press frequently is critical of the Government.[67] Due to the nation's political crisis, citizens were unable to vote for representatives to Parliament. Violence against women, societal discrimination against women, and government neglect and abuse of children remain problems. The widespread practice of rural families sending young children to the larger cities to work as unpaid domestics (restaveks) also is still a problem. Child labor persists. Vigilante activity, including killings, remained a common alternative to formal judicial processes.

The Government's effort to redress the legacy of human rights abuse from the 1991–1994 period was slightly more successful than in previous years. The 4-year investigation into the Raboteau massacre was completed in September, an indictment was issued, and by the end of the year, the case was moving towards trial. In July the Ministry of Justice disbursed about $1,700 (27,000 gourdes) in reparation money to 914 victims of the 1993 Cite de Soleil fire, which reportedly was set by the paramilitary Front for the Advancement and Progress of Haiti (FRAPH). Otherwise, no significant progress was made in addressing other human rights violations or political killings dating from the Duvalier, de facto, or post-intervention periods.[68]

It is relatively clear that the international community, particularly the United States, dramatically underestimated the Haitian challenge. After the success of the 1994 military intervention, the international community did not have a well-thought-out plan linked to the publicly stated reason for the intervention—to restore democracy—that would have given the Haitian people a good chance to successfully challenge some of those almost unresolveable problems.[69] The international community simply assumed that economic and political development and social harmony would be relatively easy to achieve. This was a dangerous illusion. In fact, there appears to be an inverse relationship between these factors. The very weaknesses of Haitian institutions and modes of operation that made the military engagement so easy and successful make the economic, political, and social challenges so difficult. The debility of Haitian institutions and their operations provided no strong basis for resisting a military invasion; neither did they, or the culture that had emaciated them, provide a foundation for democratic, political, or economic development. The society lacks a cohesive national identity and any sense of collective purpose.

Therefore, before political actors can judge whether humanitarian intervention in the guise of military force and the occupation of a country is justified, they need to have a clear understanding of the goals of intervention and whether they are justifiable. Simply because the action may be legal does not, of course, necessarily make it morally justifiable. These political actors also need to understand the problems associated with any transition to democracy and to be imaginative in trying to resolve those problems, working within the history and culture of that particular nation. Transformation requires knowledge, theory, and the courage to take steps necessary for positive reform.

To begin with, one needs a moral justification for democracy.[70] Most political actors involved in the process of consolidating democratic regimes, however, find conceptions of democracy, and all they entail, relevant only from the perspective of subjective legitimacy; that is, from the perspective of the functionality of the political system. Subjective legitimacy is the generalized belief of the population in the moral justifiability of the government and its directives. Democracy is therefore seen as an instrument to the end goal of stability. In effect, those engaged in democratic transition who propose institutional reforms are attempting to create, consolidate, and stabilize democratic structures while averting threats of reversal to authoritarian alternatives. These political actors and scholars are clearly firm partisans of democracy and take it for granted that it is the best political system. They do not, however, consider that what makes democracy the best political system is relevant to ascertaining the means for its creation and preservation. Instead, they typically adopt a perspective characterized by a results-oriented process, concluding that whatever is responsible for making democracy the morally best system of government can be identified by certain factual features: regular ways in which citizens may affect a change of government, the division of power, or respect for basic rights. Simply by identifying and replicating the phenomenon or desired results using a system in force in some paradigmatic country, such as the United States, Britain, or France, these actors seek, in a value-neutral way, the proper means for achieving or preserving that system.

This method is mistaken; indeed, it is deeply flawed. Democracy is a normative concept and cannot be identified in depth without fully articulating the evaluative conception that justifies its distinctive institutions. The inevitability of this normative inquiry is demonstrated by the inherent conflicts and tensions within the distinctive institution of democracy, making it impossible to simply identify and adopt appropriate democratic institutions. Any number of questions can be raised to prove this point. Is democracy the phenomenon of representation (the weakest form of democracy), or is a system of representation merely an auxiliary institution imposed by the difficulties of direct democracy in an open society? Is it the separation of the executive and the legislative powers, or is it instead an optimal arrangement that is not adopted in parliamentary democracies without the loss of value?

Is it the recognition of a bill of rights as a limit to majoritarian decisions imposed by independent judicial institutions? Are political parties distinctive democratic institutions, or are they unnecessary in a better-working, well-functioning democracy? Is the proportional representative system the best method of democratic representation, or is it only one of many diverse alternatives that must be chosen for technical reasons?

When we come to realize the full range of these issues, it is clear that there are no distinctive institutions of democracy outside of a value-laden theory that simply justifies a set of options. We cannot identify institutions commonly understood as democratic and work out a method for stabilizing them without systematically analyzing the moral theory that justifies them. Reality does not tell us which institutions are essential and which are contingent in relation to a normative concept like that of democracy. We are unable to determine what contingencies we can manipulate to preserve the essentials of the concept. The "realist" who thinks otherwise is mistaken, even substantially confused.

While this is not the place to discuss fully theories of democracy and their justifications, it is clear that the best means for countering some of the difficulties of moving from dictatorship to democracy is to create a polity governed by universal and impersonal principles where individual citizens, who are not identified with any particular interests but preserve the capacity to adopt different ones, make choices in a process of public justification and dialogue. This requires broad popular participation in governmental decision making and its consequent actions, led by strong participative and ideologically committed political parties and parliamentary bodies. These parties and parliaments must themselves, of course, be internally democratic, open, and disciplined.

These conclusions are based on an epistemic view of democracy and upon the utmost respect for the autonomy of each individual. In this view, autonomy consists of the exercise of self-governing capacities, such as the capacities of understanding, imagining, reasoning, valuing, and desiring. Free persons have and are recognized as having such capacities. In a political order dedicated to serving the conditions of free deliberation for its members, those members can legitimately expect of that order that it not only permit but also encourage the exercise of such capacities: that it permit and encourage autonomy. Indeed, one of the hallmarks of liberal democracy is the notion of the citizen who is not identified with any interest, but is free to choose and has an equal voice in expressing his or her choice.

Thus, it is apparent that the international community lacked a valid normative conception of democracy when it intervened in Haiti and failed to create the proper incentives in Haiti to help democracy grow. Moreover, if the international community, led by the United States, did have a coherent normative conception of democracy, it seems to have misunderstood how to apply it—to create the conditions for democracy to grow—to its actions in Haiti.

An additional serious problem afflicts the international effort in Haiti and exacerbates the failure to understand the significance of normative justifications for democracy. There seems to be a misunderstanding, even an ignorance, of the problems associated with the transition and consolidation process.[71] But before one can judge the potential for a successful transition from dictatorship to democracy in any nation undergoing this difficult process, one must understand the problems associated with it. To put it another way, this process presents difficult problems of its own that must be understood before one can create policies favorable to the creation of a democracy.

But there is a further complication. The problems of the transition process and possible solutions to them, in turn, cannot be successfully addressed without a valid justificatory theory of democracy. Theory and practice go hand in hand. As a baseline, such a democratic vision requires a continuous order of mutually assured and encouraged autonomy in which political decisions are manifestly based on the judgments of members of that society who are perceived and treated as free and equal persons. The expression of self-governing capacities must operate within both the formal institutions of politics and the affairs of daily life. The democratic order must satisfy the conditions of equal freedom and autonomy that give it definition.

What are some of the issues associated with the creation and consolidation of a democracy? There are several significant features of the consolidation of democracies that have taken place in Latin America and Haiti. The first significant feature of the consolidation is the fact that the process of democratization has taken place in many of these nations during some of the worst economic, social, and political crises in the history of these nations. In general, these crises include the commission of massive human rights violations (murder, rape, and torture), enormous debts, hyperinflation, epidemics, dramatic and surprising increases in already high rates of infant mortality, extremely high rates of unemployment, and the collapse of entire systems of social welfare.

Haiti presents an uncomfortably extreme example of many of these problems. There, the human and material resources are in such short supply, or have been degraded by such severe poverty (even destitution), illiteracy, malnutrition, disease, violence, corruption, overpopulation, rapid urbanization, deforestation, and soil erosion, as to raise serious questions about Haiti's continued survival as a society and as an independent nation-state.

Even before the crisis erupted between 1991 and 1994 over the military's refusal to restore President Aristide to power, Haiti was the poorest country in the Western Hemisphere. Its per capita income was $370 a year. In a country of approximately 7 million people, there were fewer than a thousand doctors. The life expectancy was a mere fifty-six years, one in every eight babies died before reaching the age of one, and 70 percent of all children were estimated to suffer from some form of malnutrition. At least two-thirds of the population was illiterate, and the state school system was so inefficient and small that fewer than 5 percent of eligible students were enrolled in government high schools.[72] As if these problems were not bad enough in themselves, many of the doctors, engineers, administrators, and others with the necessary skills to change Haiti had been killed or driven into exile.[73] Most of those who are in exile do not wish to risk their lives and fortunes by returning to Haiti until positive changes occur.[74] The irony is that Haiti needs these very same people to make the changes that would attract them to return. Unfortunately, these conditions have not improved since the "restoration of democracy." Some suggest that these conditions have even become more serious since the international military intervention.[75]

The most difficult obstacles to democracy in many countries, particularly in Haiti, however, may be psychological and cultural. For example, the tradition of a predatory, oppressive state has left Haitians deeply distrustful of government and of foreigners. Haiti's political culture has long been characterized as an admiration of force. Political disputes are often settled not by negotiation, but through the exercise of force, and respect for democratic procedures and obligations, including reasoned justifications for actions, is minimal.

Furthermore, there is great controversy in the international community about whether the problems associated with these transitions and the attempts to address them are leading to a change in the economic and social structures of these countries necessary to allow for a new oligopolization of the economy. To put it another way, it remains unclear whether a new oligopolization will develop that will greatly restrict the avenues of access for the powerless sectors of society to the basic goods necessary for leading a life of dignity, or whether, on the contrary, the crisis is leading to more efficient schemes of production, thereby benefiting all sectors of society. In Haiti, the unequal distribution of resources and thus general living conditions have become even more disparate since the international military intervention. The elites have obtained an even larger share of the wealth than they possessed before the intervention, and everyone else (more than 90% of the population) has been made worse off. This has led to a loss of hope; indeed, even to a sense of desperation on the part of the vast majority of Haitians.

The problem is even more difficult than it is usually perceived to be. In many of the nations in the transition process, but particularly in Haiti, the present circumstances result from a long-fought war of attrition against the vast majority by a small but ruthless ruling class. Ironically, Haiti is the product of a revolution against slavery and colonialism. It emerged as a nation in 1804 after a thirteen-year struggle against France that resulted in the destruction of the French colony of Saint Dominique.[76] Almost immediately after independence, the Haitian elites attempted to recreate the plantation economy, treating the rural masses in much the same way as the French colonial oppressors had treated them. The former slaves, however, simply refused to return to a state of slavery. Instead, they settled as small peasants on land bought or reconquered from the state or abandoned by large landowners. The urban elites then devised a dual strategy to counter this problem.

The first part of the plan was economic. The elites used the fiscal and marketing systems of the country to create wealth-producing mechanisms for themselves. They became traders, politicians, and state employees. They prospered by living off the peasants' labor. Taxes collected by the import–export bourgeoisie at the urban markets and customhouses—paid solely by the peasants—provided the entire source of government revenues. The elites then took over the state and used state revenues as their personal bank accounts.

The second part of the plan was political. The strategy was to isolate the peasants on small mountain plots and keep them away from politics. It was a brilliant but corrupt strategy. The peasants, who unknowingly subsidized the elites, had no say whatsoever in how the state was to be run. The exploitation continued throughout the nineteenth and twentieth centuries. For example, beginning in the late 1950s Papa "Doc" Duvalier came to power and exploited this plan. He used state funds as his own personal bank account to enjoy incredible economic and political power.[77] Even today, the entrepreneurial class continues to prosper at the expense of the vast majority of Haitians. Indeed, many Haitians continue to feel enslaved.

Under the best of circumstances, a nation such as Haiti cannot be changed structurally without some yielding of power by the haves, the economic elite. But, of course, rulers who profit from stasis are disinclined to risk change. Moreover, if it is to be the policy of the United States and the rest of the international community, which it appears to be, to sustain at all costs the present distribution of economic power in Haiti, hardly anything can be done that will necessarily have long-range beneficial political and social consequences and thus allow Haiti to become a democratic nation.

A second prominent obstacle that nations face in the transition process is the corrosive power of the phenomenon known as corporatism.[78]

Indeed, for the transition process to succeed, the people must dissolve the network of de facto power relationships that corporations create and jealously protect by taking advantage of the power vacuum left by representatives of popular sovereignty. Under the umbrella of authoritarian rule, a number of social groups representing particular interests sculpt a place for themselves after a bargaining process that includes their support for the present regime. Such groups include the military, religious organizations, coalitions of entrepreneurs, trade unions, and even the so-called independent press. Once democratic rule is established, these groups stubbornly resist relinquishing their power to representatives of the people.

Corporatism is usually expressed and functions in complicated ways. There is some control by the state over these interest groups and organizations, and there are a variety of official and unofficial mechanisms that are used to alter their operation. Simultaneously, however, these organizations exert enormous pressure upon government actors and agencies. This pressure allows the corporative forces to obtain favored treatment of various kinds, amounting to a legal monopoly of particular interests. Sometimes this monopoly power of corporative interests is unaccompanied by any significant state influence over these forces. In other situations, alternative legal or even constitutional privileges short of monopoly may be granted that shield organizations from the raw competitive forces of popular expression, such as a free market.

Corporatism is an insidious and powerful force, and it is very difficult to overcome. Haiti is a harsh example of the devastation created by corporatism. Between 1991 and 1994 the military corporative force assumed total power and influence and completely violated and destroyed any semblance of democratic practices and institutions. The military forces consolidated their rule by intentionally and ruthlessly suppressing Haiti's once diverse and vibrant civil society. They assassinated approximately 5,000 people, brutalized and tortured thousands of others, and forced perhaps 500,000 people to go underground.[79] The military systematically repressed virtually all forms of independent association in an attempt to deny the Haitian people any organized base for opposition.

Aristide's major accomplishment as president was to abolish the military. Recently, the democratically elected government attempted to prosecute military officials who were involved in massive human rights violations.[80] But security is an absolute necessity to pursue this strategy. With approximately 250,000 automatic weapons cached around the country, stability remains fragile.[81] The failure to understand corporative power and the fear of placing international forces in harm's way led to a failure by the multinational forces to disarm the military, in spite of the fact that such a campaign was clearly compatible with Security Council Resolution 940. Part of this misunderstanding was the belief that removal of all privately held weapons in Haiti would have seriously disturbed the balance of power in Haitian society, dangerously concentrating all firepower in the hands of a democratically elected government whose long-term commitment to the rule of law and democracy could not be guaranteed. This grave error has led to unnecessary suffering. Indeed, the international community's failure to disarm the former military forces has led to a surge in garden-variety crimes, attacks on Parliament and on the Haitian National Police, and an increasingly large number of drug-related murders committed by former military officials who have formed criminal gangs.[82]

The entrepreneurial sector constitutes another corporative source directed at the democratically elected government. It seeks to obtain a variety of privileges or protective measures and preserve those previously secured. In Haiti, the entrepreneurial sector has attempted to boycott many measures designed to achieve progressive levels of taxation. It has also pushed hard for the complete privatization of nine state-owned industries, hoping to secure them and reap huge profits.

Inextricably intertwined and connected in a multitude of ways to these two features of the transition and consolidation process (the economic, political, and social crises and the problems of corporatism) is a third factor: the failure to fulfill the requirements of the rule of law in both the formal and informal aspects of public and private life. In Haiti, as in virtually every other nation undergoing the transition from dictatorship to democracy, this failure manifests itself in the concentration of power solely in the executive branch of government, leading to massive human rights abuses and a total disregard for the functions of the other branches of government. For example, during the coup period (1991–1994), members of the Haitian armed forces systematically assassinated and tortured thousands of people, including government officials who attempted to uphold the rule of law. Indeed, the military blatantly ignored judicial orders to arrest soldiers or officers accused of human rights abuses. It ignored the basic rights guaranteed by the constitution and any laws passed by Parliament that threatened its hold on power.[83] In light of this and Haiti's history of these abuses, a Creole proverb aptly summarizes the Haitian people's view about law: "Law is paper; bayonet is steel."

The violation of legal norms, however, is not restricted to formal military or de facto government officials. Unfortunately, such behavior is a distinguishing mark of political and social life at large, and has existed throughout the nation's history. This failure to follow the rule of law is evident in both social practices and in the actions of government officials.

This tendency toward unlawfulness does not, however, only infect public officials. Unfortunately, it equally infects the general society. This mentality correlates with a general trend toward anomie in society as a whole. It manifests itself in such things as enormous black markets, tax evasion, corruption in private economic activities, nonobservance of efficient economic norms, and noncompliance with the most basic rules of society, such as elementary traffic and urban regulations.

This unlawfulness mentality is often the product and cause of collective action problems. Frequently, the combination of expectations, interests, possibilities of actions, and their respective payoffs is such that the rational course of action for each participant in the process of political or social interaction advises that person not to comply with a certain norm, despite the fact that general—in Pareto's terms—compliance with it would have been for the benefit of everybody or almost everybody. This "dumb anomie" is intimately connected with both the stunting and the reversal of economic and social development.

Therefore, for a successful transition to democracy to occur in Haiti, it is critical for the international community to help Haitians consolidate the rule of law. This is important not only to secure respect for fundamental rights and for the observance of the democratic process, but also to achieve satisfactory levels of economic and social development. But the international community seems to have misunderstood the contours of the rule of law, placing its resources almost solely into strengthening the judiciary. Even those efforts have not appreciably improved the system of justice. In point of fact, despite the international community's best efforts to help strengthen the integrity of the judicial system, it remains corrupt and inefficient. Indeed, years of corruption and governmental neglect have left the judicial system nearly moribund. For example, a shortage of adequately trained judges and prosecutors, among other systemic problems, has created a huge backlog of criminal cases, with many detainees waiting months or even years in pretrial detention before getting a court hearing. If an accused person ultimately is tried and found not guilty, there is no redress against the government for time served.[84] While it is certainly necessary to strengthen the judiciary, this is simply insufficient to achieve the goal of establishing the rule of law in Haiti.

THE ELECTORAL PROCESS

A multitude of serious economic, social, and political problems face the Haitian people in their struggle for democracy. As of August 2000, however, Haiti remains in the midst of a major, nagging political crisis—an electoral crisis—that must be resolved before these other problems can be attacked.

Indeed, the vitality of a democratic system of government is generally measured by whether free and fair elections are periodically held as suggested by the standards of advanced industrial democracies, and as required by the laws of any particular nation.[85] The measurement includes another crucial element: the degree and scope of citizen participation in these electoral activities. If this is at least a partially acceptable baseline formula for the measurement of a democratic polity, then the political system in Haiti is on the correct path toward creating the conditions for democracy to bloom. While there were undoubtedly some serious problems with the country's recent national legislative and local municipal elections, it is remarkable they took place at all, given Haiti's history. It is even more remarkable that the elections took place in an essentially nonviolent environment.

Nevertheless, the 2000 elections, for a large number of local positions and almost all national legislative positions, were met by a hailstorm of domestic and international criticism. Final results from the May, June, and July 2000 first-round and runoff elections showed Aristide's Lavalas Family Party winning eighteen of nineteen seats in the twenty-seven-seat Senate, and seventy-two seats in the eighty-three-member House of Deputies.[86] The Lavalas Family Party also won approximately 80 percent of Haiti's 133 city halls and a majority of urban and rural local assemblies.[87] Haiti's business community and several traditional religious groups joined the United Nations, the OAS, Canada, France, and the United States, among others, in condemning Haiti's method of calculating first-round Senate winners.[88] But this is only the latest twist in an electoral crisis that goes back to 1997.

Unfortunately, in Haiti, even the holding of *regular* elections is problematic. The failure to do so has caused serious political problems. Prior to the most recent elections, the last time Haitians went to the polls was in April 1997, when an election was held for a third of the Senate seats. Only 7 percent of the voters bothered to turn out. A dispute then broke out, not about the election's legitimacy, but over alleged vote rigging by supporters of the Lavalas Family Party.

Lavalas Family had hoped, but failed, to wrest control of the Senate from the Organization of People in Struggle (OPL), a group of the original Lavalas movement that had first carried Aristide to power in 1990. In protest against the alleged vote rigging, Rosny Smarth, then prime minister, resigned and the OPL–dominated parliament blocked all President Preval's subsequent nominations for prime minister, as well as most legislative business. It also failed to assure that a fresh parliamentary election took place as promised in November 1998, and its mandate clearly expired in January 1999. At that time, as required by law and the Haitian Constitution, President Preval dissolved parliament, and has been ruling by decree since then.[89]

That was only the first postponement. The elections, both parliamentary and local, were then scheduled for November 1999. President Preval formed a provisional government with one major purpose: to hold the elections. But with an election commission still not prepared to hold a poll, the elections were deferred, first to December 1999, and then to March 19, 2000. On March 3, 2000, because of organizational problems that left over 1 million voters unregistered, the elections were postponed again. On March 8, 2000, the Provisional Electoral Council (CEP) announced that the legislative and municipal elections would be held April 9, with a runoff election to be held on May 21. But the elections were again thrown into turmoil on March 10, 2000, when President Preval announced that the CEP had no authority to announce a new date. According to the election law, the election date can only be established by presidential decree.[90]

The upshot of this fiasco has been that Haiti's government has been practically paralyzed since April 1997. New budgets have not been passed, and a great deal of promised foreign money has been suspended. Total aid and loans to the country fell from approximately $534 million in 1995 to approximately $356 million in 2000, while the World Bank and the Inter-American Development Bank together have a further $570 million, equivalent to about 18 percent of Haiti's gross domestic product, on hold.[91] Many structural reforms, such as an overhaul of the judicial system and the privatization of creaking state enterprises, have been halted. The economy remains in a dire state. Formal unemployment is estimated to be 50 to 70 percent. Life is hard, almost unbearable for the vast majority of Haitians. Peasant farmers walk for an entire day from the countryside to sell a few dollars' worth of wrinkled oranges in Port-au-Prince. The city center is crumbling; its roads are cratered and thick with rubbish. Survival, for the lucky ones, often depends on remittances from Haitian relatives abroad.

Particularly alarming is the drug boost to the economy. The international community's failure to disarm the former military and paramilitary forces, the inexperience of the newly formed Haitian National Police, the weakness of the justice system, and the proximity to the Columbian coast, have made Haiti a popular transshipment point for smuggling cocaine.

In short, Haitians badly need a well-functioning, proper government. Free and fair elections are crucial for Haiti's continued survival as an emerging democratic nation. But while elections finally took place in May and July 2000, they have not resolved the crisis, but may have even exacerbated it.

Although the elections were relatively peaceful, and at least 60 percent of registered voters participated, critics challenged the methods used to tabulate the results and asserted the results to be fraudulent. American newspapers portrayed the elections as an attempt by Preval's administration to establish a totalitarian government through electoral fraud. U.S. officials opposed to Aristide, in their continuing assault on his character, claimed him to be the moving force behind the allegedly fraudulent elections.

The head of the CEP, Leno Manus, refused to sign the official results of the election and fled to the United States.[92] Emmanuel Charles and Debussy Damier, members of the opposition party Space for Dialogue, also resigned from the CEP under pressure from their party.[93] On July 6, 2000, President Preval appointed three new members to the CEP.[94] Preval's critics accused him once again of trying to create a totalitarian government, this time by an "electoral coup d'etat." The United Nations and the OAS expressed concern over the validity of the 2000 elections and there was speculation that humanitarian aid would be withheld.[95]

On June 30, 2000, the U.S. Congress passed Concurrent Resolution 126, sponsored by Senator Jesse Helms, chairman of the Senate Foreign Relations Committee and a long-term critic of the Aristide and Preval administrations, condemning electoral fraud in Haiti and encouraging the Haitian government to "end its manipulation of the electoral process and take immediate steps to reverse the fraudulent results."[96] When asked about the resolution, President Preval responded in a way that certainly offended the international community. He stated, "I don't have to respond to what the U.S. Congress says," and remarked that " a democracy is not just elections, but the setting in place of institutions and the respect for the separation of powers established by the Haitian Constitution, which in the case of elections makes the [CEP] responsible to write the electoral law, apply it, and be the judge of last resort."[97]

Runoff elections were held on July 9, 2000, with a minimum of confusion and violence. Despite low voter turnout of between 10 and 40 percent depending on the region of the country, the elections were successful. The newspaper *Haiti Progres* compared the runoff elections to the Creole proverb, "The dogs bark, the caravan passes through." Stated otherwise, despite political battles and complaints, the CEP continued to move forward. The OAS, the United States, and several candidates from opposition parties refused to participate in the runoff election because the CEP would not modify the manner in which it tabulated the first-round Senate electoral results.[98] The international community remained concerned and opposition political parties continued to cry foul.[99] On July 1, 2000, however, Senator Jesse Helms, in his role as head of the Foreign Relations Committee, in a surprising reversal of his position, decided to unblock most of the aid destined for Haiti.[100]

There are many reasons for the problems in the election process. Delays and instability in the 2000 elections can be attributed to (1) problems in, and implementation of, electoral laws; (2) international politics; (3) domestic policies; (4) lack of infrastructure and resources; and (5) scattered violence in the absence of adequate police protection. The lack of effective electoral laws that could alleviate a host of possible problems and the difficulties in interpreting existing electoral laws caused instability and delays in tabulating the results of the elections. For example, after the first-round elections of May 21, 2000, and the runoff election of July 9, 2000, controversy arose over the method used to calculate electoral results and allegations of electoral irregularities.

The 1999 Electoral Law requires that a candidate receive an absolute majority plus one vote to win an election and avoid a runoff election.[101] It is, of course, easy to apply the principle of the absolute majority (50% plus one) in the case of elections to single seats. Problems arise, however, in tabulating results in districts where there are multiple positions open because it is impossible for any candidate to receive an absolute majority. In a district with two seats open each voter would get two votes, but each voter can only vote for one candidate. Thus, if there were three candidates for two seats and 100 voters, even if a candidate received every person's vote, the candidate would only receive 100 votes out of 200 total votes, thus failing to receive an absolute majority plus one vote.

Neither the 1999 Electoral Law nor the Constitution mandates how votes in joint elections are to be tabulated.[102] The CEP asserts that the method it used to calculate electoral results in joint elections was the same method used in the elections of 1990 and 1995, without objection from the international or domestic communities. In order to tabulate votes in districts with multiple seats open, the CEP decided to take the top four candidates where there were two positions and divide their results by two in order to determine whether any candidate had a majority. The OAS recommended dividing the total number of votes in order to determine if any candidate had a majority; this method includes all of the candidates and therefore makes it more difficult to receive a majority of the votes. The CEP decided not to use this method because the CEP felt it would skew the results with "phantom votes."

The CEP asserts that the OAS method assumes that all voters actually cast two votes; however, the CEP argues that most voters do not cast two votes. The CEP claims that the assumption that all voters actually vote twice would skew results by incorporating ghost votes. Moreover, the CEP stated that it decided to use the method of the 1990 election in order to avoid confusion and controversy.[103] Using the CEP method of tabulation, after the May 21, 2000, first-round elections, Aristide's party, La Fanmi Lavalas, won sixteen of seventeen seats in the twenty-seven-seat Senate; twenty-six of twenty-seven seats in the eighty-three-seat House of Deputies; 89 out of 115 mayoral positions; and 321 out of 485 town and rural councils.[104] Under the OAS method of calculation, Lavalas would have faced runoff elections for many of the seats they won under the CEP calculations.[105]

The United States, Canada, France, the United Nations, and the OAS condemned the electoral results because they disapproved of the calculation methods the CEP used.[106] Various civic organizations, including the Haitian Chamber of Commerce, the Association of Haitian Industrialists, the Roman Catholic Bishops Conference, and the Protestant Federation, also condemned the results.

In addition to the problems with the electoral laws, domestic and international debates over the electoral laws and the integrity of the electoral process in both the domestic and international political communities caused instability and delayed the announcement of electoral results. Supporters of President Preval assert that the complaints of the opposition parties and international observers were based upon bias against La Fanmi Lavalas because the CEP used the same methods in these elections that were used and widely accepted in previous elections. Henry Carey, an assistant professor of political science at Georgia State University, however, asserts that the CEP mischaracterized the methods used to tabulate the results of the 1990 elections. Carey argues that in the 1990 election "what was done was to ignore 300,000 to 500,000 ballots and tally sheets that were lost. . . . Similar efforts were done in elections of 1995 and 1997 and virtually the entire opposition in both elections boycotted the second round" in protest.[107]

Lavalas supporters also asserted that the opinions of the OAS, the United Nations, and the entire international community are unwarranted intrusions on the internal workings of the Haitian government. This led to political protests. On Friday, June 16, 2000, and Monday, June 19, 2000, protestors angry about delays in the publication of the electoral results of the May 21, 2000, election demonstrated in Port-au-Prince, Cap Haitian, Jacmel, Gonaives, Les Cayes, St. Marc, and Camp Perrin. Groups organizing the demonstration were angry at Leon Manus, the former head of the CEP, for refusing to sign off on the results and fleeing the country because the protestors saw this move as "an attempt to halt the elections process and to invalidate the choices made by the people."[108]

Manus initially defended the electoral results. Under apparent pressure from the opposition parties and the international community, however, Manus recanted, fled the country, and went to the United States. There is some indication that employees of USAID may have helped Manus leave Haiti, which exacerbated the tension already created by his actions. In addition, some La Fanmi Lavalas supporters question the timing of a letter the OAS sent to the CEP to complain about the methods used to calculate electoral results. The OAS sent the letter several days before the final results were to be published rather than notifying the CEP of their concerns earlier.[109]

One protester commented, "There is no opposition in Haiti today—the international community is trying to create one." Many leaders of popular organizations "view[ed] the OAS's position as a pretext which is being used to disrupt the electoral process, delay the second round of voting, the seating of a Lavalas dominated parliament, leave Haiti without functioning democratic institutions, and potentially deny the Haitian people their fundamental right to choose their own leaders."[110] Thus, international objections to the methods used to calculate results created instability and delayed the announcement of electoral results. International attempts to monitor elections and the consequent development of democracy in Haiti appear to contribute to electoral instability and to limit the ability of Haiti to develop independent electoral processes.

Meanwhile, members of domestic opposition political parties rejected the electoral results as fraudulent and argued that President Preval and the Lavalas movement were enforcing an electoral coup d'état.[111] Opposition parties accused Lavalas officials of stuffing ballot boxes and mismanaging the electoral process. The opposition points to ballot boxes found littering the streets in Port-au-Prince and reports of robberies at some polls as evidence of mismanagement. Opposition political parties also charged that a million ballots mysteriously disappeared.[112] Several opposition leaders were also arrested after the elections, although the police claim the arrests were made to prevent public disturbances.[113] La Fanmi Lavalas also notes that Lavalas supporters were also arrested.[114]

Some opposition parties called for "Zero Option" or "the uprooting of Preval and the CEP and holding new presidential elections without Aristide."[115] La Fanmi Lavalas asserts that opposition parties are merely trying to delay the foundation of democratic institutions by making baseless claims.[116] Some of the opposition parties, however, are composed of former Lavalas supporters, indicating that the opposition may be broader than the traditional elite.[117] Despite the accusations of the opposition parties, most observers, including the OAS and the National Council of Electoral Observers, reported that the elections were uncommonly peaceful and the scattered irregularities did not effect the general vote.[118] Thus, the constant arguing between La Fanmi Lavalas and opposition parties creates conflicting news reports and ongoing controversy, making the establishment of democratic institutions difficult if not impossible.

The lack of infrastructure and resources also caused electoral instability and delays. Many voter bureaus (BVs) did not have adequate materials and could not open on time, which delayed the registration of voters. The locations of BVs were not well publicized and many observers of the elections expressed concern that voters were not aware that they could only vote at the BV where they had registered. In some cases polling booths were moved to different locations than their original registration site. In addition, bureaus were not as close to some communities as the Electoral Laws mandated. Delays in training employees and modifications to the format of the tally sheets also created confusion and delays.[119] In addition, large amounts of electoral materials stolen from BVs delayed the opening of BVs.

The CEP also rolled out plans to assign voters photo voter identification cards for the May 21, 2000 elections. This process was stalled by shortages of Polaroid film and problems training workers to use equipment. The identification cards were being distributed to cut down on voter fraud and improve the voting process. The best way to monitor electoral fraud and detect people with multiple electoral cards is to use a computer database. Most of the rural areas of Haiti, however, lack electricity. Many workers were not paid, causing additional delays.[120] Election officials without transportation had to carry ballot boxes on their heads for miles. Ballot boxes and ballots were left in the street in front of the central counting center in Port-au-Prince.[121] Some observers speculate that the ballot boxes were left in front of the center because workers were frustrated by the disorganization of the electoral process.[122]

Despite concerns about the May 21, 2000 election, the International Coalition of Independent Observers (ICIO) stated in a press release after the elections that most BVs they observed opened on time with sufficient resources and that voters were able to locate the correct BV. The ICIO also stated that observers from La Fanmi Lavalas and opposition parties were present at 95 percent of the BVs they visited. The ICIO expressed concern about the insufficient training of electoral workers. The ICIO, however, was not able to send observers to BVs in rural areas.[123] Other newspaper reports indicate that polling was marred by delays in opening of BVs due to a shortage of ballots and missing poll workers. According to Reuters news service, some witnesses saw armed men stealing ballots and saw Lavalas poll workers pressuring voters to elect Lavalas supporters.[124] Thus, structural problems and lack of necessary resources made the organization and implementation of these elections difficult.

Scattered violence also contributed to electoral instability. The Electoral Observation Mission of the OAS expressed concern that numerous violent incidents during the campaign would create a climate of fear. The May 21, 2000 elections, however, were remarkably peaceful and voters turned out in record numbers in most areas, with voter participation estimated at more than 60 percent. The Electoral Observation Mission expressed concern about the number of violent attacks upon the press leading up to the May 21, 2000 elections. Jean Dominique, a popular radio journalist, was murdered prior to the election and some journalists from Radio 2000 went into hiding after receiving threats.[125] It is unclear who killed Jean Dominique and for what purpose, but the murder has been linked by the press to preelection violence.[126] In his final editorial, for example, Jean Dominique spoke about suspicions that the United States was working with opposition parties to influence the upcoming elections.[127] In June 2000 the *New York Times* reported that there were fifteen politically motivated murders since March 2000.[128] In addition to violence leading up to the elections, there were reports of violence on the May 21, 2000 election day in Hinche, Verettes, Cite Soleil, and Bahon.[129] Violence has been attributed to a variety of sources, including La Fanmi Lavalas, opposition parties, and drug traffickers.[130]

But the police did take preventative measures in the days before and after the election of May 21, 2000, in order to stem violence. Police banned the sale of gasoline in containers and banned handguns, shut down roads around BVs, and closed the border with the Dominican Republic.[131] After the elections, several members of opposition parties and La Fanmi Lavalas were arrested for carrying guns or creating public disturbances.[132] The Associated Press reported that thirty-seven candidates and activists were arrested.[133] There was sporadic violence before and after the July 9, 2000, runoff elections as well. Opposition party members were accused of murdering several people in Cornillon and Les Cayes. Protestors in Artibonite and Grand Saline put up barricades and burned election materials.[134] Supporters of a losing mayoral candidate, Anse-d'Hainault, went on a rampage in a remote coastal town.[135] Although the elections in 2000 were noted for the remarkable decrease in electoral violence, scattered acts of violence continue to create instability and to discredit electoral results.

Thus, it is apparent that Haiti continues to be involved in a serious political controversy. Until this controversy dies down or is resolved, it will be difficult, even impossible, to attack the more fundamental problems of Haitian life. The Haitian people hoped that the November 26, 2000 presidential election would resolve the dilemma, although many people feared that it would simply create new controversies. Unfortunately, the election of Aristide has even exacerbated the crisis. A small but powerful opposition group has almost paralyzed the Aristide government's attempts to overcome the political crisis and move on to confront the innumerable pressing issues facing the nation.

A DIFFERENT VISION

Even with the difficulties created by the 2000 election, it is clear that the deepest roots of Haiti's problems lie not simply or most significantly in the country's politics or cultural history. Institutional reforms of the type championed by the international community, such as total privatization of state-owned industries or "judicial reform," will simply not work until the more serious problems are confronted. While the moral turpitude of the elites is real, Haiti's political problems lie in the social and economic organization of the country. To put it another way, Haiti's crisis lies in social inequality and economic maldistribution. Unless and until these difficult issues are addressed, there is little hope for positive changes for the millions of Haitians trapped in despair and destitution. If they are addressed, however, it is likely that positive changes in the political sphere will follow. The only hope Haiti has for achieving a valid democracy is the creation of a new socioeconomic arrangement, which will be difficult to initiate and even harder to maintain. The absence of material deprivation is a prerequisite for the conditions necessary to create a democracy. What steps must be taken to achieve this goal?

A real democracy means much more than holding periodic elections. It requires an environment of personal security for people to pursue their desires and their professions, to move about freely, and to explore new ideas. Democracy also means, among other things, the building of vibrant institutions of justice and law and the full blooming of civil society: a broad array of political parties, independent media, independent labor unions, and nongovernmental organizations, such as women's groups, all of which encourage political and social participation. While these choices—and democracy is always a choice—cannot necessarily be imposed by the international community, they certainly can be encouraged by it.

While many nations are reaching for democracy, what are the policy choices for changing the political economy? The overriding characteristic of the political life and discourse of nations in the transition process is a frustrated desire to escape the choice between a nationalist–populist project and a neoliberal project. The rejection of these alternatives and dictatorship has a deeper meaning than is traditionally understood. It is a revulsion against a feigned public life, which is in fact little more than a weapon or disguise of private interests. The problem is not unique to Haiti. It is reflected in the institutional structures of many developing nations. The dominant regimes of the less-developed economies, and even their critics, often start with the desire merely to imitate and import the institutional arrangements of the rich industrial democracies. They do this in the hope that from similar institutional devices, similar economic and political development will result. But such imitation has not led to these desired results. The failure of these efforts at emulation may nevertheless be useful to the development of new and experimental institutional structures, which may shed light on the suppressed opportunities for transformation. But Haiti has not yet started on this path.

The import-substituting protectionist style of industrialization and the pseudo-Keynesian public finance of a national–populist approach is unable to deal effectively with the huge problems facing these nations. Latin America, for example, still faces the problems of hyperinflation and stagnation created by irrational closed economies and massive public spending. Neoliberalism, the single-minded pursuit of foreign investment and its accompanying austerity and inequality, is unable to service the real conditions of sustained economic growth. What is needed is to somehow fix neoliberalism's major flaw: chiefly, that it does not help the poor, vast majority live dignified lives. Instead, corporative power creates wealth for a small minority, while almost enslaving the majority. If democracy-seeking governments do not spread the benefits of globalization, countries such as Haiti will remain divided between a very small ultrarich economic elite and a very large group of desperately poor and marginalized people.

Unlike neoliberalism's claim that government should play a minor role in the economy, real democratic change requires government to play an important and dynamic role. At a minimum, the international community must encourage these governments to pursue locally designed policies to draw the poor into the global economy. To achieve this minimal goal, these governments must be given incentives to pursue a vision of a political economy that is quite different than the image traditionally suggested.

In political economy terms, promising alternatives that will allow a flowering of democracy might develop in a seriously underdeveloped nation such as Haiti in a variety of rather experimental directions. Each of these experiments, of course, must be continuously monitored so they can be changed as they unfold to meet the requisite goals of democratization. This method is one of the few ways that a positive transformation may take place in Haiti. Flexibility is a key to success.

First, it is important that these nations take macroeconomic stabilization very seriously. One way of doing this is through a dramatic rise in and focusing of the tax rate, which would impose upon the privileged classes and regions of these nations the costs of public investment in people and in infrastructure. One possibility, and I believe a promising one, would be to impose a direct, consumption-based tax— taxing, in a steeply progressive way, the difference between income and savings—as the means to finance the state and promote capital formation and productive investment.

Second, there must be a major push to train the poor majority in a variety of skills needed in the global economy. Democratic-minded governments must aggressively attack and overcome the internal division of these nations into two or more economies that are only tentatively and hierarchically connected. What is needed is the consolidation and development of a technological vanguard in both the public and private sectors, and the use of the vanguard to lift up and transform the immense, backward second economy. This approach would also suggest attempting joint public–private ownership of enterprises and encouraging decentralized capital allocation and management. One idea would be to change both the organization of firms (by making them more democratic) as well as the character of regional economies within the country. But these ideas must be developed by a deliberate economic program helped by the international community. Indeed, the world community must help train people in a variety of highly technical skills that will allow the less-developed nations an opportunity to compete in world markets.

Third, if the breakdown of corporative control of the economy is to succeed, the strict requirements of capitalism must be imposed on so-called free market capitalists through the privatization of the private sector. This should allow for real competition. It requires parliament to pass laws and the executive to enforce them, opening the market so everyone can compete on a somewhat level playing field. It may also be necessary to develop public companies to compete with the private ones and impose upon them the requirements of serious competition and independent financial responsibility.

The last part of the plan is educational. There must be a massive investment in people and infrastructure, financed by taxes on the people who possess the wealth. There must be a priority of such claims upon the budget, backed by procedural devices with executory force. In addition, preventive public health, sanitation, and food supplementation need to be given preference. The people must be educated; free public schools must be opened to everyone. There must also be a shift of the control of education away from the memorization of facts and toward an emphasis upon the mastery of generic practical and conceptual capabilities.

In the organization of government, politics, and civil society, the alternative to nationalist–populist or neoliberal projects may take the form of a public-law counterpart to the political economy I have just outlined, animated by the same concerns and moving toward the same goals. This, of course, means experiments should be attempted in these areas as well. For example, structural reforms require at least two sets of institutional innovations. First, a merger of the electoral characteristics of presidential regimes is needed, posing a periodic threat to oligarchic control of political power. There must be a facility for rapid resolution of impasse through priority accorded to programmatic legislation, liberal resort to plebiscites and referenda, and perhaps the vesting of power in all branches of government to provoke anticipated elections in the face of impasses over the direction the country should take. Second, measures must be taken to heighten the level and broaden the scope of political mobilization in society, especially through strengthening of political parties, public financing of campaigns, increased free access to television and radio, and the breakup of any broadcasting cartel. Direct democracy must be encouraged at all levels of society.

The macropolitics of institutional change must be complimented by a micropolitics confronting the logic of habitual social interactions. The typical elements of this logic include a predominance of patron– client relations, with their pervasive mingling in the same associations and encounters of exchange, power, and sentimental allegiance. There is frequently an oscillation between rule formalism and personal favoritism, and each creates the opportunity and need for the other. There is also a stark contrast between the treatment of "insiders" and "outsiders," and the consequent shortage of impersonal respect and reliability.

A democratic system must be capable of challenging and changing both the established arrangements of the economy and the polity, and the intimate habits of sociability. In this task, those who yearn for democracy must combine a strategic approach to the satisfaction of recognized material interests with the visionary invocation of a reordered society. In Haiti, as in other nations striving for democracy that are trapped in these impoverished visions and systems, nothing is more important than encouraging the belief in the people that structural change is possible. The international community, as well as the Haitian government, must encourage such beliefs and actions.

More than six years after the deployment of the multinational force, it is clear that Haiti's struggle for internal security and economic, social, and political development—its attempt to become a democratic nation—will continue to be a tortuous one. Unsettled political conditions, weak management of the economy, public indifference to the electoral process, and grinding poverty underscore how poorly international intervention has succeeded in helping to create the conditions for democracy. Some may, therefore, conclude that only Haitians can overcome the legacy of their history. Even if one ultimately reaches this conclusion, it is also correct to add that the international community is essential if Haitians are to achieve their goal. But only correct international incentives directed at the real problems will lead to a democracy in Haiti. So far, those incentives have simply not been properly employed.

NOTES

1. Aristide actually received a substantially higher percentage of the vote. Many of the ballots in his favor, however, had to be discounted because voters failed to mark them properly. This was due to the high illiteracy rate among the electorate. In point of fact, virtually every one of the ballots that had to be discounted were votes for Aristide. See Cathy Maternowska, interview with author, Miami, Florida, 8 November 1993. Maternowska, an anthropologist who lived in Haiti from 1985 to 1993, worked extensively with the poor of Haiti and was an observer of the 1990 election.

2. In addition to the smooth functioning of the election process itself, voter turnout was an astounding 75 percent, despite formidable logistical challenges. The dirt roads and mountain paths of rural Haiti, where over 75 percent of the population lives, made the distribution of election materials treacherous and uncertain. The high illiteracy rate among Haitians compounded the already difficult challenges of registering and voting. Despite these difficulties, approximately 3.2 million Haitians registered to vote and more than 2.4 million voted on election day. Moreover, despite these logistical problems, virtually all observers who monitored the voting, both international and domestic, attested that the elections were free and fair and that the voters experienced no threats, intimidation, or harassment. See ibid. See also Council of Freely Elected Heads of Government, National Democratic Institute for International Affairs, *The 1990 General Elections in Haiti* (1991).

3. See OAS, "The Santiago Commitment to Democracy and the Renewal of the Inter-American System," OEA/Ser. P/XXI.O.2, adopted at the Third Plenary Session, 4 June 1991, p. 1; "Representative Democracy," AG/RES. 1080 (XXI-0/91), adopted at the Fifth Plenary Session, 5 June 1991.

4. No strong multilateral or regional efforts have been made to institute democracy in Cuba. While still formally a member of the OAS, Cuba was suspended from the organization in 1962.

5. See Graham Greene, *The Comedians* (New York: Viking Press, 1966).

6. S.C. Res. 940, U.N. SCOR, 49th Sess., 3413th mtg. at 23, U.N. Doc. S/RES/940 (1994).

7. Christopher Marquis, "What Next for U.S. on Haiti? The Options Aren't Good," *Miami Herald*, 30 October 1993, p. A28.

8. See Tim Weiner, "Key Haiti Leaders Said to Have Been in C.I.A.'s Pay," *New York Times*, 1 November 1993, p. A1.

9. These sources continued to spread false and unsubstantiated information about Aristide and his government after Aristide had been reinstated. The worst of these rumors suggested that Aristide and his associates were involved in numerous political murders. The accusations continue through today. Aristide is now being portrayed as the power behind the throne, a

murderer, and either a drug dealer or a leader who gets paid off by drug dealers. For a discussion of these and other issues about the opposition to the Aristide and Preval governments in the United States, see Irwin P. Stotzky, *Silencing the Guns in Haiti: The Promise of Deliberative Democracy* (Chicago: University of Chicago Press, 1997).

10. The Permanent Five includes China, France, the Soviet Union (now Russia), the United Kingdom, and the United States.

11. For a discussion and analysis of the U.S. occupation of Haiti, see Hans Schmidt, *The United States Occupation of Haiti, 1915–1934* (1971).

12. Antoine Rougier, "La Théorie de l'Intervention d'Humanité," *Revue Génerale De Droit International Public* 17 (1910): 472. This formulation is also adopted by other writers in the post-Charter era. See, for example, Ann Van Wynen Thomas and Aaron Joshua Thomas Jr., *Non-Intervention: The Law and Its Import in the Americas* (Dallas: Southern Methodist University Press, 1956), 372.

13. Fernando R. Tesón, *Humanitarian Intervention: An Inquiry into Law and Morality*, 2d ed. (Irvington-on-Hudson, N.Y.: Transitional Press, 1997), 5.

14. In this chapter, I do not discuss in depth all of the formal international legal requirements and permutations for a valid humanitarian intervention. The topic is unbounded and the literature is substantial. See, for example, Danish Institute of International Affairs, *Humanitarian Intervention: Legal and Political Aspects* (Copenhagen, Denmark: Danish Institute of International Affairs, 1999); Lori Fisler Damrosch, ed., *Enforcing Restraint: Collective Intervention in Internal Conflicts* (New York: Council on Foreign Relations Press, 1993); Richard B. Lillich, ed., *Humanitarian Intervention and the United Nations* (1973); Laura W. Reed and Carl Kaysen, *Emerging Norms of Justified Intervention* (Cambridge, Mass.: Committee on International Security Studies, American Academy of Arts and Sciences, 1993); Natalino Ronzetti, *Rescuing Nationals Abroad through Military Coercion and Intervention on Grounds of Humanity* (1985); Nigel S. Rodley, ed., *To Loose the Bands of Wickedness: International Intervention in Defense of Human Rights* (New York: Macmillan, 1992); Tesón, *Humanitarian Intervention*; Hugo Caminos, "The Role of the Organization of American States in the Promotion and Protection of Democratic Governance," *Recueil des cours* 273 (1999): 107; Jost Delbrück, "A Fresh Look at Humanitarian Intervention under the Authority of the United Nations," *Indiana Law Journal* 67 (1992): 887; Christopher M. Goebel, "Population Transfer, Humanitarian Law, and the Use of Ground Force in U.N. Peacekeeping," *New York University Journal of International Law and Politics* 25 (1993): 627; Dino Kritsiotis, "Repraising Policy Objections to Humanitarian Intervention," *Michigan Journal of International Law* 19 (1998): 1005; Ved P. Nanda, Thomas F. Muther, Jr., and Amy E. Eckert, "Tragedies in Somalia, Yugoslavia, Haiti, Rwanda and Liberia: Revisiting the Validity of Humaitarian Intervention under International Law. Part II," *Denver Journal of International Law and Policy* 26 (1998): 827; David J. Scheffer, "Toward a Modern Doctrine of Humanitarian Intervention," *Universitiy of Toledo Law Review* 23 (1992): 253; Glenn T. Ware, "The Emerging Norm of Humanitarian Intervention and Presidential Decision Directive," *Naval Law Review* 44 (1997): 1; Julie Jackson, "An Update on: *Self-Determination and Humanitarian Intervention in a Community of Power* by James A. Nafziger," *Denver Journal of International Law and Policy* 26 (1998): 917.

15. See Robert M. Cassidy, "Sovereignty versus the Chimera of Armed Humanitarian Intervention," *The Fletcher Forum of World Affairs* 21 (1997): 47.

16. See U.N. Charter, art. 2, para. 1.

17. Ibid., art. 2, para. 4.

18. See ibid., art. 2, para. 7.

19. Ibid.

20. Ibid., ch. VII.

21. Ibid., art. 39.

22. Ibid., art. 51.

23. See Cassidy, "Sovereignty," 53–54.

24. See U.N. Charter, preamble; art. 1, para. 3; art. 55, para. c.

25. Ibid., preamble.

26. Ibid., art. 1, para. 3.

27. Although unlikely, it is possible that a situation could arise where there is no government for a territory where a severe internal conflict exists. From a purely legal standpoint, the U.N. Charter would arguably allow humanitarian intervention without a threat to international peace. Practically speaking, however, in this type of situation the United Nations would likely still request permission to intervene from the controlling powers and treat them as sovereign authorities.

28. See U.N. Charter, ch. IX.

29. Ibid., art. 55, para. c.

30. Ibid., art. 56.

31. See generally U.N. GAOR, 3d Sess., U.N. Doc. GA/RES/217A(III) (1948). The preamble states, "Whereas the peoples of the United Nations have in the Charter reaffirmed their faith in fundamental human rights, in the dignity and worth of the human person and in the equal rights of men and women and have determined to promote social progress and better standards of life in larger freedom."

32. "To the end that every individual and every organ of society . . . shall strive by teaching and education to promote respect for these rights and freedoms and by progressive measures, national and international, to secure their universal and effective recognition and observance." Ibid.

33. See generally ibid. It appears almost impossible to achieve these goals solely through state action. Civil society—the private sphere—must also work toward these same goals.

34. In considering human rights on an international scale, there remains the problem of their universality. Most scholars agree that human rights are universal, but that recognition of human rights changes from state to state. See Alex Y. Seita, "Globalization and the Convergence of Values," *Cornell International Law Journal* 30 (1997): 447. Proof that human rights are universal can be found in contemporary U.N. conventions addressing human rights. See W. Michael Reisman, "Sovereignty and Human Rights in Contemporary International Law," *American Journal of International Law* 84 (1990): 866. Reisman contends that the Universal Declaration of Human Rights is now accepted as customary international law and is upheld by various regional pacts professing the same ideals. See pp. 868–869. For example, at the World Conference on Human Rights in 1993, all 171 participating states adopted the Vienna Decla-

ration and Programme of Action. For provisions of the document, see U.N. World Conference on Human Rights, *Vienna Declaration and Programme of Action*, art. 5, U.N. Doc. A/CONF.157/23, pt. 1 (1993). The Declaration states,

All human rights are universal, indivisible, and interdependent and interrelated. The international community must treat human rights globally in a fair and equal manner, on the same footing, and with the same emphasis. While the significance of national and regional particularities and various historical, cultural and religious backgrounds must be borne in mind, it is the duty of States, regardless of their political, economic and cultural systems, to promote and protect all human rights and fundamental freedoms.

35. Richard Falk has suggested a method for resolving this dilemma. He contends that the sovereign rights of any particular state are necessarily limited. When massive human rights abuses take place, the legal identity of a sovereign state ceases to exist. Falk explains this loss of power in two ways: the resulting illegitimacy of the territorial government or, alternatively, the existence of anarchic conditions of brutality and chaos. Either of these conditions results in the nonrecognition of the government as a sovereign authority. He concludes that without recognition of sovereignty, a state's sovereignty cannot be violated by intervention. See Richard Falk, "The Complexities of Humanitarian Intervention: A New World Order Challenge," *Michigan Journal of International Law* 17 (1996): 491. One could push Falk's theory even further to argue that a state is endowed with a defeasible right of sovereignty, contingent upon a minimum standard of treatment of its subjects. If state action falls below this standard, for example, by violating the human rights of the people living within its borders, the state forfeits its sovereignty and therefore becomes subject to external intervention.

36. See Hugo Grotius, *De Jure Belli ac Pacis* (Washington, D.C.: Carnegie Institution, 1913–1925).

37. See "Reports of the International Civilian Mission to Haiti," in "Notes by the Secretary-General," Annex, U.N. Docs. A/47/960 (1993), A/48/532 and Add.2 (1993); "Report of the Secretary-General," U.N. Doc. A/48/931 (1994); "Report of the Secretary-General on the Question of Haiti," U.N. Doc. S/1994/742 (1994); "Report of the Secretary-General on the United Nations Mission in Haiti," U.N. Doc. S/1994/765 (1994). See also Douglas Farah, "Aristide's Backers: Latest Plan Falls Short," *The Washington Post*, 2 May 1994, p. A1; Janet Reitman, "Political Repression by Rape Increasing in Haiti," *The Washington Post*, 22 July 1994, p. A10.

38. See S.C. Res. 841, U.N. SCOR, 48th Sess., 3238th mtg., p. 119, pmbl., U.N. Doc. S/RES/49 (1993); S.C. Res. 940.

39. See S.C. Res. 841, p. 119. This statement reiterated an earlier Security Council statement on Haiti. On February 26, 1993, the Security Council issued a statement noting that the humanitarian crisis in Haiti, including mass displacements of population, were "becoming or aggravating threats to international peace and security." "Note by the President of the Security Council," U.N. Doc. S/25344 (1993).

40. The Security Council also deplored "the fact that, despite the efforts of the international community, the legitimate government of President Jean-Bertrand Aristide has not been reinstated." S.C. Res. 841, p. 119.

41. See S.C. Res. 940.

42. Ibid. The vote on the resolution was twelve to zero, with abstentions by Brazil and China.

43. See U.N. Charter, art. 2, para. 4.

44. After the passage of Security Council Resolution 940, the United States undertook a serious public relations campaign in which it provided extensive details about an impending invasion, and constantly raised the spectre of the use of force to restore democracy, in the hope of frightening the Haitian military authorities into stepping down. For example, on August 4, 1994, when asked at a press conference why he sought U.N. approval for military intervention in Haiti, President Clinton replied,

Let me say I think all Americans should be pleased that the United Nations stated, with a firm voice that includes many voices from our own area, that we should keep on the table the option of forceably [sic] removing the dictators who have usurped power in Haiti and who have trampled human rights and murdered innocent people. Let me remind you all of what our interests are there: We have Americans living and working there, several thousand of them. We have a million Haitian-Americans in this country who have family and friends there. We have an interest in promoting democracy in our hemisphere. We have an interest in stabilizing those democracies that are in our hemisphere. For the first time ever, 33 of the 35 nations in the Caribbean and Central and South America are governed by popularly elected leaders but many of those democracies are fragile. As we look ahead to the next century, we need a strong and democratic Latin America and Central America and Caribbean with which to trade and grow. So those are our fundamental interests. ("News Conference of President Clinton [3 August 1994])," reprinted in *New York Times*, 4 August 1994, p. A16)

On September 15, 1994, in a nationally televised address, President Clinton, explaining why "the United States was leading the international effort to restore democratic government in Haiti," called upon the Haitian authorities to "leave now or we will force you from power." "Speech of President Clinton (15 September 1994)," reprinted in *New York Times*, 16 September 1994, p. A10, and *The Washington Post*, 16 September 1994, p. A31. With an invasion imminent, President Clinton dispatched to Haiti a delegation led by former President Carter with a mandate to negotiate the manner in which the military authorities would relinquish power. They met on September 17–18 and, in a dramatic breakthrough, the Carter delegation reached an agreement with the Haitian military leaders. This occurred shortly after President Clinton ordered the commencement of the invasion. Thus, sixty-one U.S. Army transport and refueling planes launched from North Carolina had to be recalled. See Douglas Jehl, "Showdown in Haiti," *New York Times*, 19 September 1994, p. A1; Calvin Sims, "Mission to Haiti," *New York Times*, 22 September 1994, p. A15.

45. The United States even called the military blockade of Haiti "Operation Support Democracy." John F. Harris, "From Sailing 7 Seas to Sealing 1 Coastline," *The Washington Post*, 19 June 1994, p. A23.

46. See, for example, Tesón, *Humanitarian Intervention*.

47. Universal Declaration of Human Rights, art. 21(3), G.A. Res. 217A (III), U.N. GAOR, 3d Sess., pt.1, p. 75, U.N. Doc. A/810 (1948).

48. See "The Santiago Commitment."

49. Algeria is the prime example.

50. This is not such a far-fetched possibility. Colombia, for example, presents serious concerns for its neighbors. Its two most consuming problems—the drug trade and a brutal, nearly forty-year civil war—are getting worse. They increasingly threaten neighboring countries. Venezuela, one of the largest suppliers of oil to the United States, is seen as particularly vulnerable. The Clinton administration has unveiled a $1.3-billion plan to help Colombia, which includes $955 million in security assistance. The plan risks dragging the United States into a costly counterinsurgency war and close alliance with Colombia's military forces. See "Dangerous Plans for Colombia," *New York Times*, 13 February 2000, p. A16.

51. See Tom Fawthrop and James Pringle, "Prince Removed by Hun Sen in Cambodia Coup," *Times* (London), 7 July 1997; Keith B. Richburg, "Hun Sen Gains Prominent Ally," *The Washington Post*, 17 July 1997, p. A25.

52. See Fawthrop and Pringle, "Prince Removed."

53. See Stotzky, *Silencing the Guns*.

54. For a discussion of some of these problems and possible solutions to them, see discussion in parts 2, 3, and 4 of this chapter.

55. See S.C. Res. 940.

56. See Colin Powell, *My American Journey* (New York: Random House, 1995), 434.

57. For example, Powell quotes Madeline Albright as chafing at the constraints his policy imposed on U.S. policy in Bosnia. See ibid., 576.

58. See 50 U.S.C. §§1541–1548 (1988). The act was passed in 1973 to restrict the president's ability to introduce U.S. military forces into hostilities without Congressional approval.

59. The Clinton administration never publicly argued that Security Council authorization substituted for Congressional approval, but the administration's timing and actions strongly suggest this position. It is important to note that the Clinton administration did not take the legal position that Congressional consent was superfluous because Security Council authorization sufficed. See John J. Kavanagh, "U.S. War Powers and the United Nations Security Council," *Boston College International and Comparative Law Review* 20 (1997): 180–182. Such a position would surely have caused a Congressional uproar. Instead, the administration claimed that the planned deployment was consistent with the sense of Congress as expressed in the Defense Appropriations Act of 1994, that it satisfied the requirements of the War Powers Resolution, and that the operation was "not a war in the constitutional sense." See Marian Nash, "Contemporary Practice of the United States Relating to International Law," *American Journal of International Law* 89 (1995): 122, discussing the War Powers Act and the deployment of military forces into Haiti.

60. This report is to some extent biased against the Preval government. Nevertheless, it is accurate enough to quote at length because it summarizes many of the problems facing Haiti. In other footnotes I will note some of the inaccuracies.

61. The implication in this report is that President Preval was violating, rather than upholding, the rule of law. Contrary to this implication and the claims of many, President Preval did not dissolve the Haitian parliament in January 1999. Haiti's Election Law of 1995 explicitly states that this parliament's

term would expire on January 11, 1999. The Haitian Constitution also prohibits any extension of the term of any parliament. On January 11, 1999, therefore, President Preval simply announced his intention to respect the law and honor the constitution. His January 1999 choice for prime minister, Jacques Edouard Alexis, had previously been approved by both the Haitian Senate and Haiti's Chamber of Deputies.

62. This is not entirely accurate. For example, the Special Investigative Units helped investigate and successfully prosecute the killer of Antoine Izméry, one of the high-profile political murders. More recently, these units have been involved in the investigation of the Raboteau Massacre. For a description of these cases, see note 80; Stotzky, *Silencing the Guns*.

63. If one looks at Port-Au-Prince, it appears that the vast majority of people are unemployed.

64. Although Haiti's economy grew by 4 percent in 1998, millions of Haitians lead very difficult lives. Investment has been hard to attract. International analysts note that external pressure on Haiti to lower tariffs, for example, has caused the widespread impoverishment of countless small rice farmers, and has transformed Haiti from self-sufficiency in rice production to almost complete dependence on imported rice. Increasingly, U.S. and other experts are acknowledging the devastating impact of their "structural adjustment" program on countries like Haiti.

65. Approximately $500 million in international assistance is being withheld because of the election crisis. See Trenton Daniel, "Political Situation Remains Cloudy," *Haitian Times*, 16–22 August 2000, p. 9.

66. The report fails to note that there are marked contrasts between Haiti pre-1994 and today. Impartial human rights organizations documented the killing by the then-coup regime of some 5,000 Haitian men, women, and children between 1991 and 1994. In the six and a half years of restored democracy, human rights organizations can point to not one case of state-sponsored killing in Haiti. A small number of inexperienced or rogue members of the Haitian National Police have tortured, killed, or been involved in corruption, as have some members of the New York, Los Angeles, and other metropolitan police forces in the United States. In Haiti, as in the United States, these individuals have been suspended and charged. And, as is the case in the United States, the government of Haiti abhors these acts, has publicly condemned them, and takes action against perpetrators. For example, on August 21, 2000, the Haitian government began the trial of former police chief Coles Rameau and five other policemen accused of executing eleven unarmed people in the Port-au-Prince slum of Carrefour Feuilles on May 28, 1999. On September 11, 2000, a jury convicted the former police chief and three other former policemen of manslaughter and the judge sentenced them each to serve three years in prison. The judge also fined each of the former officers 26,000 gourdes (approximately $1,180). Two other police officers were acquitted after a three-week trial that marked the first time that a Haitian government in power had brought to trial government officials accused of human rights violations. See "Haitian Police Jailed for Slum Killing," *Reuters Press*, 12 September 2000. Today, the violent death of any politically active Haitian is immediately termed a "political murder," whether there is persuasive evidence or even indications

of other motives. Haitians of all political persuasions are exercising their freedom of speech and assembly. They fearlessly skewer political figures of all persuasions. No one is thrown in jail for their political views. The 1998 U.S. Human Rights Report found no political prisoners in Haiti. As is the case in Russia and the Middle East, both burdened by turbulent pasts, political divisions run deep in Haiti. In any event, the victim list transcends ideology. Preval and Aristide supporter Jean Dominique, Aristide supporter Deputy Feuille, and Cedras supporter Mireille Bertin have all, over the past six years, met the same tragic fate as State Duma Deputy Galina Staravoitova of Russia, Prime Minister Rabin of Israel, and nationalist lawyer Rosemary Nelson in Ireland.

67. The assassination of Jean Léopold Dominique, the preeminent investigative reporter and commentator in Haiti, on April 3, 2000, sent shock waves throughout the hemisphere, and continues to cause problems in Haiti. See Trenton Daniel, "Protestors Demand Justice for Slain Journalist," *Haitian Times*, 26 July–1 August 2000, p. 3.

68. U.S. Department of State, Bureau of Democracy, Human Rights, and Labor, *1999 Country Reports on Human Rights Practices: Haiti* (Washington, D.C.: U.S. Government Printing Office, 2000).

69. This is the point at which theory becomes important. Contrary to most people who favor democracy, I believe that justificatory theories of democracy are essential for creating solutions to the problems. See Stotzky, *Silencing the Guns*.

70. For a thorough discussion and analysis of theories of democracy and suggested policies derived from some of these theories, see ibid.

71. For an analysis of different characterizations of the process of transition, see Guillermo O'Donnell, Phillipe C. Schmitter, and Laurence Whitehead, eds., *Transitions from Authoritarian Rule: Latin America* (Baltimore: Johns Hopkins University Press, 1986); Juan J. Linz and Alfred Stepan, *The Breakdown of Democratic Regimes* (Baltimore: Johns Hopkins University Press, 1978).

72. See Larry Rohter, "Haiti Is a Land Without a Country," *New York Times*, 14 August 1994, p. E3. The state of education, a key to development, is one of the major reasons that Haiti remains one of the poorest countries in the world. Teachers remain wholly inadequate to the task of educating the millions desiring to improve their lives. For example, in December 1996 and January 1997, Haiti's approximately 1,200 grade school teachers took a simple test, and almost all of them failed it. Only 400 could alphabetize a list of words; only 41 could arrange fractions by size. This ignorance is reflected in the students. More than half of the children between six and twelve cannot read. In addition, classrooms are extremely overcrowded—some have more than 200 students—and most classrooms do not have benches, chalkboards, or even doors. See Michael Norton, "Teacher Strike Highlights Education Crisis in Haiti," *Miami Herald*, 13 January 1997, p. A8.

73. Indeed, there are sizable populations of exiled Haitians in New York, Montreal, Paris, and Miami.

74. Confidential interviews by author with various exiled Haitians (1981–2000).

75. Confidential interviews by author with various U.N. officials, Haitian government officials, and human rights workers stationed in Haiti (1994–2000).

76. For a general discussion of the history of Haiti, see David Nicholls, *From Dessalines to Duvaliér: Race, Colour, and National Independence in Haiti* (New York: Cambridge University Press, 1979); see also Michel-Rolph Trouillot, *Haiti, State Against Nation: The Origins and Legacy of Duvalierism* (New York: Monthly Review Press, 1990); Stotzky, *Silencing the Guns*.

77. For analysis of all of these points, see Stotzky, *Silencing the Guns*. See also Michel-Rolph Trouillot, *Haiti*.

78. For an interesting discussion of the concept of corporatism and its relationship to state and society in Latin America, see James M. Malloy, ed., *Authoritarianism and Corporatism in Latin America* (Pittsburgh: University of Pittsburgh Press, 1977). For a discussion of corporatism, see Irwin P. Stotzky, "Suppressing the Beast," *University of Miami Law Review* 53 (1999): 883.

79. Confidential interviews by author.

80. For example, in August 1995, a mid-level member of the paramilitary group FRAPH was convicted of the murder of Antoine Izméry, a prominent businessman and supporter of Aristide. There have been ongoing investigations of human rights offenses committed by the de facto regime between 1991 and 1994 since the return of Aristide in 1994. On September 20, 2000, after an investigation that started shortly after President Aristide's reinstatement in 1994, the Haitian government began the prosecution of dozens of former military leaders for the massacre of at least fifteen residents of a poor neighborhood in Gonaives in April 1994. The Raboteau slayings were part of a series of attacks undertaken by the coup leaders to break support for Aristide. At the trial, only twenty-two of the defendants actually appeared in court. On November 9, 2000, sixteen of these twenty-two defendants were convicted of taking part in the massacre. Twelve of the sixteen, including the military commander of the town at the time of the massacre, Captain Castera Cénafils, and a grassroots figure turned paramilitary leader, Jean Tatoune, were sentenced to life in prison with hard labor. The other four defendants received sentences of up to nine years imprisonment. Six defendants were acquitted. All of the convicted defendants also were ordered to pay the equivalent of $2,300—a large amount in Haiti—to a fund to benefit the families of the victims. On November 16, 2000, a Haitian court sentenced the thirty-seven defendants who did not appear in court, and were being tried in absentia, to life in prison with hard labor. The absent defendants include coup leaders Raoul Cedras and Philippe Biamby, both of whom received asylum in Panama; former Port-au-Prince police chief, Michel Francois, who is in Honduras; and paramilitary leader Emmanuel Constant, who cut a deal with the CIA and lives in New York City. Prosecutors alleged that they masterminded the attack. Lawyers were not allowed to defend the absent defendants. Judge Napla Saintil tried them without a jury exclusively on the basis of a 172-page bill of accusation presented to the court by the Haitian government prosecutors. The absent defendants will be arrested if they return to Haiti, but would have the right to a new trial if they return. See Marie-Andre Auguste, "Haitian Court Sentences 30 Officers," *Associated Press*, 16 November 2000. Moreover, the Haitian government has asked a number of nations, including the United States, to extradite several former military officials who have been indicted in Haiti for committing murders during the coup period.

81. Confidential interviews by author.

82. See Stotzky, *Silencing the Guns*.

83. Ibid.

84. U.S. Department of State, *1999 Country Reports*.

85. This factor is, of course, insufficient as an absolute measurement for a democracy. It is, however, an important factor in determining the legitimacy of a democratic nation.

86. See Michael Norton, "Haiti's Election Results Official," *Associated Press*, 16 August 2000.

87. Ibid. President Preval made the election results official on August 16, 2000, by publishing them in the official publication, *Le Moniteur*. On August 28, 2000, nineteen senators and eighty-two members of the Chamber of Deputies were sworn in and the Haitian parliament held its first session since January 11, 1999, when it dissolved as required by law and the Haitian Constitution. The presidential election took place as scheduled on November 26, 2000. Former President Aristide, strongly favored to win the presidency, indeed lived up to this prediction. He won the election by an overwhelming majority, estimated by some observers as 91.7 percent of the votes cast. Nevertheless, as is always the case in Haiti, controversy ensued, this time about the number of voters that turned out and voted. Some opposition parties claim that only between 15 and 20 percent of the registered voters actually cast their votes, while the Provisional Electoral Council argues that the number is 60.5 percent.

88. See Michael Norton, "Haitian Groups Condemn Election," *Associated Press*, 24 June 2000.

89. For a discussion of the legality of these actions under the Haitian Constitution and laws, see Ira J. Kurzban, "President Preval Seeks to Uphold the Law and Resume Elections in Haiti," 26 January 1999 (memorandum on file with author).

90. See Jennifer Bauduy, "Haitian President Denounces New Election Plan," *Reuters Press*, 10 March 2000; Don Bohning, "Haiti Vote Suffers Setback," *Miami Herald*, 11 March 2000, p. 3A; "Haiti Again Sets New Election Dates," *Reuters Press*, 8 March 2000; "Haiti Election Delay Prompts Concern," *Reuters Press*, 6 March 2000; "Just Weeks Away, Haiti's Election Cloaked in Doubt," *Reuters Press*, 23 February 2000; Michael Norton, "Haiti Postpones Elections," *Associated Press*, 3 March 2000; Michael Norton, "Haiti Sets New Election Dates," *Associated Press*, 8 March 2000; "O.A.S. Hopeful as It Starts Observing Haiti's Vote," *Reuters Press*, 2 March 2000; "U.N. Chief Concerned About Delay in Haiti Elections," *Reuters Press*, 6 March 2000.

91. Confidential interviews by author with Haitian government officials (1998–2000).

92. See Leon Manus, "Declaration," 21 June 2000 (on file with author).

93. See Emmanuel Charles, "Resignation Letter," 6 June 2000 (on file with author).

94. See "Second Round of Elections to Go Forward on Sunday, July 9," *Haiti News Summary*, 7 July 2000.

95. The *New York Times* reported that the United States shut down a training program for Haiti's National Police Force because of the refusal of the Haitian government to change the disputed election results. See "Haiti: Police

Aid Cut," *New York Times*, 4 August 2000, p. A8. By mid-August, however, the international community had started to take a more subdued stance. For example, the OAS now claimed that it was up to the Haitian people to resolve the electoral crisis, not the international community. The United States did not agree. Instead, it intervened to keep the pressure on the Haitian government. Several newspapers reported that during an OAS meeting in Washington held on September 6, 2000, the Clinton administration warned Haiti's government that it risked losing tens of millions of dollars in U.S. aid unless it voided the results of the election. The threatened measures included the withdrawal of approximately $20 million in financial support for the November presidential election, denial of U.S. recognition for the recently installed parliament, and a recommendation that international lending institutions not extend new financing to the Haitian government. Nevertheless, the United States would continue to contribute nearly $70 million a year for education, development, and infrastructure programs. That aid, however, would be channeled through nongovernmental groups and used only for private-sector programs. See George Gedda, "U.S Warns Haiti on Election Set Up," *Associated Press*, 6 September 2000; David Gonzalez, "U.S. to Withhold Money for Haiti's Presidential Election," *New York Times*, 6 September 2000, p. A10; Esther Schrader, "Haiti Risks Losing U.S. Aid Over Condemned Elections," *Miami Herald*, 3 September 2000, p. 3A.

96. See S. Con. Res. 126, 106th Cong., (2000). 2d Session, placed on Senate calendar by Senator Helms, Committee on Foreign Relations, 30 June 2000.

97. "With Second Round, Haiti Blows Off Foreign Bluster," *Haiti Progres*, 12–18 July 2000. Available at <www.haiti_progres.com> (on-line only).

98. Ibid.

99. George Gedda, "U.S. Faults Haitian Election," *Associated Press*, 10 July 2000.

100. "Helms Unblocks Aid to Haiti," *Miami Herald*, 1 July 2000, p. A8.

101. See Haiti Electoral Laws, arts. 53–54 (1999).

102. See CEP letter in response to OAS letter, 5 June 2000 (on file with author).

103. See Provisional Electoral Council of Haiti, "Clarification Written Under Seal and Signed by CEP," 30 June 2000 (on file with author); see also Leon Manus, letter to OAS, 5 June 2000 (on file with author).

104. See "With Second Round." La Fanmi Lavalas won even more seats after the second round runoff elections.

105. See "Demonstrations Rock the Capital," *Haiti News Summary*, 22 June 2000.

106. See Norton, "Haitian Groups."

107. Henry Carey, "Carey Comments on Pierre's Comment on the Elections," Haiti mailing list organized by Robert Corbett, 25 June 2000.

108. See "Demonstrations Rock the Capital."

109. Ibid.

110. Ibid.

111. Ibid.

112. See "Candidate Is Killed in Haiti in Post-Election Violence," *Miami Herald*, 24 May 2000, p. 5A.

113. See "Police Free Arrested Haiti Opposition Ex-Senator," *Reuters Press*, 26 May 2000.

114. See "With Second Round."

115. Ibid.

116. Ibid.

117. See "Police Free Arrested Haiti Opposition Ex-Senator."

118. See "What's Behind the Arrests in Haiti," *Haiti Progres*, 31 May–6 June 2000. Available at <www.haiti_progres.com>.

119. See "The Legislative, Municipal, and Local Electoral Process in Haiti, May 2000," Interim report of the Electoral Observation Mission of the OAS, Port-au-Prince, Haiti.

120. See "It Is Time for a New CEP," *Haiti Progres*, 15–21 March 2000. Available at <www.haiti_progres.com>.

121. See Michelle Faul, "Haiti: Elections," *Associated Press*, 23 May 2000.

122. Confidential interviews by author with poll workers (10 July 2000); see also Henry Carey, "Haiti's Elections Not Perfect, but Improving," *Miami Herald*, 12 June 2000, p. 7B.

123. See International Coalition of Independent Election Observers, "Press Release," 23 May 2000.

124. See "Police Free Arrested Haiti Opposition Ex-Senator."

125. See "The Legislative, Municipal, and Local Electoral Process.

126. See Don Bohning, "Haitian Widow Vows to Press On," *Miami Herald*, 30 May 2000, p. 1A.

127. See "Elections, and Violence, Now Seem Certain for Monday," *Haiti Progres*, 17–23 May 2000. Available at <www.haiti_progres.com>.

128. See David Gonzalez, "Aristide's Party Wins Control of Haitian Senate—Rivals Decry Tactics," *New York Times*, 31 May 2000, sec. A, p. 7.

129. See OAS Electoral Observation Mission in Haiti, "Press Release," 24 May 2000.

130. See Mark Fineman, "Haitian Terror Takes Toll on Today's Election," *Los Angeles Times*, 22 May 2000, pt. A1, p. 1.

131. See Ives Marie Chanel, "Haiti Holds Legislative, Municipal Elections," *IPS*, 20 May 2000.

132. See "With Second Round, Haiti Blows Off Foreign Bluster."

133. See Michael Norton, "Haiti Arrests Opposition Candidates," *Associated Press*, 7 June 2000.

134. See "With Second Round, Haiti Blows Off Foreign Bluster."

135. See Michael Norton, "Six Wounded in Haiti Vote Violence," *Associated Press*, 7 July 2000.

CHAPTER 8

Rethinking U.S. Policy toward Fidel Castro: Can Implementation of Best Business Practices Better Promote Political and Economic Liberalization in Cuba?

Edward Drachman

Previous chapters have discussed a variety of methods used by the United States and other countries seeking to promote democracy and human rights. This chapter focuses on the case of Cuba.

Two major ways that countries deal with Cuba have not in any significant way brought about political and economic liberalization of the Castro regime. Neither the policy of isolation and sanctions tried by the United States nor the policy of constructive engagement tried by such countries as Canada has led to improvement in Cuba's human rights record or more free enterprise on the island. It is thus understandable that countries should look toward another policy that might be more effective in these areas. Whereas traditional government-to-government diplomacy has failed as a liberalizing mechanism, private business should be afforded the opportunity to play a potentially influential role. Investment in Cuba should be made only if both the foreign business itself and the Cuban government adopt a socially and politically responsible code of conduct. Implementation of the Arcos Principles for Cuba, a code of "best business practices" based on previous codes such as the Sullivan Principles for South Africa and the MacBride Principles for Northern Ireland, is a third way of dealing with Cuba that may offer better hope of liberalizing Cuban society through its focus on worker rights. Pushed by such diverse NGOs as Pax Christi of The Netherlands and the National Policy Association, the Arcos Principles are being considered at the highest levels of foreign governments and business operations. Indeed, for the past few years Washington has urged both U.S. firms and foreign companies to adopt best business practices throughout the world. Success of the Arcos Principles will depend on both the political will of the public and private sectors in the United States and acceptance by Cuba of foreign investment with political strings attached.

U.S. POLICY TOWARD CASTRO'S CUBA:
A BACKGROUND

The U.S. government under President Dwight Eisenhower first looked upon the Cuban Revolution of 1959 with a cautious "wait and see" attitude. Many Americans considered Castro a romantic revolutionary, another George Washington who would lead the Cuban people to freedom. When Castro made an unofficial visit to the United States in April 1959, the American people and the media generally gave him high marks. They were impressed when he said in a press conference in New York on April 23, "We want to establish in Cuba a true democracy, without any trace of Fascism, Peronism or Communism. We are against every kind of totalitarianism." Americans, in general, expected Castro to establish a humanistic form of liberal democracy that emphasized "liberty with bread and without terror." But Vice President Richard Nixon, after a two-and-a-half-hour private talk with Castro during his five-day visit to Washington, thought otherwise. Together with State Department and CIA officials, he warned Eisenhower that Castro was cozying up to Communists and not to be trusted. Cuban exiles in the United States, moreover, were arguing that Castro was becoming a dangerous leader who had to be overthrown. In March 1960 Eisenhower authorized the CIA to train a Cuban exile force for invasion of the island. A chain of events was souring the relationship between Washington and Havana. Castro's extensive land reform program, his nationalization of property held by American citizens without compensation, his restriction of human rights; his declaration that he was a Marxist–Leninist, and his increased ties to the Soviet Union led to a confrontational U.S. policy toward Cuba.

After early U.S. efforts to forcibly remove Castro failed, nine U.S. presidents, from Eisenhower through Clinton, chose to isolate Cuba economically and politically. President Eisenhower rejected Havana's request for loans, eliminated the Cuban sugar quota (sugar was Cuba's main source of revenue), and in January 1961 formally severed diplomatic relations with Cuba. On April 16, 1961, Castro declared Cuba a socialist state. The next day, U.S.–supported Cuban exiles invaded Cuba in a failed attempt to overthrow the Cuban leader. From this point on, relations between the United States and Cuba took a nosedive. On January 22, 1962, the United States pressured the Organization of American States to suspend Cuba. Cuba responded by calling for armed revolt throughout the hemisphere against what it termed repressive capitalist regimes. In February, President John F. Kennedy imposed a trade embargo against Cuba. This meant that the United States would no longer sell Cuba goods or services. Before this embargo, the Cuban economy was tied tightly to the United States. Indeed, it was highly dependent on the "Colossus to the North." But when the United States stopped trade and investment and urged other countries to do the same, the Soviet Union and other communist states rushed to fill the breach. They also built up military power on the island.

During the Cold War, the United States saw Cuba with its ties to the Soviet Union and active support for communist-led guerrillas in the Third World (primarily in Latin America and Black Africa) as a threat to its national security. During the 1980s, President Ronald Reagan was angered by Castro's aid to communist guerrilla groups in Central America, particularly Nicaragua, El Salvador, and Guatemala, and to Soviet-backed groups in Angola and Ethiopia. He was also perturbed that in 1980 Castro had allowed over 100,000 Cubans to sail to the United States through the port of Mariel, many of whom had just been released from jails and mental asylums. Consequently, in 1982 Reagan increased U.S. isolation of Cuba. He closed a loophole in the embargo by clamping down on U.S. businesses that were trading indirectly with Cuba through foreign firms.

With the end of the Cold War, the dissolution of the Soviet Union, and the Pentagon's conclusion that Cuba no longer poses a security threat in the region, continuation of the embargo has come under renewed questioning, scrutiny, and debate. Critics have called it a relic of the Cold War. Dropping the embargo, they claim, would be the best way to move the communist island toward democracy and capitalism. Castro, then, could no longer claim that Cuba's economic problems were caused by "Yanqui imperialism." Nor could he use the embargo as an excuse to crack down against Cuban human rights activists, many of whom languish in jails. Critics add that with increased trade and other contacts with the United States, Castro would likely see that economic and political liberalization would be in his own best interest, as well as that of the Cuban people.

Supporters of the embargo are led by the politically powerful alliance of right-wing Republicans in Congress and the conservative Cuban exile community that speaks largely through the Cuban-American National Foundation (CANF). They believe that with the cessation of

Soviet aid to Cuba the embargo will finally have a chance to succeed. They also make these arguments for the embargo:[1]

1. Castro is responsible for the suffering of the Cuban people, not the United States.

2. Castro continues to train and provide support to thousands of international terrorists, such as the Tupamaros in Peru.

3. A free flow of trade and tourists will not influence Castro to improve his human rights record. Note, for example, the fact that the People's Republic of China (PRC) has emphasized economic growth through foreign trade and investment without corresponding advances in human rights. Indeed, after the collapse of the Soviet Union, Castro visited the PRC and has looked to it as a possible model for Cuba.[2]

4. Loosening or removing the embargo will not influence Castro to improve human rights in Cuba, for he is committed to both securing his power and the socialist revolution.

5. U.S. business will continue to lose out to investors from other countries. But why should the United States put business profits over human rights principles, like they do in the PRC?

6. Admittedly, the embargo harms innocent Cuban people, but maintaining it will lead to a faster demise of the odious Castro regime.

7. Maintaining the embargo gives hope to Cuban human rights activists and their supporters who need to know that outsiders care and want to help them.

Thus far, this conservative anti-communist alliance has won the day. In the 1990s, the United States hardened its policy toward Cuba. In October 1992, President George Bush signed the Cuban Democracy Act (CDA). Also known as the Torricelli Bill (named after its sponsor, Democratic Congressman Robert Torricelli of New Jersey), the CDA strengthened the U.S. embargo by stopping foreign subsidiaries of U.S. businesses from trading with Cuba and urging countries that received U.S. foreign aid to stop helping Cuba economically. The goal of the CDA was to pressure Castro to make peaceful democratic reforms. Yet it also aimed to decrease the isolation of the Cuban people by allowing more communication (by mail and telephone) between the United States and Cuba and shipment of medicines and other humanitarian aid from the United States.

On October 24, 1996, Cuban jet fighters shot down two small planes in the Florida Straits flown by members of Brothers to the Rescue. A month later, President Bill Clinton signed the Cuban Liberty and Democratic Solidarity Act (CLDSA). In effect, the president surrendered to Congress his authority to ease or lift the embargo. The CLDSA is known popularly as Helms–Burton after its sponsors, Senator Jesse Helms

(R–N.C.) and Representative Dan Burton (R–Ind.). Senator Helms, powerful and influential chair of the Senate Foreign Relations Committee, quipped that its message to Cuba is "Farewell Fidel!" The act seeks to isolate Cuba further by punishing foreign companies that invest in American-owned property that Castro seized after the Revolution, by allowing the State Department to deny entry visas to top officials of companies that use or otherwise benefit from this confiscated American property, and by giving American citizens the right to sue these foreign companies for payment of damages.

Arguably, Helms–Burton has become the main source of conflict between the United States and Cuba. Castro has regularly upbraided the United States for its embargo. He terms it a "blockade" because it means "economic warfare" against Cuba. He also points at glaring inconsistencies of the "blockade: "Those who blockade us have [had] good relations with South Africa [under apartheid], excellent relations with Chile [under General Augusto Pinochet's military dictatorship] where thousands of people have been killed . . . and Argentina [under authoritarian military rule] where thousands of people are missing." And when the United States deals with the Middle East, Castro complains, "it discusses only one thing: oil, never democracy."[3] As a symbol of Cuba's contempt for the "blockade," Castro constructed a billboard cartoon just outside the U.S. Interest Section in Havana. This cartoon depicts Uncle Sam with a slightly cocked hat reaching across the Straits of Florida toward Cuba. He faces a Cuban who has no fear and shows defiance.

Helms–Burton has also caused significant friction between the United States and its allies, notably countries of the European Union (EU) and Canada. They claim that it amounts to an illegal secondary boycott because it penalizes foreign firms that do business in Cuba, and that it violates free trade agreements under the oversight of the World Trade Organization. The United States counters that Helms–Burton is legal and justifiable based on requirements of U.S. national security. Differences between the United States and the EU over Helms–Burton have eased, at least for the time being, with the EU's agreement to press harder for human rights concessions in Cuba. U.S.–Canadian relations, however, remain somewhat strained over the issue.

U.S. POLICY OPTIONS TOWARD CUBA

Few people expected that at the start of the twenty-first century Castro would still be in power and the embargo would still be in place. It seems clear that at least by autumn of 2000, the embargo had not achieved its main goal of influencing Castro to move toward political and economic liberalization or peacefully removing him from power.

Nor, it seems, had the Clinton administration's quite limited implementation of the so-called Track 2 option (Track 1 refers to government-to-government relations) fared much better. This option, with specified examples in U.S. legislation, includes fostering relations outside of government through people-to-people contacts and support for nongovernmental organizations like the church. The papal visit to Cuba in January 1998 did offer some hope for liberalization, evidenced, for example, by the Cuban government's acquiescence to reestablish Christmas as an official holiday. But Castro has stiffly opposed cultivation of relationships by Americans with Cuban human rights groups such as the Cuban Committee for Human Rights (CCPDH), an independent group formed to promote human rights and democratic reform. Castro has cracked down on this group, imprisoning many of its leaders. The policy of constructive engagement adopted by U.S. allies such as Canada and countries of the EU (i.e., normalizing relations while exerting gentle pressure on Castro to undertake political reform), has also not achieved this goal.[4]

The United States could consider other options, such as full normalization of relations with Cuba. This would entail, inter alia, establishing formal diplomatic relations with Cuba; dropping the embargo unconditionally; abandoning all efforts at subversion of the Castro regime; welcoming Cuba back into key regional organizations of the Western Hemisphere, such as the OAS, the Caribbean Community, and the Common Market (CARICOM); giving Cuba economic aid and Permanent and Normal Trade Relations (PNTR) status; and returning to Cuba the U.S. naval base at Guantanamo Bay, which was taken at the end of the Spanish–American War when Cuba was weak and defenseless. Some argue that the United States no longer keeps this base as a strategic necessity, but as an irritant to Castro. At the same time the United States would make these overtures to Castro, through negotiation and diplomacy it could keep up pressure on the Cuban regime to liberalize its political and economic policies. Supporters of this option cite the precedents of U.S. recognition of the PRC in 1979 and Vietnam in 1997. It is just a matter of time before the United States and Cuba establish normal diplomatic relations, but this is not yet politically feasible. In the interim, there is another option that is more viable politically and possibly more effective in achieving political and economic liberalization in Cuba. The United States should increase its efforts to urge foreign companies to adopt and implement best business practices (also known as Corporate Codes of Conduct and Model Business Principles).[5] At the same time, the United States should signal Castro that when the time is right, American companies will be prepared to enter Cuba on the same basis. Adoption of best business practices would not only have a positive influence in Cuba, but also on foreign companies that need to improve their own ethical performance record.

BEST BUSINESS PRACTICES: AN OVERVIEW

Generally speaking, until recently, businesses around the globe have considered promotion of human rights the responsibility of government. Multilateral government organizations such as the United Nations, the Organization for Economic Cooperation and Development (OECD), and the International Labor Organization (ILO) have all established codes of responsibility as a way to check global activities of transnational corporations (TNCs).

The United Nations formulated a code of conduct for TNCs in the 1970s mainly in response to pressure by the Group of 77. This organization of developing countries pressed the industrialized world to change what it considered oppressive economic policies that were propelling them into a state of indefinite poverty and dependency. There was also concern that private corporations were being used by government for nefarious purposes, such as the role played by ITT in the 1973 overthrow of President Salvador Allende of Chile. The U.N. Code, never formally adopted, remains largely a statement of principle. For example, it requires that TNCs "shall respect human rights and fundamental freedoms in the countries in which they operate. In their social and industrial relations, transnational corporations shall not discriminate on the bases of race, colour, sex, language, social, national and ethnic origin or political or other opinion."

The OECD established its Guidelines for Multinational Enterprises in 1976. The concern then was also corporate interference in a country's political affairs. The main features of this code include recognition of the right of labor to organize and bargain collectively, and prohibition of on-the-job discrimination. In the absence of enforcement procedures, the code is considered mainly advisory.

The ILO, a specialized agency of the United Nations, has long advocated international labor standards and corporate responsibility. With tripartite representation of workers, employers, and government representatives, it is responsible for monitoring labor conditions, setting standards, and research and technical cooperation. Its 1977 Tripartite Declaration of Principles Concerning Multinational Enterprises and Social Policy outlines ethical guidelines for corporations, governments, and workers. It also focuses on job creation, employment standards, and working conditions. Although it provides for a complaint procedure before a Standing Committee on Multinational Enterprises that can investigate and report on code violations by individual companies, like the OECD code it is has no enforcement provision. Instead, both OECD and ILO officials must resort to jawboning or adverse media publicity.

Businesses have faced several main choices in dealing with regimes that systematically violate human rights: do no business at all, which could mean divestment or pulling out existing business; do business in accordance with the requirements of each country ("when in Rome, do as the Romans do"); or do business with conditions. In this last instance, the goal is to use business operations as a lever to promote human rights.

Over the last two decades several individual leaders, often with government backing, have sponsored codes of conduct for businesses to use in the workplace. The "lever approach" to improve human rights has been utilized by a number of U.S. companies across the globe. Among the best known are the Sullivan Principles, adopted in 1977 to push for racial equality in South Africa; the MacBride Principles, issued in 1984 to work against anti-Catholic discrimination in employment in Northern Ireland; the Slepak Principles, developed in 1987 to stop anti-Semitism in the workplace in the Soviet Union; and the Miller Principles, developed in 1991 to improve human rights in the PRC, including the disputed area of Tibet.[6]

The Sullivan Principles are perhaps the most important and illustrative. They were developed in March 1977 by the Reverend Leon H. Sullivan, pastor of the Zion Baptist Church in Philadelphia and a member of the board of directors of General Motors Corporation. His principles aimed at U.S. corporations doing business in South Africa under apartheid. Their goal was to apply pressure on the South African government to end apartheid through adoption of employment practices that prohibited racial discrimination in hiring, employee housing conditions, and promotion. In 1971 the board of directors of General Motors rejected his proposal that the company divest from South Africa until the end of apartheid. Soon, advised by some black South Africans and others that an attempt be made to "marshal the resources of U.S. and other multinational companies into true forces of change," Sullivan developed his activist principles. When he announced his principles, Sullivan stressed that twelve major U.S. corporations doing business in South Africa had already signed and agreed to follow them. They were later modified and elaborated upon in response to changing conditions. As time passed and apartheid seemed to have staying power, Sullivan was disappointed that his principles did not seem to be making the significant impact he had hoped for. He was far from optimistic even when the U.S. government passed the 1986 Comprehensive Anti-Apartheid Act that obligated U.S. corporations to abide by his principles. In June 1987, in frustration Reverend Sullivan turned away from his code-of-conduct strategy and called on U.S.

businesses to withdraw completely from South Africa. He also asked Washington to impose a total trade embargo against South Africa until that government formally ended apartheid and gave a meaningful commitment to blacks and coloreds for equal political rights. Many believed that the Sullivan Principles contributed to the collapse of legal apartheid in the early 1990s. How important its role was, however, needs further study.

The experience of the Sullivan Principles notwithstanding, in the 1990s, largely in response to increased globalization of the marketplace, more attention focused on the responsibility of private business in promoting human rights. Corporate codes of conduct were developed to make progress in targeted areas, such as child labor, health and safety in the workplace, environmental safeguards, and worker rights—especially the establishment of free labor unions with free collective bargaining; open hiring, promotion, and treatment of workers without prejudice based on race, ethnicity, language, religion, gender, sexual orientation, or political belief; and payment of fair wages.

The pressure on companies to become better corporate citizens— either separately or as members of business associations—has come from competitors, labor unions, consumer groups, investors, religious associations, human rights organizations, and worker-rights advocates.[7] Companies often find it in their interest to be seen publicly as "socially responsible." Indeed, the idea is for the combination of social responsibility and self-interest to become a "win–win" proposition for the companies and their workers. Companies in such diverse areas as footwear (Nike, Reebok), restaurants (Starbucks), and photographic equipment and supplies (Polaroid) have developed their own codes of conduct, as have business associations like the American Apparel Manufacturers Association (AAMA).[8]

Sometimes codes of conduct are developed by umbrella groups. An important example is the Rugmark Campaign. In September 1994, the newly established U.S.–based Child Labor Coalition joined forces with carpet industry representatives from India, the South Asian Coalition on Child Servitude, and the Indo–German Promotion Council to form the Rugmark Foundation. Companies that made rugs were encouraged to obtain the Rugmark label for their products, which signifies they do not exploit child labor.

One of the most active umbrella groups in the Western Hemisphere is the Coalition for Justice in the Maquiladoras (CJM).[9] This is an association of more than 100 religious, environmental, labor, Latino, and women's organizations whose goal is to pressure U.S. TNCs operating along the U.S.–Mexican border to adopt socially responsible practices within the maquiladora industry. Its standard of conduct principles, issued in spring 1991, was drawn from existing Mexican and U.S. federal laws and ILO labor standards. The standard focuses on stopping environmental contamination, abiding by good health and safety practices, improving standards of living, and following fair employment practices, all with a commitment to community economic development and improvements in quality of life. Among its most important methods of enforcement are shareholder pressure, legislative advocacy (both in the United States and Mexico), and publicity (through publication of a quarterly newsletter, booklets, videos, and reports).

Although this standard has made only a modest impact, due mainly to the not so cooperative attitude of both the Mexican government and participating U.S. companies, its success should best be judged in the long term. What it has done is set an important precedent. Adoption of standard of conduct principles can at least begin to make an impact in influencing both U.S. companies and governments in Latin America to treat workers more freely, fairly, and safely. Indeed, this standard, along with other codes of corporate responsibility already discussed, could possibly serve as a model for U.S. companies and others around the world to conduct business in Cuba.

THE NEED FOR FOREIGN INVESTMENT AFTER THE COLLAPSE OF THE SOVIET UNION

With the collapse of the Soviet Union and communist regimes in Eastern Europe, long-term Soviet-bloc aid that had kept the Cuban economy afloat stopped short. Until then, virtually the entire Cuban economy was dependent on the Soviet bloc, which accounted for most of its foreign investment and about 85 percent of its foreign trade.[10] When this situation ended, Cuba entered the "Special Period" wherein Castro desperately tried to save the Cuban economy from collapse. Holding steadfast to the principles of socialism ("socialism or death," he insisted), he would not be enticed to return Cuba fully to its capitalist ways, which in his mind had previously led his country down the road to exploitation and degradation. Yet out of necessity, Castro did make some concessions to capitalism.

Castro decided to reorient the Cuban economy by attracting significantly more Western tourists and Western investment, especially to build hotels. Before the 1959 Revolution, Cuba was a major tourist destination in the Caribbean, with Americans comprising about 80 percent of the 300,000 visitors a year. But with restrictions on tourists imposed by the U.S. government (technically, they could travel to Cuba but not spend their money there, as this would violate the Trading with the Enemy Act of 1964), Cuba—at least for the time being—had to look elsewhere. In 1988, just before the collapse of the Soviet empire, 309,000 tourists to Cuba spent about $189 million on the island. By 1995, about 800,000 tourists spent more than $1 billion in Cuba. As a high priority, Castro was banking on turning its world-class beach area at Varadero into a "red hot" tourist destination.[11]

To attract Western investment and gain access to modern technology, in September 1995 the Cuban government decided to allow 100-percent foreign ownership of businesses. Until then, Cuba had preferred to retain majority control of joint ventures.[12] The new law also authorized the creation of duty-free zones and guaranteed foreign investors that their properties would not be expropriated except for reasons of critical national interest, and then only with proper compensation.[13]

These accommodations with capitalism, accompanied by Castro's decision in November 1995 to allow Cuban citizens to buy and sell foreign currencies, especially U.S. dollars, breathed new life into Cuba's economy, which slowly began to recover.[14] Castro even began to allow small private businesses to operate, such as small farmers and in-home family-run restaurants called *paladares* (with no more than twelve employees). The worst of the food shortages abated, but the economy, though no longer in tatters, still tottered. Indeed, some foreign investors, taking note of the loopholes in the 1995 law (e.g., it allowed 100-percent foreign ownership of the real estate, but not the land underneath) and frustrated by the anticapitalist stance of the Cuban government, pulled back. Some even left the island.[15] Businesses in Canada and countries in the EU, however, tended to step up their activity in Cuba. But would this make a major impact in Cuba? If the Cuban economy were to significantly improve, it probably needed to attract heavier foreign investment. The obvious source would be the United States. But how could this happen?

CODES OF CONDUCT FOR FOREIGN BUSINESSES: THE ARCOS PRINCIPLES

With more and more foreign investment coming into Cuba, Cuban human rights activists began to see this as an opportunity to help the Cuban people while also possibly weakening Castro's grasp over them. During the second quarter of 1994, Rolando H. Castaneda (an Inter-American Development Bank senior operations officer) and George Plinio Montalvan (former chief economist of the OAS) sent a document to Gustavo Arcos Bergnes, executive secretary of the CCPDH in Cuba, through the good offices of several persons, among them Dr. Ricardo Bofill (president of the CCPDH). They proposed a set of "Principles for Foreign Investment in Cuba." Their goal was not only to search out the opinion of Mr. Arcos, but also to call them the "Arcos

Principles." They wanted the Arcos family name, with three members actively involved in the Cuban people's struggle for human rights, to lend credibility to their endeavor.[16]

The following Arcos Principles were patterned after the Sullivan, MacBride, Slepak, and Miller principles already discussed, and drew upon international human rights standards:

1. Respect for the dignity of the Cuban people and due process of law.
2. Respect for basic human rights. Equal rights and nondiscrimination of the Cuban people in access to and use of facilities and in the purchase of goods and services, especially those normally reserved for foreign visitors and residents.
3. Equal and fair hiring and employment practices, with nondiscrimination for reasons based on political considerations, sex, race, religion, or age.
4. Promotion of fair labor standards and the right of Cuban workers to form labor unions and to receive fair wages.
5. Improvement of the quality of employees' lives outside the workplace in such areas as occupational safety and health, culture, and environmental protection.

The intent of the Arcos principles is to help improve the human rights situation in Cuba by focusing on labor rights.[17] In some instances, they are consonant with laws and provisions of the Cuban Constitution (e.g., all Cubans should have equal access to and use of all public areas). What is needed in these cases is adherence by the Cuban government. In other instances (e.g., the right of Cuban workers to form their own associations and belong to independent trade unions) they call for the Cuban government's compliance with international labor conventions on human rights to which it is a signatory.

Cuba systematically violates fundamental human rights conventions of the ILO, such as the freedom of association and the right to organize, the right to bargain collectively, and the right to nondiscrimination. A Cuban state agency (Cubalse) selects "suitable" workers for joint ventures, based mainly on their revolutionary Communist Party credentials. Furthermore, Cuban workers assigned to all embassies and diplomatic residences are chosen by the state security apparatus. Cuban workers are exploited because foreign companies must pay their salaries in dollars to Cubalse, which in turn pays the workers in almost worthless pesos. In effect, the Cuban government makes a handsome profit on the backs of Cuban workers, who receive only a small fraction of their wages.[18] Cuban workers, for the most part, still covet these jobs because they have access to dollars through tips. Indeed, many Cuban professionals moonlight in tourist industry jobs for precisely this purpose. For example, it is common practice for a medical doctor to drive a cab in off hours. Tips in dollars from cab rides in one evening often equal a doctor's monthly salary in pesos.

The authors of the Arcos Principles and the organizations dedicated to human rights and promotion of democracy that cosponsored them believe that businesses that invest and operate in Cuba have been blocking or delaying required reforms. Supporters decided to appeal to both current and prospective investors to sign and abide by the Arcos Principles. They hoped that multinational companies operating in Cuba would exhibit the same sense of social responsibility that helped bring about democracy in South Africa."[19] A Special Unit for Responsible Foreign Investment would be established to implement the principles. The International Society for Human Rights headquartered in Germany and its Pan American Committee would coordinate the project's activities in Europe and Latin America, respectively. It was expected that signatories and organizations that support the Arcos Principles would help monitor the principles, report on their performance, finance the costs of implementation, and present an annual progress report to at least one human rights organization in Cuba, preferably the CCPDH.

A "fundamental short-term objective" of the sponsors of the Arcos Principles was to help resolve "the disagreement between the government of Cuba and our citizens." Moreover, the sponsors argue that by going along with requirements of the Cuban government, foreign businesses violate human rights. Thus, they are actually complicit in government repression of Cuban workers. According to ILO Convention 95, foreign businesses can be held coresponsible for these human rights practices as they accept them, profit by them, or at least in a de facto manner condone them.[20] The sponsors took no position on whether there should be foreign investment in Cuba, although if they had their druthers they would prefer that there would not be any.[21] Instead, they wanted the principles to improve the conditions of Cuban workers, which would also protect the interests of investors.[22]

NGOs in Europe and North America have taken the initiative and assumed a leadership role in the adoption and implementation of the Arcos Principles and other voluntary codes of conduct. In the forefront is the Catholic human rights group Pax Christi Netherlands and the North American Committee (NAC) of the National Policy Association (NPA).

LEADERSHIP EFFORTS BY PAX CHRISTI NETHERLANDS TO ADVANCE THE ARCOS PRINCIPLES

The Latin America Desk of Pax Christi Netherlands has focused most of its attention on influencing activities of companies operating in countries of the EU that are doing business in Cuba or contemplating doing so. For example, on November 29, 1997, Pax Christi convened European NGOs in Rome for the second meeting of the European Platform for Human Rights and Democracy in Cuba. The platform's communiqué called upon European investors to "voluntarily subscribe [to] and comply with the so-called 'Arcos Principles' that include guarantees for Cuban workers rights."[23]

On December 3, 1998, Pax Christi Netherlands convened a roundtable meeting in the European Parliament in Brussels on foreign investment and human and labor rights in Cuba. Present were representatives of trade unions, private-sector organizations, human rights NGOs, members of the European Parliament (MEPs), academics, a former Cuban government official, and a representative of the independent Cuban trade unions. The challenge of this meeting was "to come to a coherent strategy on investments in Cuba that can count on significant social and political support in Europe."[24] The participants agreed on several issues, most notably the following:

1. The Cuban government is a dictatorship with a repressive state security system. Conference participants noted that the elite in Europe seemed "poorly informed" on violations of labor union rights in Cuba. There is a continuing need, therefore, "to keep feeding the public debate on Cuba in Europe with facts and information."

2. Foreign investors in Cuba can be held accountable for their complicity "in gross and systematic violations of fundamental human rights."

3. Foreign investors in Cuba should be encouraged to adopt the best business practice approach based on such examples as the Arcos Principles. To date, no individual business had signed the Arcos Principles or any other code. Conference participants underscored the "significant role" that could be played by international private-sector and trade union networks in promoting best business practices in Cuba.

4. The European Commission should help promote standardization of codes of conduct and independent monitoring of implementation of these codes.

The EU had been trying to use business and trade as levers to pressure the Cuban government to undertake human rights reforms, but this effort was generally considered too meek and ineffective by human rights organizations like Human Rights Watch/Americas.[25] Perhaps stung by such criticism, on December 2, 1996, the EU adopted a "Common Position" that called upon all fifteen member states and the EU Commission to push harder for human rights and democratic change in Cuba.

The United States, meanwhile, was also taking the EU to task for not going far enough to improve human rights in Cuba. The conflict escalated when the United States threatened to impose sanctions against European businesses operating in Cuba through the Helms–Burton law. The EU, in turn, angry at the extraterritorial application of Helms–Burton, threatened to bring a legal challenge before the WTO. The dispute was defused when on April 11, 1997, the United States reached an understanding with the EU. The United States agreed not to invoke Helms–Burton as long as the EU discouraged investments in U.S. properties that Cuba nationalized after the 1959 Revolution, and stepped up pressure on Castro to improve human rights. Then in London, on May 18, 1998, the United States and the EU concluded the Understanding with Respect to Disciplines for the Strengthening of Property Protection.[26]

At the Brussels meeting in December 1998, the EU seemed to be moving toward a more proactive approach in its dealings with Cuba. The EU Human Rights Commission circulated a draft report that indicated increased attention to human rights around the globe. The draft contained a section on codes of conduct for business. Several items are particularly noteworthy. First, the EU should adopt a corporate code of conduct obliging EU-based companies to abide by internationally recognized human rights practices in operations outside the EU. This is possible under EU law, for in 1977 the Council had adopted a code of conduct for businesses in South Africa. Second, the adoption of voluntary codes by many private-sector companies was welcomed. Third, the Council was called upon "to develop a joint position on voluntary codes of conduct, on the lines of the code of conduct for arms exporters, taking due account of the fact that 'self-policing' is not always the answer." Last, private companies were urged "to take a more proactive approach in relation to the right of employees to freedom of expression and to freedom of association."[27]

Whether there will be a successful follow-up to the Brussels conference is uncertain. There seems a good chance that the EU will focus more on the issue of best business practices for Cuba. How many individual businesses will start signing on to these practices is difficult to say. Pax Christi noted that, regrettably, representatives of individual businesses were "scarcely present" at the Brussels meeting. In postconference letters to the heads of the International Confederation of Free Trade Unions (ICFTU), the World Confederation of Labor (WCL), and members of the European Parliament, the group "strongly recommended" that representatives who are sent to Cuba should meet with independent trade unions such as the six unions that are forming the Confederacion de Trabajadores Libres. The letter also asked the ICFTU and WCL to push for adoption of best business practices on behalf of Cuban trade unions that cannot do this themselves. Pax Christi Netherlands has thus been making a very serious effort to get businesses to adopt codes of conduct for operations in Cuba. It has been joined in this leadership role by other organizations, notably the North American Committee.

LEADERSHIP EFFORTS OF THE NORTH AMERICAN COMMITTEE IN ADVANCING THE ARCOS PRINCIPLES

The National Policy Association is a nonpartisan nonprofit research institution founded in 1934 on the conviction that the private sector should be a major player in discussion of the making of public policy that deals with economic and social issues. The NPA provides a forum for business, labor, agricultural, and academic leaders to discuss and debate important issues. The NPA also conducts research, holds conferences, and publishes reports that recommend to policy makers and the public what it considers effective strategies and solutions. Much of this work is done in its six policy committees, one of which is the North American Committee. The NAC was founded in 1957 as a private-sector network of business, labor, and academic leaders from both Canada and the United States. Mexico was included after the signing of the North American Free Trade Agreement (NAFTA). The goal of the NAC is "to advance the economic and social policy interests of the three member countries through private-sector dialogue and research."[28]

According to Charles A. Barrett, vice president of business research of the Conference Board of Canada, the NAC began to focus on the "Cuba question" in 1996.[29] In June of that year it issued a statement that opposed the Helms–Burton Act. The NAC maintained that "the international private sector has a role in promoting adherence to universal standards of human rights [and] that unilateral government sanctions are not necessarily the best way to achieve this goal."[30] The NAC sought to avoid partisanship politics. Moreover, it wanted to defuse inflammatory rhetoric that traditionally engulfed discussion of policy toward Cuba and to seek a consensus among the committee's three participating member countries. Thus, it considered what the private sector could do to advance commonly shared goals: promotion of democracy, protection of human rights, and improvement of the lives of the Cuban people. Adoption of a voluntary code of business conduct seemed a more sensible policy approach. It was hoped that other countries would also subscribe to this suggested code.

Barrett maintains that the private sector can play a "crucial role" in development around the world. Adoption of a voluntary code of business conduct, he argues, can heighten the level of awareness of the role of private business in economic development and promotion of civil society. A code could be especially effective in countries such as

Cuba, where workers rights are systematically violated. Accordingly, on July 7, 1997, the NAC recommended for public discussion the "Business Principles for Private Sector Involvement in Cuba." These principles, based on the Arcos Principles, were much more succinct and presumably would be easier to implement.[31] The NAC believes that promotion of its principles for Cuba is consistent with the global trend toward increased corporate social responsibility.[32] To further this effort, it sponsored a conference on best business practices in Cuba that was held in Mexico City in the summer of 2000.

The goal of the NAC is to encourage companies doing business in Cuba to voluntarily accept its principles. They should abide by Cuban laws and regulations except where these preclude adherence to the principles. In such instances, they should encourage changes. Barrett points out that the Cuban government, which desperately needs foreign investment, has already been forced to implement some economic reforms, such as allowing foreign investors to earn profits of more than 50 percent in their joint ventures with the government. He takes note, however, of very serious problems faced by foreign businesses in Cuba, including the requirement of entering joint ventures, proscription of creating partnerships with Cuban citizens, selection of employees only from a government-approved list, a two-tiered payment system (dollars to the contractual government agency, which pays pesos to Cuban employees), and the ban against organization of independent trade unions. These severe problems notwithstanding, Barrett believes that there is a trend toward more openness and accountability of both the private sector and governments taking place in both the hemisphere and the world at large. Adoption of a socially responsible code of conduct for business operating in Cuba is thus a "realistic goal."[33] To what extent, though, is this policy realistic for the United States?

ORIGINS AND DEVELOPMENT OF THE U.S. GOVERNMENT'S MODEL BUSINESS PRINCIPLES

The idea for model business principles for U.S. companies arose in 1994 in the aftermath of a disputatious annual review of extending PNTR status to the PRC. Presumably, renewal would be determined by the administration's determination that China had taken sufficient positive steps toward improvement of human rights. Business groups led the push for renewal of MFN, whereas human rights groups, underscoring a lack of progress in human rights and labor conditions, argued for its revocation. Although President Clinton had campaigned to hold China accountable on human rights, he decided to delink human rights issues from China's MFN status. To cushion the political impact of this decision, the next year Clinton called upon U.S. companies to develop their own codes of conduct for foreign operations. These would be based on a general set of model business principles outlined by the U.S. Department of Commerce that did not specifically target China. Included were somewhat blandly and weakly worded measures, such as a call for fair employment practices, respect for the right of association and the right to organize and bargain collectively, and opposition to political coercion in the workplace.[34] Moreover, these principles did not mention the responsibility of companies to pay a living wage, and there was no enforcement mechanism.[35] Despite these problems, stipulation of the model business principles concept down the road could influence companies doing business in Cuba.

ADVANTAGES AND DISADVANTAGES OF POSSIBLE U.S. ADOPTION OF MODEL BUSINESS PRINCIPLES FOR CUBA

Whether the United States should pursue the model business principles option for Cuba depends on how well this satisfies several criteria:

1. Support by the U.S. business community.
2. Consistency with U.S. foreign policy goals toward Cuba.
3. Acceptability in U.S. domestic politics.
4. Receptivity by President Castro and the degree of effectiveness if agreed upon.

After a brief discussion of each criterion, an assessment of how well the model business principles option satisfies it will be made on a scale of 1 (weakest) to 5 (strongest). This will be followed by an overall assessment of the four criteria.

Support by the U.S. Business

Some U.S. businesses, most notably the National Association of Sugar Mill Owners of Cuba, oppose the lifting of the U.S. embargo. Nick Gutierrez, a lawyer and secretary for this Florida-based group comprising former sugar farm owners whose property was expropriated by Castro, calls those favoring an end to the embargo "naked business interests that don't care about the human rights situation in Cuba." He adds that lifting the embargo now would be a grave mistake because "the walls [around Castro] are closing for his regime, and that's why he's trying so desperately to lift the embargo."[36]

In general, however, U.S. businesses want to enter Cuba as soon as possible.[37] They are upset that they will be at a competitive disadvantage by entering "late in the game." Some groups, like the U.S.–Cuba Business Council, endorse U.S. investment with preconditions that include establishment of a free-enterprise economy, enforcement of contracts, and protection for and expansion of private property, all of which are most unlikely to occur as long as Castro remains in power.

Most business groups, however, want an unconditional end to the embargo. Among the most vocal are the U.S. Chamber of Commerce, USA Engage (a coalition of businesses, agricultural groups, and trade associations), and the U.S.–Cuba Trade and Economic Council (a New York City–based organization that provides information for U.S. companies planning future business operations in Cuba). Statements by two leaders of the U.S. Chamber of Commerce are illustrative. According to Dennis Sheehan, chair of the Chamber's International Policy Committee, "The nearly four-decade U.S. embargo of Cuba has done nothing to accelerate the current regime's removal from power. Instead, our 'allies' castigate U.S. policy toward Cuba, while U.S. businesses and their workers bear the burden of lost opportunities to other competitors." Willard Workman, Chamber vice president for international affairs, added this conclusion: "An open economy is the first step to democracy. The best thing to do is send 1,000 American businesspeople to Cuba to cut deals and make it happen."[38] Florida-based companies seem especially well positioned and poised to enter the potentially lucrative Cuba market. For example, Neal Ganzel, the Jacksonville Port Authority public relations director, believes trade with Cuba "certainly will be a boon" for his city. He continued, "A whole lot of Cubans in this country will want to be shipping to their family and friends and business associates what they cannot get [in Cuba]."[39] Overall, therefore, U.S. business wants to enter Cuba and probably would subscribe to model business principles (assessment: 4.5).

U.S. Foreign Policy Goals

Human rights has long been a concern of U.S. foreign policy.[40] In the 1970s, President Jimmy Carter elevated human right issues to a higher plane, convinced that they were the "soul" of American foreign policy. Subsequent administrations, influenced more by the Cold War, emphasized improvement of human rights records, especially of communist countries. At times, Congress has linked trade, economic aid, and arms sales to a government's progress in human rights. For example, the Jackson–Vanik amendment to the U.S. trade act of 1974 denied MFN to nonmarket economy countries that restricted the right of their citizens to emigrate. Yet the United States has not been consistent in its methods for influencing governments to improve their human rights records. Both strategic international and domestic political factors have been important. For example, the Jackson–Vanik amendment was adopted largely for U.S. domestic political reasons. Senator

Henry Jackson (D–Wash.), a strong anti-Communist with presidential ambitions, sought to win the support of American Jewish voters who considered free emigration of Jews from communist countries, especially the Soviet Union, one of their highest priorities. Yet the application of Jackson–Vanik at times rested on strategic grounds. In 1979 the United States refused to grant MFN trade status to the Soviet Union (even though in that year it let a record number of Soviet Jews leave the country). The same year, though, it granted MFN status to the PRC. At that time, the United States was playing its "second China card." Extending formal diplomatic recognition to the PRC was one way to check the power of the Soviet Union in Asia. Moreover, in 1978 the United States granted MFN trade status to Romania, led by President Nicolae Ceausescu. President Carter even called Ceausescu "a great leader of a great country."[41] The U.S. goal was to influence Romania, which already was resisting Soviet domination, to continue to exert its independence within the Soviet-bloc countries of Eastern Europe.

Human rights was somewhat of a priority of the Clinton administration, at least in some areas. When Clinton supported the reorganization and renaming of the State Department Human Rights Bureau as the Bureau of Democracy, Human Rights, and Labor, he seemed to be placing more emphasis on worker-rights issues. Although the development of model business principles came in the aftermath of his delinking of MFN to China with progress in human rights, these principles could be applied to future business operations in Cuba. On January 28, 1997, the U.S. Agency for International Development issued "Support for a Democratic Transition in Cuba," with a preface by President Clinton. One section implies that the practice of model business principles could be applied to Cuba:

Recognizing the important role of civil society in transition countries, external donors have directed considerable portions of their assistance to and through indigenous independent NGOs in transition countries, often using NGOs from their home countries as intermediaries. When Cuba begins its transition, the panorama of Cuban NGOs likely to attract external support will include formerly repressed independent NGOs. NGOs formerly controlled by the government, and newly created NGOs. Examples include labor unions, professional and business associations, cooperatives, community organizations, social service organizations, women's groups, environmental organizations, human rights organizations, and private think tanks.[42]

Administration advisors on Cuban policy have made more direct references in support of possible U.S. application of model business principles to Cuba. Although they are quick to stress continued U.S. opposition to investment in Cuba, they call upon those companies already doing business there to adopt model business principles.

Public remarks by Stuart E. Eizenstat, appointed special representative of the president for the promotion of democracy in Cuba, and by Michael Ranneberger, the State Department's special coordinator for Cuban affairs, point to the importance the administration attaches to the possibility that model business principles could be one element of a multipronged multilateral push for political and economic reform in Cuba that would also involve cooperation with NGOs and intergovernmental organizations. While their reference is to non–U.S. companies, there is a hint that at some future date U.S. companies might also employ this practice, most likely after the embargo officially ends. When Eizenstat was appointed on August 16, 1996, he told the press,

We're looking for concrete and specific measures [to effect a peaceful transition to democracy in Cuba]. Among the kinds of things that we will be exploring are greater pressure on the Cuban regime for political and economic reform and respect for human rights; *encouraging voluntary business principles* for companies doing business in Cuba, like the Sullivan principles; promoting greater cooperation among United States, European, Canadian and Mexican and other Latin NGOs and assisting in the development of a civil society; channeling assistance to groups promoting change in Cuba—human rights groups, dissidents and independent journalists; using European, Mexican and Canadian and Latin governments and non-governmental groups to channel humanitarian aid through legitimate non-governmental institutions rather than through the Cuban government itself; . . . strengthening our cooperation in international fora, such as the U.N. General Assembly [to deal with] the question of Cuban human rights abuses.[43]

And in a speech on the Cuban transition process given at Tulane University on November 9, 1998, Ranneberger expanded on the model business principles theme:

A significant element of the multilateral effort to promote democracy is growing movement to promote "best business practices" in Cuba. I want to be clear that the U.S. opposes investment in Cuba. Virtually the only opportunities for investment are in joint ventures with the government, which therefore supports and prolongs the current oppressive regime. We recognize, however, the reality that some foreign companies have nevertheless chosen to invest in Cuba, and those companies should be urged to pursue best business practices.[44]

Ranneberger went on to list organizations that had been pushing for adoption of model business principles for Cuba: the NAC, Pax Christi, the AFL–CIO, Dutch and British employer associations, and the Transatlantic Business Dialogue.

The potential of a U.S.–EU joint initiative toward Cuba that might involve application of model business principles is also worth noting. In February 1998 the secretaries of labor in the United States and the

EU convened the first "U.S.–EU Symposium on Codes of Conduct." Several U.S. and European companies and NGOs discussed the effectiveness of model business principles in improving global working conditions. One interesting twist was that in June 1997 legislation was introduced in the U.S. Congress to give companies that subscribe to the bill's code of conduct preference in government contracts and foreign trade and investment assistance. This would be a modern version of "Dollar Diplomacy," as businesses would be given enticements to invest for both political gain and economic profit. Although this bill has not been passed, it does indicate what inducements the U.S. government might offer U.S. businesses contemplating investment in Cuba when the political climate becomes more favorable (assessment: 4).

Acceptability in U.S. Domestic Politics

In an interview broadcast on the BBC on January 8, 1999, Robert McNamara, secretary of defense under the Kennedy administration, which initially imposed the embargo on Cuba, criticized it as a "total failure." He mentioned that former secretaries of state Henry Kissinger, Lawrence Eagleburger, George Shultz, and Cyrus Vance, and establishment organizations like the Council on Foreign Relations, had all changed their position on the embargo and now wanted it lifted.

In fall 1998, Kissinger, Eagleburger, and Shultz joined with a bipartisan group of senators led by John Warner (R–Va.) and other prominent government officials, such as former defense secretary Frank Carlucci, to undertake a comprehensive review of U.S. policy toward Cuba. This meant a probable recommendation to drop the embargo that has been the cornerstone of U.S. policy. The premise of this group was that U.S. policy toward Cuba should be similar to U.S. policy toward China (i.e., that increased contact leads to increased openness).

The push to end the embargo reflects the serious divisions within the Republican Party. The Kissinger–Warner group represented what may be termed the probusiness wing that has long wanted the embargo to end.[45] Walter Mead, staff director of the the Council of Foreign Relations task force on Cuba, pointed to a different source of support for an end to the embargo: "There is a growing concern in the internationalist wing of the Republican Party over the proliferation of unilateral sanctions."[46] On January 2, 1999, cochairmen of this task force Bernard W. Aronson and William D. Rogers wrote that "it is time for the United States to reorient its policy away from Fidel Castro and toward preparing for a democratic transition in Cuba. . . . Today, the United States must nurture and strengthen the fragile civil society that is tentatively but persistently beginning to emerge in Cuba." Aronson and Rogers, both Democrats who had served in Republican administrations, underscored what they termed a "developing bipartisan consensus" for a change in U.S. policy toward Cuba.[47] Opposed to these two wings is the strongly anti-Communist right wing of the Republican Party, dominated by the powerful Senate Foreign Relations Committee chairman Senator Jesse Helms. This group wants to keep the pressure on Castro and does not want to be criticized as "soft on Communism," though it does support humanitarian aid that goes directly to the Cuban people (e.g., from the Catholic Church).

Many liberals in the Democratic Party want the embargo to end. For example, Arthur Schlesinger, Jr., advisor to President Kennedy on Cuba, believes that "a better policy would be to repeal Helms–Burton, lift the embargo and drown the regime in American tourists, investments, and consumer goods." He argues that in 1963 President Kennedy considered a possible rapprochement with Cuba when Castro reduced his connection with the Soviet Union and stopped fomenting revolution in the hemisphere. As Castro is no longer involved in these activities, Schlesinger concludes, "Preserving the American embargo after its justification has disappeared only provides Mr. Castro with an all purpose alibi [for economic shortcomings]."[48]

Criticism of the U.S. embargo emanates from a variety of religious, humanitarian, and political forces. When Pope John Paul II visited Cuba in January 1998, he called for an end to the embargo that was causing so much pain and suffering among innocent Cuban people. The U.S. Catholic Church is on record as officially opposing the embargo. In a 1992 letter to the Bush administration criticizing the tightening of the embargo by the Torricelli Act, the U.S. Catholic Conference argued that embargoes "are acts of force . . . morally unacceptable, generally in violation of the principles of international law, and always contrary to the values of the Gospel."[49] Bishop Thomas Wenski, the auxiliary bishop of the Roman Catholic Archdiocese of Miami, has stated publicly that "the embargo cannot be sustained morally," and that lifting it "would be both smart policy and a powerful humanitarian effort."[50] Humanitarian groups like the New York–based Madre makes a similar argument against the embargo, and Randall Robinson, president of Trans/Africa Forum, in a visit to Cuba in January 1999, charged that the embargo caused disproportionate harm to Afro-Cubans.[51]

Two of the more outspoken Democratic Party critics of U.S. Cuba policy are Senator Christopher Dodd (D–Conn.) and Representative Charles B. Rangel (D–N.Y.). Dodd, after a six-hour discussion with Castro in Havana in December 1998, called for a review of U.S. policy and new talks with Cuba, arguing that Washington's four-decade policy of isolating Cuba had not worked. Rangel's criticism has been much sharper. In 1996 testimony on Helms–Burton before the Senate Foreign Relations Committee, Rangel said, "I am convinced that our national interests will clearly be served by changing our policy. And I am equally convinced that lowering the barriers to trade, cultural and scientific exchange is also the best way to promote democracy in Cuba."[52] Like McNamara in his BBC interview and other critics of U.S. policy, Rangel charged that domestic political considerations kept Clinton from making major policy changes.

In March 1998, President Clinton announced some modest changes in U.S.–Cuba policy, including allowing Cuban Americans to send remittances to family members in Cuba of up to $1,200 a year, and streamlining and expediting the issuance of licenses for the sale of medical supplies to Cuba. Then, in the first week of January 1999, the president outlined more changes. Among the most notable were resumption of direct postal service; authorization for any U.S. citizens to send up to $1,200 a year to Cubans; permission for U.S. firms to sell fertilizer, pesticides, and agricultural equipment to independent farmers and privately owned restaurants; and permission to the Baltimore Orioles to explore the possibility of playing two exhibition baseball games against the Cuban national team in spring 1999.

Proceeds from these baseball games, the United States insisted, should not go to the Cuban government but to the Cuban people. Castro, shortly after the proposal was made, hinted at Cuban government acceptance if proceeds went to help Cuban doctors aid victims of Hurricane Mitch in Central America.[53] An agreement was soon reached for the Orioles to play a game in Havana on March 28, and for the Cubans to play in Baltimore in May. Cuban American groups objected strongly. Members of the Alliance of Young Cubans and CANF staged protests at Orioles Grapefruit League games in Florida, contending that the United States should not use baseball to simulate the appearance of normalcy in Cuba. They added that the timing of this game could not be worse, for it would come on the heels of a show trial of four of Cuba's best known human rights activists who had been accused of sedition. The Orioles responded that individual players who objected to playing in Havana could sit out. The dispute continued, and playing the games remained highly controversial.

Some political pundits in the United States viewed President Clinton's proposed changes as a significant step toward improving U.S.–Cuban relations. There was talk, for example, of the potential success of "baseball diplomacy," reminiscent of the "ping pong diplomacy" that paved the way toward resumption of U.S. diplomatic relations with the PRC in the 1970s. Others, however, played down Clinton's announced changes, contending they only nibbled around the edges of the embargo and thus were essentially window dressing.

At the same time that President Clinton announced these changes, he rejected the proposal to establish a bipartisan commission to review all aspects of U.S. policy toward Cuba. His main reason was domestic political considerations. The strongest, most implacable, and most politically influential opposition to change in U.S. policy toward Cuba comes from the Cuban American community. It is based mostly in Florida and New Jersey, two states with important electoral votes. Three Cuban Americans in Congress wield almost a veto power over proposed U.S. policy changes toward Cuba. Reps. Lincoln Diaz-Balart (R–Fla.), Robert Menendez (D–N.J.), and Ileana Ros-Lehtinen (R–Fla.) maintain a consistent hard-line approach. When the idea of a bipartisan review commission was floated in the fall of 1998, these members of Congress immediately wrote a fiery letter of opposition to President Clinton, arguing, "We are concerned that some people in the business community care nothing at all about the absolute lack of political freedom, human rights, or independent, organized labor in Cuba."[54]

Rep. Ros-Lehtinen, perhaps, has been most outspoken. For example, in a televised discussion on the legitimacy of the Helms–Burton Act, she lambasted Art Eggelton, Canada's trade minister, for his country's policy of engagement toward Cuba. Eggelton defended his country's considerable business activity in Cuba. He also criticized the Helms–Burton Act as both illegal under international law (because of its extraterritorial application) and diplomatically unwise. Ros-Lehtinen went on the offensive, asking "Why do Canada and other countries deal with Castro?" She then answered her own question:

Because even though it's immorally wrong, they feel free to do it because they have no problems with, let's say, worker complaints. See, the Canadian government doesn't pay the Cuban worker. They pay the illegitimate Cuban regime. Castro then pays the worker in undervalued pesos that are actually almost worthless, so the Canadian Government is wonderfully happy they don't have to deal with pesky workers' rights, they don't have to deal with any environmental regulations, they don't have to deal with any kind of safety inspection in their hotels. They are free to do business with a dictator, and they're just as pleased as punch.[55]

The Cuban American exile community is not so monolithic as it once was. The hard-line group, led by the Washington-based Center for a Free Cuba (directed by Frank Calzon) and the Miami-based Cuban American National Foundation, has steadfastly resisted any changes in U.S. policy.[56] It was the CANF, for example, that influenced Congress to set up Radio Marti in 1983 in order to broadcast "truthful" news and entertainment to the Cuban people. Yet there have been some cracks in the hard-line CANF approach. One reason is the recent death of Jorge Mas Canosa, CANF's chairman, who influenced Washington to keep as much pressure on Castro as possible. Mas reportedly even boasted that he had often rewritten White House briefings on Cuba.[57]

The new leadership of the Cuban exile community subsequently has shown a little less zeal for this position. Important generational differences among Cuban Americans have also emerged. Younger Cubans no longer routinely back the embargo, but tend to be more open to changes. Even though they oppose Castro, they increasingly disagree over the best way to deal with him. More and more, they see the embargo as hurting innocent Cuban people more than helping to remove Castro from power or to liberalize his rule.

Some Cuban Americans have openly called for an end to the embargo. This is now a priority of the Washington-based Cuban Committee for Democracy. So far, however, the hard-line Cuban Americans prevail. U.S. policy toward Cuba probably will not change until they endorse it. President George W. Bush does not ne4ed to be reminded that he eked out victory in Florida and won the 2000 presidential election only with significant support from Cuban American voters. Thus, for the forseeable future, President Bush will continue to support the embargo. When a change in U.S. policy does come, most likely only then will adoption of model business principles by U.S. companies that will operate in Cuba be given serious consideration (assessment: 2).

Castro's Receptivity to Model Business Principles

There is an obvious additional question that must be addressed in assessing the possibility that U.S. businesses would adopt model business principles when they enter Cuba. How receptive would Castro be toward model business principles, and if agreed upon, how effective would they be?

There is no question that Castro both needs and wants more foreign investment. In November 1998, for example, at the opening of the sixteenth annual Havana International Trade Fair, he touted Cuba as a safe and attractive location for serious foreign investors. He pointed out, "You want to invest, and our desire is to create the best possible conditions so that you may invest." Cuba, he contended, would be a safer place to invest than many other places because the capitalist global economy had turned the world into "a huge casino." By contrast, Castro pointed out, Cuba's state-run economy did not accept speculative capital, so in Cuba there is "total and absolute security to investors."[58]

But how far will Castro be willing to go in attracting businesses that insist on following the Arcos Principles or similar ones, such as those proposed by the NAC or the U.S. government? It is unlikely the Cuban government would accept these principles as long as the United States maintained its embargo. This was certainly indicated by Cuba's official reaction to President Clinton's January 1999 proposed changes in U.S. policy toward Cuba.

Ricardo Alarcon, the legislative leader who is Castro's main spokesman for negotiations with the United States, called Clinton's initiatives a "deceptive maneuver" that aimed to deflect almost unanimous worldwide opposition to the embargo. This included repeated, almost unanimous votes by the U.N. General Assembly urging the United States to scrap the embargo. Alarcon also charged that Clinton's initiatives were a smoke screen for the president's rejection of the proposal for a bipartisan commission to review the embargo. He suggested that the proposal to allow money to be sent to Cubans by any American could serve as a cover for the Cuban exile community to send more money to Cuban counterrevolutionaries so they could "look for ways to manufacture traitors." Alarcon argued that the initiatives were actually "an attack on an ideological plane, a political plane, without giving in reality anything, trying to confuse and trick you. I'm sure all of our people sincerely are going to reject this new face of the war against Cuba." Alarcon devoted much of his speech to spotlighting those liberal legislators and advocacy groups in the United States and other countries that have protested the embargo. He concluded that some day the United States will have to abandon "this blockade, this criminal policy."[59]

The embargo is clearly the main impediment to improved U.S.–Cuban relations. The fall of the embargo probably would greatly increase the chances for agreement on model business principles. Even when this does happen, while Cuba remains communist—with or without Castro—the chances of Havana's acceptance of all these principles at one time is highly unlikely. When the embargo ends, presumably Castro would invite U.S. businesses to operate in Cuba. The United States, still aiming to effect political and economic liberalization of the Cuban regime, might insist that U.S. businesses entering Cuba abide by model business principles. If Castro wants U.S. businesses badly enough, at this point he may agree to one or more of the principles. The most likely possibilities are those that deal with environmental and health and safety regulations. Castro could also accept a modified request for payment of Cuban workers: At the outset, perhaps a fifty–fifty arrangement could be agreed upon, with the Cuban government retaining 50 percent of wage payments and Cuban workers receiving the other 50 percent in dollars. With the Cuban economy becoming increasingly dependent upon dollars, and with more and more dollars being sent to the Cuban people from relatives and friends in the United States, Castro may be willing to accept this arrangement. He would attract business from the United States and other countries that subscribe to the principles while at the same time, with more dollars available to more Cubans, allow more steam to blow off from a disgruntled populace. The least likely principles for Castro to accept would be those that deal with formation of independent labor unions and the right to free collective bargaining. In his view, these principles would unacceptably weaken the Cuban government's economic and political control over the people.

U.S. businesses that subscribed to model business principles in Cuba would probably abide by them. It would be in their interest to do so, especially if they received special inducements from the U.S. government, such as tax benefits. Would Castro abide by those best business principles he did accept? Would business operations have to be carefully monitored for mutual compliance? If so, perhaps international monitors (say, from the OAS) would be most politically palatable to both sides. The hope is that both Castro and foreign businesses would look at the principles as a "win–win" situation. If so, there would be little incentive for either side to break its side of the bargain (assessment: 3).

Total Average Assessment: 3.38.

CONCLUSION

The United States has maintained its embargo against Cuba since 1962. This position has been largely supported by a combination of the hard-line Cuban American exile communities in Florida and New Jersey and anti-Communist right-wing Republicans in Congress. Cuban Americans in Congress have been especially influential. They argue that with cessation of Soviet aid, Cuba is now much more vulnerable to the embargo. The United States just has to "stay the course" for the embargo to do its job and force Castro to liberalize politically and economically or leave office.

The United States now stands virtually alone in imposing sanctions and isolating Cuba. Most of the rest of the world recognizes the Castro regime and conducts business in Cuba, all the while resisting extraterritorial application of U.S. laws such as Helms–Burton that seek to tighten the embargo. Helms–Burton has caused friction with U.S. allies such as Canada, Mexico, and the EU. They have chosen a policy of constructive engagement (i.e., to conduct business in Cuba while pressuring the Cuban government to improve its human rights record). Neither U.S. policy nor that of its allies has brought about this improvement. It is necessary, therefore, to look for other alternatives that might be more fruitful.

In the last few years of the Clinton administration, U.S. Cuba policy began to focus on preparing for the peaceful transition to political and economic liberalization after Castro passes from the scene. Since then Washington has been trying to build up an independent Cuban civil society that can serve as a basis and catalyst for peaceful change. But how best to do this? One option that has received serious attention, both inside and outside Washington, is use of the private business sector.

In considering operations in authoritarian regimes such as Cuba, private business has three main options: no investment (or divestment if operations are already there), investment in accordance with each country's customs and laws, and investment only under its own specified conditions. It is this third option that deserves more attention from the U.S. government. Utilizing a modern-day version of "Dollar Diplomacy," the United States should intensify efforts to urge foreign businesses to go to Cuba, and when there, to abide by a voluntary code of conduct that would require improvement in worker rights. At the same time, Washington should signal Castro that U.S. businesses are prepared to do the same. This would be a prelude to eventual establishment of U.S.–Cuban relations.

The Commerce Department has already drawn up its list of best business practices. It did so in 1995 after President Clinton's decision the previous year to delink extension of PNTR status to the PRC with progress in human rights. These principles were initially aimed at U.S. companies doing business in China. Yet with inclusion of goals to stop sweatshops and acts harmful to the environment and health and safety of workers, and with support for creation of independent labor unions and free collective bargaining, Washington hoped that U.S. companies would apply its version of model business principles around the world.

Since their formulation, U.S. government pointmen on Cuban policy such as Stuart Eizenstat and Michael Ranneberger proposed application of model business principles to non–U.S. companies now doing business in Cuba. The hope is that private companies can exert more effective influence on the Cuban regime than foreign governments. Presumably, implementation of a corporate code of conduct could also lay the groundwork for the entry into Cuba of U.S. businesses when the embargo ends.

Both private individuals and private-sector groups have drawn up sets of best business practices specifically for Cuba. The Arcos Principles were developed by Cuban human rights leaders in 1994 and have received some attention. The NAC drew up its code based on the Arcos Principles. The NAC and Pax Christi Netherlands have exerted leadership, mainly in Europe and the United States, in getting businesses to subscribe to a politically and socially responsible business code.

Thus far, few businesses have expressed interest in codes of conduct. Yet implementation of a code could strengthen the independent Cuban civil society (the so-called Track 2 approach) and encourage private business and the rule of law.[60] This would be part of a multipronged and multilateral policy toward Cuba. For these reasons and others, a code would be consonant with the goals of U.S. foreign policy. Most businesses in the United States want the embargo to end so they can enter the Cuban market. They probably would subscribe to model business principles if this were their ticket to the Cuban economy. Liberal Democrats, humanitarian groups in the United States, the Vatican, and a host of religious leaders have all called for an end to the embargo.

Thus far, an alliance of hard-line Cuban American groups such as CANF with the strongly anti-Communist right wing of the Republican Party has successfully lobbied to keep the embargo. The Cuban government has indicated that the embargo is the main obstacle to improved relations with the United States. Once the embargo is lifted, for pragmatic reasons Castro will probably invite U.S. business into his country. It is at this point that model business principles could play an important role in Cuban society. It is unlikely that Castro would accept all of the Arcos Principles, but he might agree to some, especially if he decides he needs U.S. business to help rescue his country's ailing economy. Businesses that adopt a code could thus spur reform in Cuba.[61]

In desperate need of an economic boost, Castro has grudgingly made some concessions to capitalism. Faced with continued economic crisis, Castro could make even more concessions. A change in U.S. reporting on Cuba could help the progress of reform. Havana has complained that reporting on Cuba has been too limited, unfair, and one-sided. Major newspapers like the *New York Times* have focused almost exclusively on Cuba's human rights problems, it charges, while neglecting advances in education, medicine, health, and the like.[62]

Adoption of best business practices, accompanied by more balanced U.S. reporting, may be just the right fillip to effect political and economic liberalization in Cuba. Economic liberalization by itself, as evidenced in both communist countries like the PRC and non-communist countries like Singapore, does not necessarily lead to political liberalization. Changes brought about by a corporate code of conduct, however, could make an important difference in the long-run. Although adoption of such a code would be no panacea, it could make a significant positive impact on Cuban society.

NOTES

1. See, for example, Adolpho Levya De Varona (executive coordinator of the Endowment for Cuban American Studies), "Propaganda and Reality: A Look at the Embargo Against Castro's Cuba," The Cuban American National Foundation, September 1996. Available at <www.canf.org>.

2. See Tad Szulc, "Castro's China Model," *New York Times*, 29 February 1996, p. A21.

3. "Conversations with Castro," *Vanity Fair*, March 1994, pp. 138–135, 166–170.

4. For an excellent assessment of Canada's policy toward Cuba, see John M. Kirk, *Canada–Cuba Relations: The Other Good Neighbor Policy* (Tallahassee: University Press of Florida, 1997).

5. The option of model business principles is based on voluntary compliance by both the United States and Cuba with the prospect of mutual gain. It stands in sharp contrast to the option of sanctions. For a discussion of this option, see Jacob Heilbrunn, "The Sanctions Sellout," *New Republic*, 25 May 1998, pp. 21–26.

6. The MacBride Principles, issued by the Washington-based Irish National Caucus, were named after Sean MacBride, Nobel Prize–winning Irish human rights activist who founded Amnesty International; the Slepak Principles, issued by the Slepak Foundation (a Philadelphia-based nonprofit organization whose goal was "making human rights a priority issue that must be placed at the forefront of any exchange between the United States and the Soviet Union"), were named after Vladimir Slepak, a member of the original Moscow Helsinki Monitoring Group; and the Miller Principles were contained in a bill introduced in the U.S. Congress by U.S. Representative John Miller (R–Wash.). The MacBride, Slepak, and Miller Principles were influenced by and patterned after the Sullivan Principles. For a discussion of these codes of conduct, see Jorge F. Perez-Lopez, "Promoting International Respect for Worker Rights through Business Codes of Conduct," *Fordham International Law Journal* 17 (1993): 1–47; Lance Compa and Tasha Hinchiffe-Darricarrere, "Enforcing International Labor Rights through Corporate Codes of Conduct," *Columbia Journal of Transnational Law* 33 (1995): 663–668.

7. Among the most important groups pushing for adoption of corporate codes of conduct are the following: Business for Social Responsibility (Washington, D.C.), Interfaith Center for Corporate Responsibility (New York City), the AFL–CIO, Amnesty International, Human Rights Watch, and the National Labor Committee Fund in Support of Worker and Human Rights in Central America.

8. See, for example, Richard Rothstein, "The Starbuck Solution: Can Voluntary Codes Raise Global Living Standards?" *The American Prospect* 27 (July–August 1996): 36–37.

9. See *Coalition for Justice in the Maquiladoras: 1997 Annual Report* 8 (1998) (entire issue). For additional information, contact the Coalition for Justice in the Maquiladoras, 3120 W. Ashby, San Antonio, Texas 78338.

10. See Antonio Jorge and Robert David Cruz, "Foreign Investment Opportunities in Cuba," in *Cuban Communism*, ed. Irving Louis Horowitz and Jaimie Suchlicki (New Brunswick, N.J.: Transaction, 1998), 299–313.

11. See Larry Rohter, "Cuba, Eager for Tourist Dollars, Dusts Off Its Vacancy Sign," *New York Times*, 19 October 1995, p. A14. By 1998, over 1 million tourists spent $1.5 billion in Cuba.

12. A 1982 Cuban law allowed foreign private investment in the form of joint ventures, but generally with no more than 49-percent foreign ownership.

13. See Jose De Cordoba, "Cuba Law to Allow Foreign Ownership of 100% of Firms," *The Wall Street Journal*, 5 September 1995, p. A11.

14. Larry Rohter, "Cuba Allowing Citizens to Buy and Sell Foreign Currencies," *New York Times*, 8 November 1995, p. A3. Robert P. Walzer, Eduardo Kaplan, and John Bussey, "Notes from Havana: Cubans Pursue a Tenuous Economic Balancing Act," *The Wall Street Journal*, 27 September 1998, p. A14.

15. Teo A. Babun, Jr., "Cuba's Investment Boom That Never Was," *The Wall Street Journal*, 1 March 1996, p. A15.

16. Gustavo Arcos was a hero of the Cuban Revolution. He later became Cuba's ambassador to Belgium. Soon, because of this political beliefs in support of political pluralism, he was recalled to Havana and jailed. He was released several years later and became a leader in the struggle for human rights in Cuba. For more details on Arcos's life published on the anniversary of Castro's attack against Batista's army barracks in 1953, see Frank Calzon, "Ask Castro About Gustavo Arcos Today," *Miami Herald*, 16 July 1988, p. 12A.

17. Cuban government violation of labor rights (among other human rights) is well-documented. The *Human Rights Watch World Report 1999* (New York: Human Rights Watch, 1998) on Cuba points out, for example, three disturbing violations: strict government control over labor rights and refusal to legalize independent unions and agricultural cooperatives, adoption of several laws that tightly control labor rights in businesses backed by foreign investment, and maintenance of its extensive system of prison agricultural camps.

18. See Pax Christi Netherlands, "Foreign Intestments in Cuba and Human and Labor Rights," meeting, 15 December 1996.

19. For a good analysis of the South African sanctions issue, see "The United States and South Africa: The 1985 Sanctions Debate," in *Making American Foreign Policy*, ed. Gregory F. Treverton (Englewood Cliffs, N.J.: Prentice Hall, 1994), 48–78.

20. Complicity of foreign investors with the Cuban government in exploitation of the Cuban people has also been underscored by groups such as the American Institute for Free Labor Development. In a 1995 report it contended, "The growing number of partnerships between foreign investors and Cuban government agencies has not improved the lot of workers or provided them with greater autonomy. Instead, *the Cuban government has used the exploitation of working people in the absence of freedom of association as a lure to attract investors*, often to the detriment of workers in neighboring countries." See American Institute for Free Labor Development, AFL–CIO, *Foreign Investors: Oiling the Cuban Government Machine* (Washington, D.C., 1995), 1–2, italics added.

21. See Sebastian A. Arcos, "Trading with Dictators Only Strengthens Them," *Miami Herald*, 29 May 1998, p. A25. Sebastian Arcos, an activist with CCPDH, died from cancer in December 1998.

22. Cuban Dissidence Task Group, "Letter to Foreign Investors," 10 April 1997.

23. Press release, Pax Christi Netherlands. Available at <http://antenna.hl/paxchristi/cubaenme2.html>.

24. Pax Christi Netherlands, report on meeting "Foreign Investments in Cuba and Human and Labor Rights" to members of the European Parliament, Utrecht, The Netherlands, 15 December 1998.

25. Human Rights Watch/Americas said, "Profiting from this shameful arrangement [of European companies' joint ventures in Cuba] can be justified only if investors press Castro to repeal laws that violate the basic international

principles governing modern labor relations." See Christopher Marquis, "Rights Group: EU Economic Policy in Cuba Unjustified," *Miami Herald*, 26 September 1996, p. 14A.

26. For details of this understanding, see Alan P. Larson, Assistant Secretary of State for Economic and Business Affairs, "US–EU Understanding and the Protection of American Property Rights in Cuba," remarks at the Institute for U.S.–Cuba Relations, Washington, D.C., 23 July 1998. Available at <http://www.state.gov/www/policy>.

27. EU, Human Rights Commission, drafted document.

28. "The North American Committee (NCA) Promotes Business Principles and Opposes Secondary Boycotts," 7 January 1998 conference, the National Press Club, Washington, D.C.

29. The Conference Board is Canada's largest and most important independent applied economic and management research institute. Its 800 members provide an independent perspective on public policy issues such as trade and investment in Cuba.

30. NAC, "Principles for Private Sector Investment in Cuba," press release, 7 July 1997; and statement passed by NAC Executive Committee, 27 June 1997.

31. The NAC principles said that companies should

1. Provide a safe and healthy workplace.

2. Employ fair employment practices, including avoidance of child and forced labor and discrimination based on race, gender, national origin, religious beliefs, or political beliefs or affiliation.

3. Work to gain the right to recruit, contract, pay, and promote workers directly, not through government intermediaries.

4. Respect employees' right to organize freely in the workplace and to choose a union to represent them in negotiations with management.

5. Maintain a corporate culture that respects free expression consistent with legitimate business concerns, and does not condone political coercion in the workplace.

6. Support the strengthening of legal procedure in Cuba, encouraging respect for due process, human rights, and the international conventions of which Cuba is a signatory (from NAC press release, "Trilateral Group Urges Private Sector to Play a Role in Promoting Human Rights in Cuba," 7 July 1997).

32. An interesting development occurred in 1997 when the Council on Economic Priorities, a U.S.–based think tank, joined forces with influential companies such as Avon and Toys-R-Us to launch Social Accountability 8000. This concept, similar to the ISO 9000 standard for quality control, stipulates a set of certifiable labor and human rights standards based on conventions of the ILO, the U.N. Universal Declaration of Human Rights, and the U.N. Convention on the Rights of the Child.

33. For more details on Barrett's views on best business principles for Cuba, see "Principles for Private Sector Involvement in Cuba," luncheon address to AmCham Cuba, the National Press Club, Washington, D.C., 25 September 1998; and "Adopting a Code of Socially Responsible Business Practice," *Looking Ahead* 20 (June 1998): 10–12. This article is part of a collection of articles based on a conference held in January 1998. It was cosponsored by the NPA, the Conference

Board of Canada, the Instituto Tecnologico Autonomo de Mexico (Mexico's leading business organization), and the Washington office of the Germany-based Friedrich Ebert Foundation, which is concerned with international and social issues of interest to German government, business, and labor institutions.

34. See "Administration Releases Details on Voluntary Business Principles," *Daily Labor Report*, no. 104 (31 May 1995): A-4; Bureau of Democracy, Human Rights and Labor, *Promoting the Model Business Principles*, Department of State publication 10486 (Washington, D.C.: Bureau of National Affairs, 1997).

35. See "The Battle's On: Corporate Codes of Conduct," *Interhemispheric Resource Center Bulletin* 47–48 (October 1997): 6–7.

36. Quoted by Juan Forero, "Driving against the Embargo," The Star-Ledger Network, NJ, 5 January 1999; full text available at <http://usaengage.org/news/990105starledger.html>.

37. See Jim Carner, "Wish You Were Here: Marxist Cuba Beckons and U.S. Capitalists Champ at the Bit," *New York Times*, 22 April 1998, pp. D1, D4.

38. U.S. Chamber of Commerce, "Time to End Embargo on Food and Medical Sales to Cuba Says U.S. Chamber," 13 January 1998. Available at <www.uschamber.org>.

39. "First Coast Firms See Market of Millions in Cuba," *Jacksonville Business Journal*, 1 December 1997. Available at <http://jacksonville.bcentral.com>.

40. For a good overview of human rights in U.S. foreign policy, see Felice D. Gaer, "Human Rights: What Role in U.S. Foreign Policy?" In *Great Decisions 1998* (New York: FPA), 31–39.

41. Remarks of Jimmy Carter, ibid.

42. U.S. AID Report, "Support for a Democratic Transition in Cuba," 28 January 1997. Available at <www.USAID.gov/countries/cu/english.htm>.

43. Remarks of Stuart E. Eizenstat, Special Representative of the President for the Promotion of Democracy in Cuba, Associated Press, 16 August 1996 (italics added).

44. Remarks of Michael Ranneberger, Special Coordinator for Cuban Affairs, U.S. Department of State, Associated Press, 16 August 1996.

45. See Michael S. Lelyveld, "Policy Shift Toward Cuba Floated," *Journal of Commerce*, 15 October 1998, pp. 1, 4A; Thomas W. Lippman, "Group Urges Review of Cuba Policy," *The Washington Post*, 8 November 1998, p. A10.

46. See *Independent Task Force Report, U.S.–Cuban Relations in the 21st Century* (New York: Council on Foreign Relations, 1999).

47. Bernard W. Aronson and William D. Rogers, "Bringing Cuba in from the Cold," *New York Times*, 2 January 1999, p. A11.

48. Arthur Schlesinger, Jr., "Cuba Embargo No Longer Makes Sense," Letter to the Editor, *New York Times*, 21 February 1997.

49. Remarks of Stuart E. Eizenstat, Special Representative of the President for the Promotion of Democracy in Cuba, Associated Press, 16 August 1996 (italics added).

50. Quoted by Mireya Navarro, "Miami Generally Welcomes Easing of Ban," *New York Times*, 6 January 1999, p. A8.

51. Randall Robinson, "Forty Years of Hostility: Consequences of the United States Economic Embargo in Cuba," *Trans Africa Forum*, 1999; available at <transafricaforum.org/reports/cuba>.

52. U.S. Senate, Committee on Foreign Relations, Subcommittee on Western Hemisphere and Peace Corps Affairs, testimony of Rep. Charles B. Rangel on the Cuban Liberty and Solidarity Act, 1st sess., 14 June 1996, 69–70.

53. Thomas W. Lippman, "U.S. Ready to Play Ball with Cuba," *The Washington Post*, 5 January 1999, p. A1.

54. See Anthony Boodle, "Cuban Legislators Slam U.S. Cuba Policy Review," *Reuters Report*, 25 November 1998; available at <cubanet.org>.

55. Charles Krause, "Ill Trade Winds," interview on the PBS television broadcast *The News Hour*, 11 July 1996. For more on Canada's policy toward Cuba, see John M. Kirk and Peter McKenna, *Canada–Cuba Relations: The Other Good Neighbor Policy* (Tallahassee: University Press of Florida, 1997); Gillian McGillvray, *Trading with the "Enemy": Relations in the 1990s*, Georgetown University Cuba Briefing Paper Series (1997).

56. Creation of CANF in 1981 was advocated by Richard Allen, President Reagan's first national security adviser. Allen envisioned CANF a lobbying vehicle for Cuban exiles to influence U.S. Cuba policy as effectively as American Jews had utilized the American Israel Political Action Committee to lobby in Washington on behalf of Israel. See Mirta Ojito, "Castro's Foe's Legacy: Success, Not Victory," *New York Times*, 30 November 1997, sec. 4, p. 5.

57. See Timothy Ashby, "Cuban-American Economists Grip US Politics and Policy," *Christian Science Monitor*, 9 November 1995, p. 19.

58. "Dispatch from Havana," *Reuters*, 1 November 1998.

59. See James C. McKinley, Jr., "Cuba Attacks as 'Deceptive' Clinton's Easing of Embargo," *New York Times*, 10 January 1999, p. A6.

60. See Eliot Richardson, "A Blueprint for Better Relations between the US and Cuba," *Christian Science Monitor*, 28 September 1995, p. 19. Richardson, who held several Cabinet posts in the Nixon and Ford administrations, was chair of the Inter-American Dialogue's Task Force on Cuba. The Inter-American Dialogue is a leading U.S. center for policy research and exchange on hemispheric affairs that seeks to develop and promote new policy approaches for U.S.–Cuban relations. The president of the Inter-American Dialogue has also advocated beefing up the U.S. Track 2 strategy, especially people-to-people exchanges and support for NGOs that were part of the 1997 Canadian–Cuban accord. See Peter Hakim, "Setting the Stage for Transition in Cuba," *Christian Science Monitor*, 30 January 1997, p. 19.

61. See Susan Kaufman Purcell, "Cubans Need U.S. Pressure for Reform," *The Wall Street Journal*, 21 June 1996, p. A15.

62. See "Freedom of the Press, American Style," *Granma International*, 24 May 1998, p. 15. An editorial in this Cuban government-controlled newspaper criticizing U.S. press coverage of the visit to Cuba by Canada's Prime Minister Jean Chretien dripped in sarcasm: "Of course, the editors may have considered it much more important to cover the massacres in elementary schools, serial rapes, or pleas to legalize drug use, all of which undoubtedly boost newspaper sales." The article concluded, "It would be interesting to see how the U.S. media reports Clinton's opinions on Cuban government policies on health care and education. I am almost certain that they will not write about the U.S. blockade's success in deteriorating those services."

CHAPTER 9

Conclusion

Richard S. Hillman, John A. Peeler,
and Elsa Cardozo Da Silva

This book reveals the complexity of democratic transitions, the importance of support for human rights, and the way in which democracy and human rights are linked in Latin America and in much of the world. The aspects treated in the first section illustrate the multifaceted nature and variety of considerations involved in the analysis of Latin American political, economic, and social realities regarding these topics. The second part of this book contains an explicit investigation of democracy and human rights promotion. These chapters demonstrate the interrelationships between democracy and human rights as they are manifested in particular cases, as well as throughout the Latin American region and the world. The era of democratization has opened great potential for the achievement of regimes that protect citizens' rights. In Latin America, this is occurring in a context of past abuses. Military dictatorships and authoritarianism led to repressive rule, denigration of Native American rights, suppression of political dissent, use of torture, disappearances, extrajudicial executions, and socioeconomic systems that deny the opportunity for large segments of the population to lead dignified lives.

The "Dirty War" in Argentina, abuses under Pinochet's regime in Chile, treatment of Haitian workers in Dominican *bateyes*, Brazilian military crackdowns and treatment of Indians in the Amazon Basin, the tradition of violence in Colombia, and conditions in Venezuelan and Peruvian jails are just a few historic examples of political and legal abuses. Every country within the region exemplifies the massive social and economic impoverishment that essentially militates against human dignity.

Past experiences and new openings pose challenges for those interested in promoting and protecting human rights in Latin America. In the past, human rights violations were systematic expressions of dictatorial regimes. Today, every country in the region has signed the International Treaty on Civil and Political Rights and the American Convention on Human Rights. Moreover, the Inter-American Human Rights Court and the Inter-American Commission on Human Rights have been active and supported by democratic regimes. Yet violations persist despite these positive developments. In fact, cultural and social discrimination is widespread. In a socioeconomic perspective, "Latin America is the world's most unequal region" (Basombrío 2000, 8).

These issues are clearly reflected in this book. Moreover, the chapters demonstrate how social, economic, and cultural rights are inextricably interrelated with civil and political rights, particularly in Latin America, where extreme inequality and weak democratic traditions have resulted in contradictory approaches to the analysis of democratization and protection of human rights.

One troubling perspective questions the ability of democracy to advance economic, social, and cultural rights due to the primacy of short-term political considerations. According to this interpretation, conservative politicians, entrepreneurs, international technocrats, and sectors of the armed forces that seek long-term neoliberal economic measures are undermined by political populism. This perspective is based on the idea that only economic development can ensure social, economic, and cultural rights, which are constrained by the discontinuities of elections that frequently change leaders and policies.

Another disquieting perspective suggests that democracy and civil and political rights are not significant in an environment characterized by massive poverty. Accordingly, "it makes little sense to worry about 'formal democracy' when we should be striving for 'real democracy,' understood as equal access to basic economic, social, and cultural rights for the majority of the population" (Basombrío 2000, 9).

Paradoxically, both approaches raise a dilemma that pervades Latin American political discourse in the era of democratization. Indeed, economic conditions largely influence the efficacy and legitimacy of political institutions and are apparent in the polarization between political and socioeconomic rights. People want their governments to provide conditions under which their quality of life improves. Neither the inability to deliver on populist promises nor the austerity inherent in long-term solutions satisfies growing expectations on the part of citizens in Latin American countries. Political and economic stability, therefore, is linked to democratization, "a process that involves the inclusion of citizens into social life and its benefits, equal opportunities, structural changes in this respect, and participation at the various levels that affect individual and collective life" (Garretón 2000, 25).

Each chapter of this volume reflects the interrelationships between politics and economics and democracy and human rights. The challenges deriving from these linkages are highlighted in the first part and the prospects for promoting and supporting them are treated in the second part of this book.

In the first part, Louis N. Bickford outlines the major challenges that confront postauthoritarian Latin American human rights movements. He signals comparatively the confessions of those involved in human rights abuses in Argentina and the arrest of Chile's Pinochet in London as examples of new initiatives that have energized the movement. The past, however, remains the primary battleground for the constructive articulation of human rights concerns.

In addition, Elsa Cardozo Da Silva points to the need for a less governmental and more societal approach to democratic governability: the social construction of democracy. Despite new developments in civil society, however, both Colombia and Venezuela have continued to deal with the problems of governability according to a very "governmental" approach. Again, how to overcome the past is a central issue. Accordingly, from now on democracies must be built by societies that value democratic principles and possess a comprehensive idea of socioeconomic democracy. Two social practices that are slowly creating and recreating new patterns of democratic behavior are national decentralization and regional integration.

Isabel Ribeiro de Oliveira shows how the Human Rights National Plan has made a positive contribution despite entrenched authoritarianism in Brazilian political culture. Ribeiro de Oliveira, like Cardozo Da Silva, suggests that a citizen's consciousness of his or her rights constitutes a source of power in resisting authoritarian decisions.

The second part of this book explores the ways in which democracy and human rights might be most effectively promoted, supported, and protected. Christopher Sabatini posits that institutional weakness, corruption, the increasing violation of political and human rights, and the growth of personalistic, corrupt governments threaten to undermine democracy in Latin America. Defending democracy in Latin America as well as the rest of the world in the future therefore entails more than ensuring fair elections and preventing the interruption of elected governments. María Teresa Romero adds to this idea by illustrating that Venezuela does not constitute the only challenge for American policy on democracy in Latin America. Peru, Paraguay, Haiti, Colombia, and Ecuador are also cause for concern. She points out that many doubts emerge about the reality of Latin American democracies and about the dangers they face. Insufficient participation in the elections and the possibility of alternate governments, the lack of an independent and impartial judicial administrations, the absence of guarantees for the exercise of fundamental liberties, separation of powers, and legal control over the rulers are elements that remain conspicuously absent in many Latin American democracies. Moreover, tremendous social inequalities, corruption, drug traffic, terrorism, the disrepute of political parties and people's apathy, political assassinations, constitutional organizations' dissolution or annulment of their actions, prolongation of mandates without a judicially defined base, electoral fraud, and prohibiting a legally elected government from exercising its authority are issues that must be addressed. In the face of such challenges, Romero asks, How should the United States proceed against typical military threats? Or prevent them? How is it possible to reconcile the traditional principle of defense of democracy with the nonintervention principle? She concludes that in the specific case of Venezuela, and due to the potential decomposition of its democratic process, the United States has a responsibility to influence the Venezuelan process without intervening in such a way as to violate Venezuelan sovereignty.

Irwin P. Stotzky shows how the United States has, in fact, intervened in order to preserve democracy in Haiti. His analysis reveals that, beyond elections, an environment of personal security is essential. He defines democracy to include

the building of vibrant institutions of justice and law and the full blooming of civil society: the broad array of political parties, independent media, independent labor unions, and nongovernmental organizations, such as women's groups, all of which encourage political and social participation. While these choices—and democracy is always a choice—cannot necessarily be imposed by the international community, they certainly can be encouraged by it.

In agreement with the pervasive themes throughout this book, Stotzky suggests that the macropolitics of institutional change must be complemented by a micropolitics confronting the logic of habitual social interactions. A democratic system must be capable of challenging and changing both the established arrangements of the economy and the polity, and the intimate habits of sociability. He concludes that in Haiti, as in other nations striving for democracy that are constrained by the past, encouraging people to believe in the possibility of structural change is extremely important. The international community, as well as the Haitian government, must encourage such beliefs and actions that would be appropriate in realizing them. International intervention can thus be considered in a complex framework of legality, legitimacy, and efficacy.

Edward Drachman proposes the kind of action inherent in Stotzky's imperative. Drachman suggests that the United States should urge American and foreign enterprises to conduct business in Cuba under a voluntary code of conduct that would require improvement in worker rights. This would be a prelude to eventual establishment of U.S.–Cuban relations. The Commerce Department has already drawn up its list of best business practices, which were initially aimed at U.S. companies doing business in China. Yet with inclusion of goals to stop sweatshops and acts harmful to the environment and health and safety of workers, and with support for creation of independent labor unions and free collective bargaining, Washington hopes that U.S. companies will apply its version of model business principles around the world. Most businesses in the United States want the embargo to end so they can enter the Cuban market. The Cuban government has indicated that the embargo is the main obstacle to improved relations with the United States. Once the embargo is lifted, for pragmatic reasons Castro will probably invite U.S. business into his country. It is at this point that model business principles could play its most important role in Cuban society.

In sum, each chapter reaffirms the essential linkages between procedural democracy and substantive human rights and the need for rights-protective political attitudes and institutions. The contributions to this volume highlight the complex and ambivalent relationships between democracy and human rights, and the contradictions and challenges of promoting them. Bickford's poignant study of the human rights movement in Chile points up the irony that human rights organizations struggle more for survival and identity in a democratic regime than in the authoritarian regime in which they emerged. Yet insofar as the democracy cannot or will not come to terms with Chile's past, it remains complicit in violations of human rights. The chapters by Cardozo Da Silva and Ribeiro de Oliveira each explore how democracies (in Venezuela, Colombia, and Brazil) may fall considerably short of fully respecting and protecting human rights. The crisis of democratic governance in Venezuela is particularly interesting because the failure of the old, *puntofijista* democracy was a failure to fully incorporate and protect the poor majority, while the new populist democracy of Chávez is emphatically majoritarian in its rhetoric while showing troubling tendencies to disregard rights of minorities and procedural safeguards.

How can democracy and human rights best be promoted by outside actors? The chapters of Part II expose the difficulties of doing so. Sabatini tells a tale of imperfect and inconstant advocacy of human rights and democracy by the international community. Both Romero and Drachman are specifically concerned with U.S. policy, and both ask why the United States has not done more in the specific cases of Venezuela and Cuba. Stotzky, on the other hand, looking at the Haitian case, suggests that the United States, as the leader of the international community, has imposed its will too much, failing to allow the Haitians to find their own way to democracy. All of the authors in the second part are critical of basic errors and shortcomings in international promotion efforts: Those who support such efforts will be hard put to draw much optimism from these chapters.

Nevertheless, strong consensus among the experts contributing to this volume emerges around several important considerations. First, in order to achieve efficacious democratic governance, a social construction of democracy must reorient political cultures that have been influenced by the legacies of past authoritarianism and in some cases histories replete with egregious abuses of human rights. Second, initiatives must derive from domestic as well as international agents, including under particular conditions external intervention that respects national sovereignty but does not rule out the use of diplomatic, legal, and even military methods. In this regard, a proactive multilateral approach prevents after-the-fact justification. Finally, an era of democratization at the advent of the twenty-first century presents great opportunities as well as challenges for individuals, states, and the international community to contribute to the achievement of democratic governments that protect the rights of human beings according to the Universal Declaration.

REFERENCES

Basombrío, Carlos. 2000. "Looking Ahead: New Challenges for Human Rights Advocacy." *NACLA* 34: 7–11.

Brown, Seyom. 2000. *Human Rights in World Politics.* New York: Longman.

Carothers, Thomas. 1999. *Aiding Democracy Abroad: The Learning Curve.* Washington, D.C.: Carnegie Endowment for International Peace.

Donnelly, Jack. 1998. *International Human Rights.* 2d ed. Boulder, Colo.: Westview Press.

Garretón, Manuel Antonio. 2000. "From Authoritarianism to Political Democracy: A Transition That Needs Rethinking?" In *Democratic Culture and Governance: Latin America on the Threshold of the Third Millennium,* edited by Luis Albala-Bertrand. Montevideo, Uraguay: UNESCO/HISPAMERICA.

Index

About the Editors
and Contributors

Louis N. Bickford, Associate Director, Global Studies Program, University of Wisconsin, Madison.

Elsa Cardozo Da Silva, Professor of International Relations and Associate Director of the Institute for the Study of Democracy and Human Rights, Central University of Venezuela.

Edward Drachman, Professor of Political Science, State University of New York, Geneseo.

Richard S. Hillman, Professor of Political Science and Director, Institute for the Study of Democracy and Human Rights, St. John Fisher College/Central University of Venezuela.

John A. Peeler, Professor and Chair, Department of Political Science, Bucknell University.

Isabel Ribeiro de Oliveira, Professor of Political Science, Federal University of Rio de Janeiro, Brazil.

María Teresa Romero, Professor of International Relations, Central University of Venezuela.

Christopher Sabatini, Director, Latin America and the Caribbean, National Endowment for Democracy, Washington, D.C.

Irwin P. Stotzky, Professor of Law and Director, Center for the Study of Human Rights, University of Miami School of Law.